MS. MARVEL
FISTS OF JUSTICE

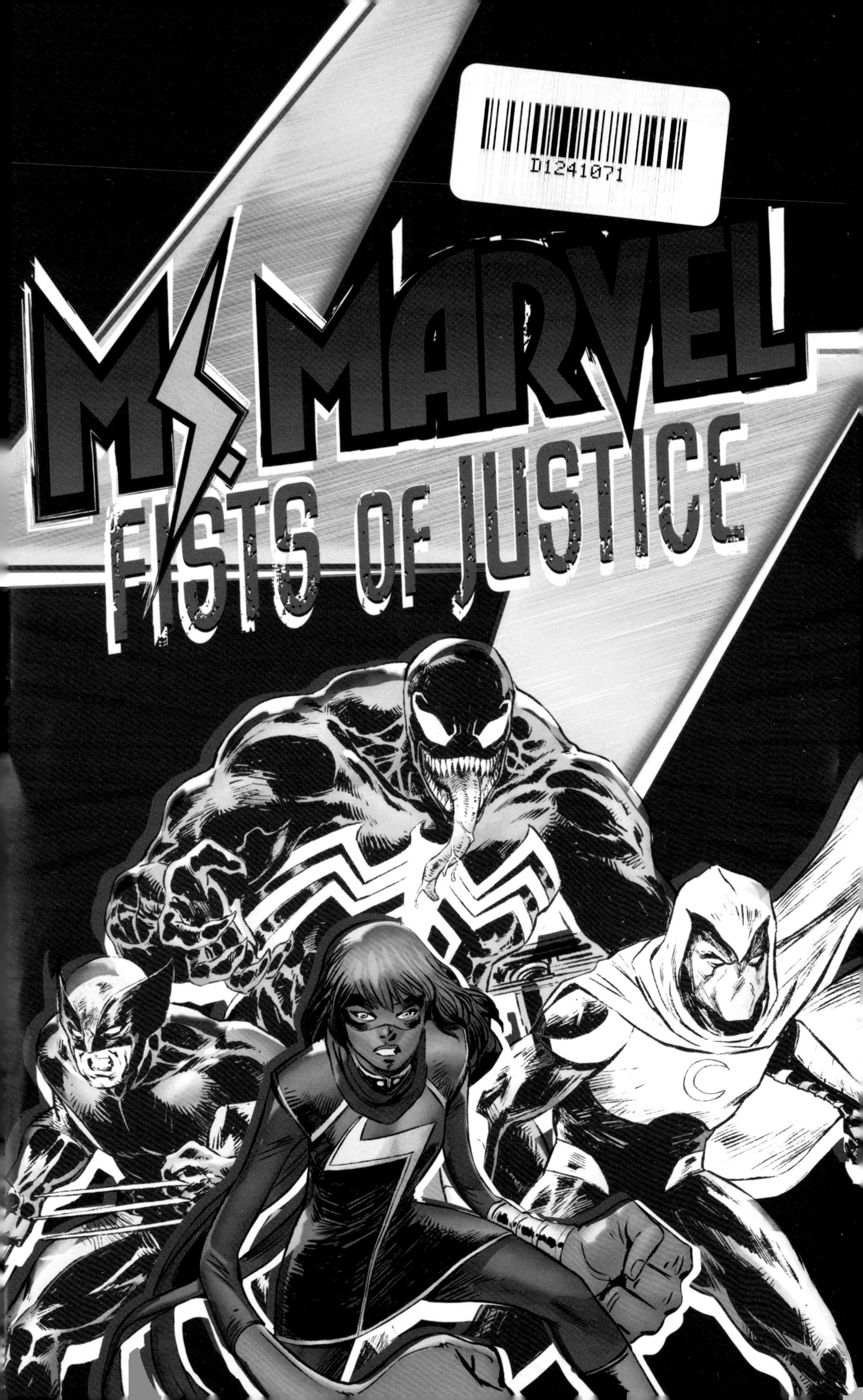

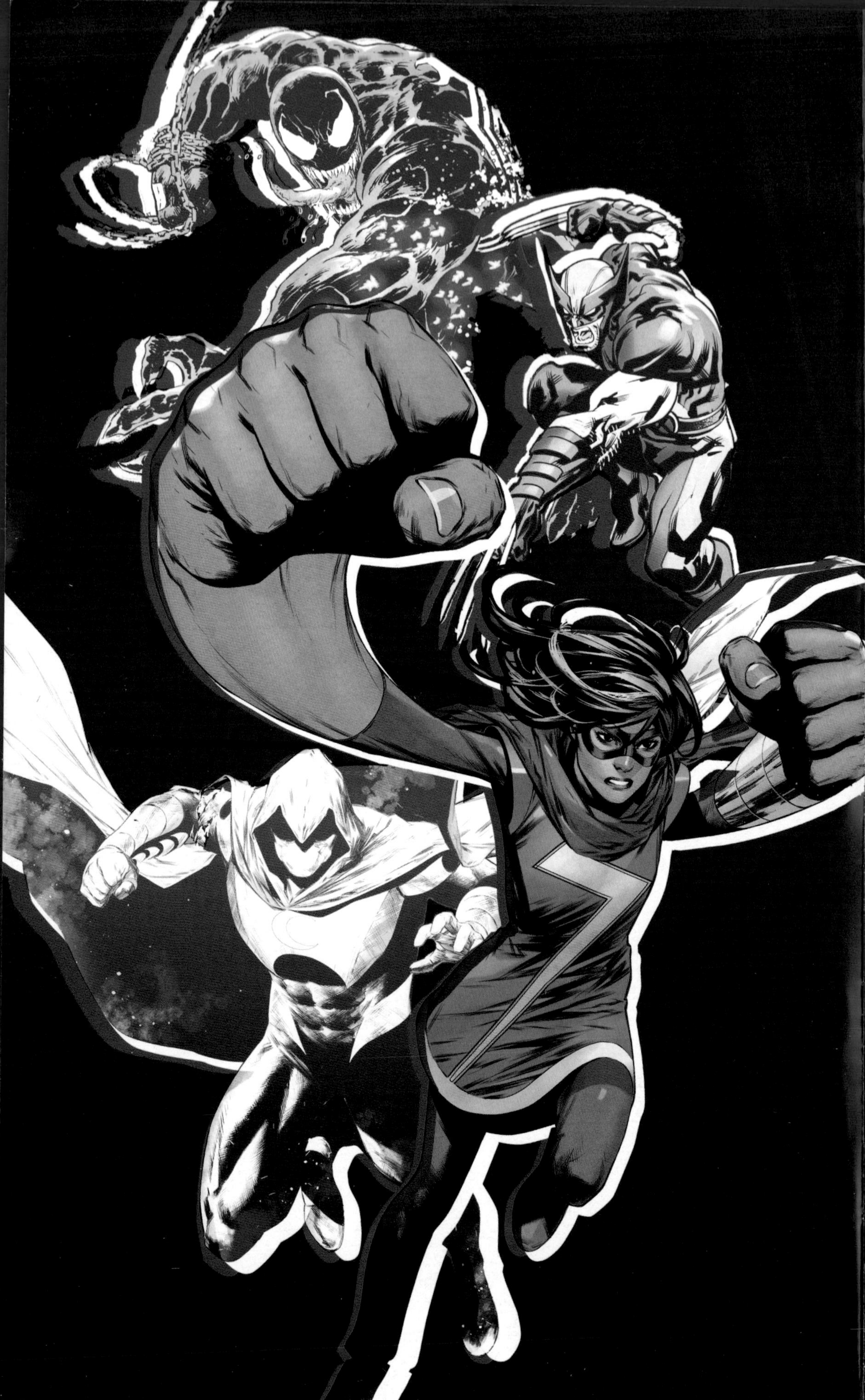

MS. MARVEL
FISTS OF JUSTICE

JODY HOUSER
WRITER

ZÉ CARLOS (WOLVERINE),
IBRAIM ROBERSON (MOON KNIGHT) &
DAVE WACHTER (VENOM)
ARTISTS

ERICK ARCINIEGA
COLOR ARTIST

VC's TRAVIS LANHAM
LETTERER

SARA PICHELLI &
FEDERICO BLEE
COVER ARTISTS

DREW BAUMGARTNER
ASSISTANT EDITOR

MARK BASSO
EDITOR

DANIEL KIRCHHOFFER
COLLECTION EDITOR

MAIA LOY
ASSISTANT MANAGING EDITOR

LISA MONTALBANO
ASSOCIATE MANAGER, TALENT RELATIONS

JENNIFER GRÜNWALD
DIRECTOR, PRODUCTION & SPECIAL PROJECTS

JEFF YOUNGQUIST
VP PRODUCTION & SPECIAL PROJECTS

STACIE ZUCKER
BOOK DESIGNER

ADAM DEL RE
SENIOR GRAPHIC DESIGNER

DAVID GABRIEL
SVP PRINT, SALES & MARKETING

C.B. CEBULSKI
EDITOR IN CHIEF

MS. MARVEL: FISTS OF JUSTICE. Contains material originally published in magazine form as MS. MARVEL & WOLVERINE (2022) #1, MS. MARVEL & MOON KNIGHT (2022) #1 and MS. MARVEL & VENOM (2022) #1. First printing 2022. ISBN 978-1-302-94838-2. Published by MARVEL WORLDWIDE, INC., a subsidiary of MARVEL ENTERTAINMENT, LLC. OFFICE OF PUBLICATION: 1290 Avenue of the Americas, New York, NY 10104. © 2022 MARVEL No similarity between any of the names, characters, persons, and/or institutions in this book with those of any living or dead person or institution is intended, and any such similarity which may exist is purely coincidental. **Printed in the U.S.A.** KEVIN FEIGE, Chief Creative Officer; DAN BUCKLEY, President, Marvel Entertainment; DAVID BOGART, Associate Publisher & SVP of Talent Affairs; TOM BREVOORT, VP, Executive Editor; NICK LOWE, Executive Editor, VP of Content, Digital Publishing; DAVID GABRIEL, VP of Print & Digital Publishing; SVEN LARSEN, VP of Licensed Publishing; MARK ANNUNZIATO, VP of Planning & Forecasting; JEFF YOUNGQUIST, VP of Production & Special Projects; ALEX MORALES, Director of Publishing Operations; DAN EDINGTON, Director of Editorial Operations; RICKEY PURDIN, Director of Talent Relations; JENNIFER GRÜNWALD, Director of Production & Special Projects; SUSAN CRESPI, Production Manager; STAN LEE, Chairman Emeritus. For information regarding advertising in Marvel Comics or on Marvel.com, please contact Vit DeBellis, Custom Solutions & Integrated Advertising Manager, at vdebellis@marvel.com. For Marvel subscription inquiries, please call 888-511-5480. **Manufactured between 11/4/2022 and 12/6/2022 by SEAWAY PRINTING, GREEN BAY, WI, USA.**

10 9 8 7 6 5 4 3 2 1

MS. MARVEL & WOLVERINE

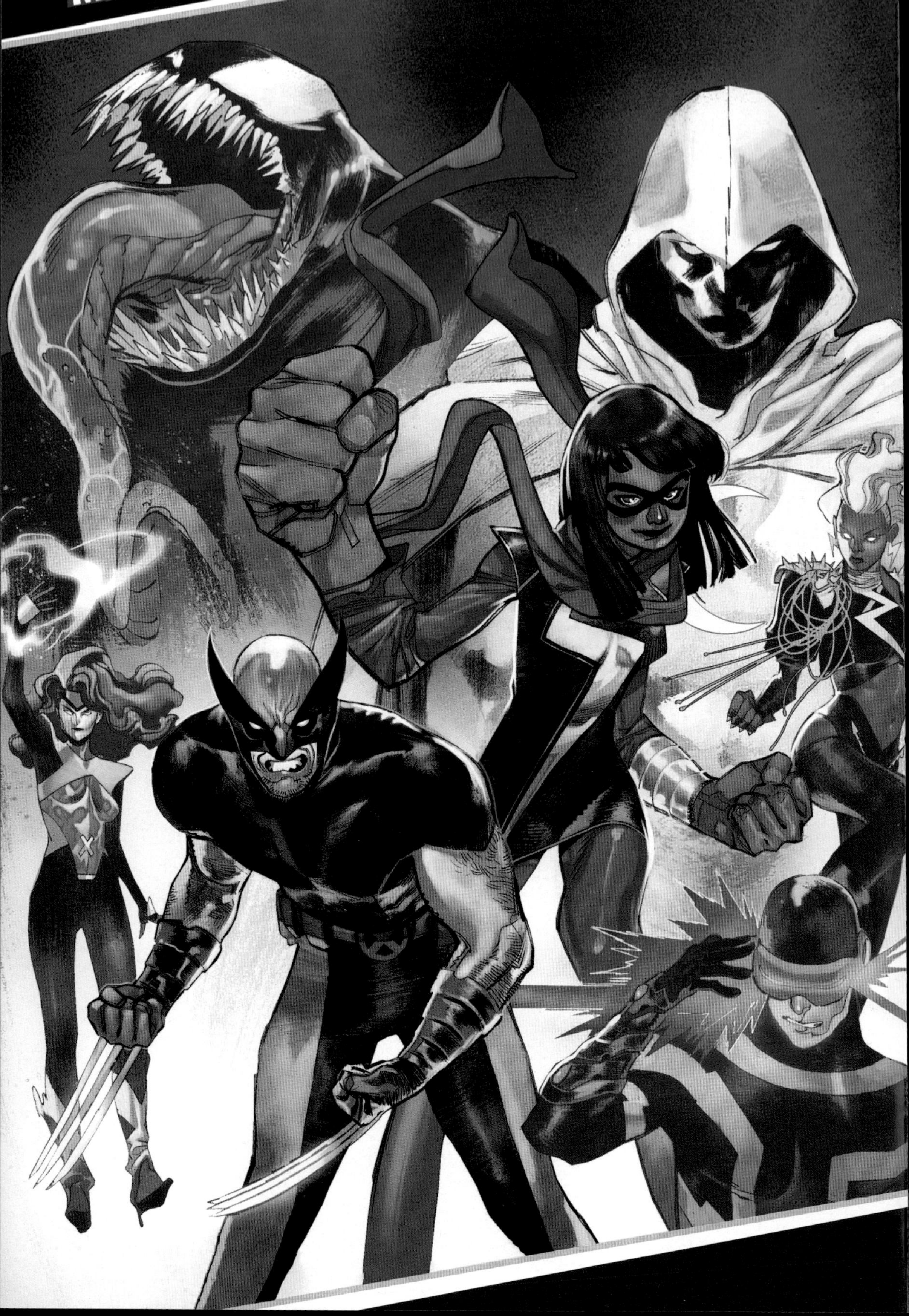

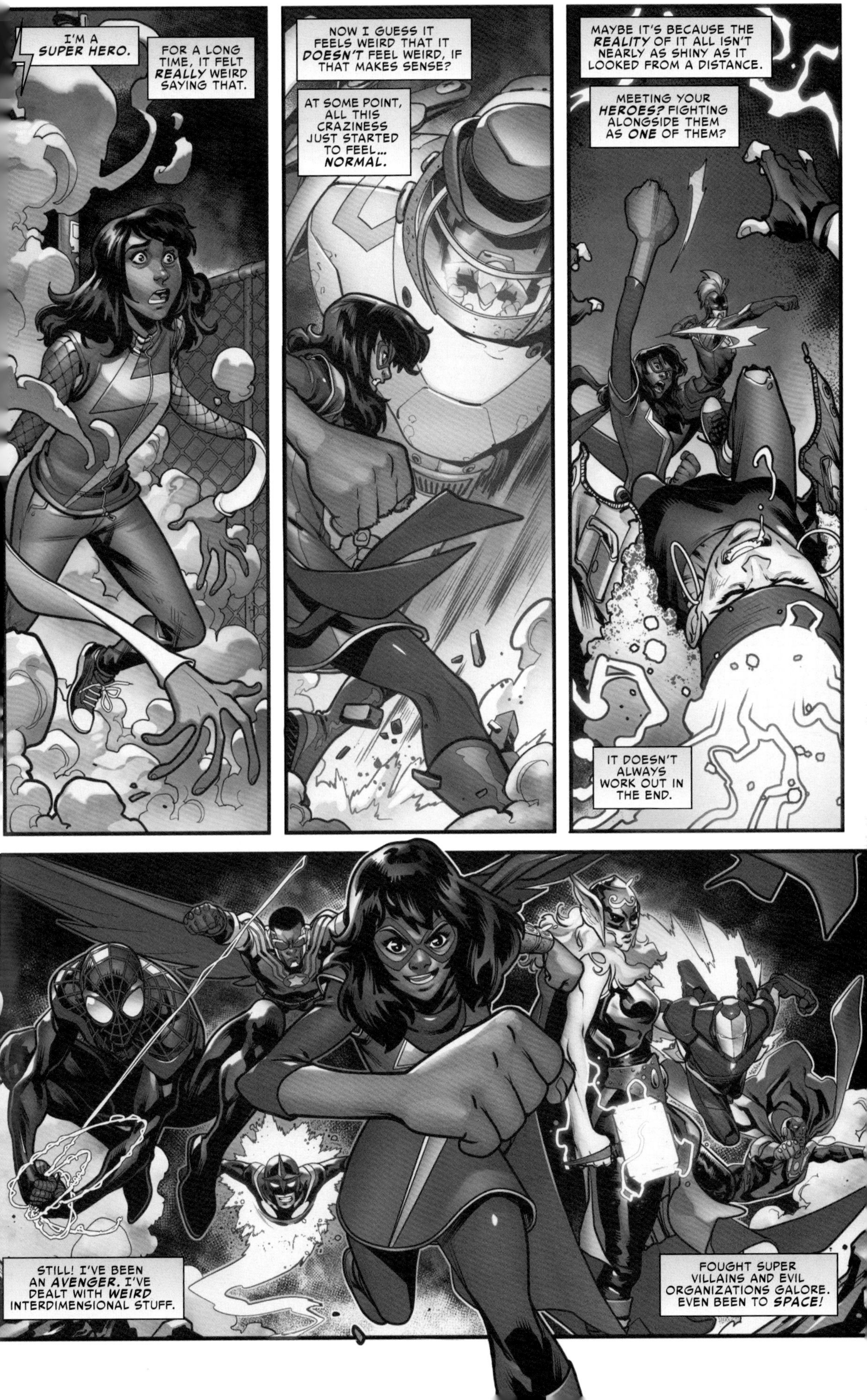
I'M A SUPER HERO.
FOR A LONG TIME, IT FELT REALLY WEIRD SAYING THAT.
NOW I GUESS IT FEELS WEIRD THAT IT DOESN'T FEEL WEIRD, IF THAT MAKES SENSE?
AT SOME POINT, ALL THIS CRAZINESS JUST STARTED TO FEEL... NORMAL.
MAYBE IT'S BECAUSE THE REALITY OF IT ALL ISN'T NEARLY AS SHINY AS IT LOOKED FROM A DISTANCE.
MEETING YOUR HEROES? FIGHTING ALONGSIDE THEM AS ONE OF THEM?
IT DOESN'T ALWAYS WORK OUT IN THE END.
STILL! I'VE BEEN AN AVENGER. I'VE DEALT WITH WEIRD INTERDIMENSIONAL STUFF.
FOUGHT SUPER VILLAINS AND EVIL ORGANIZATIONS GALORE. EVEN BEEN TO SPACE!

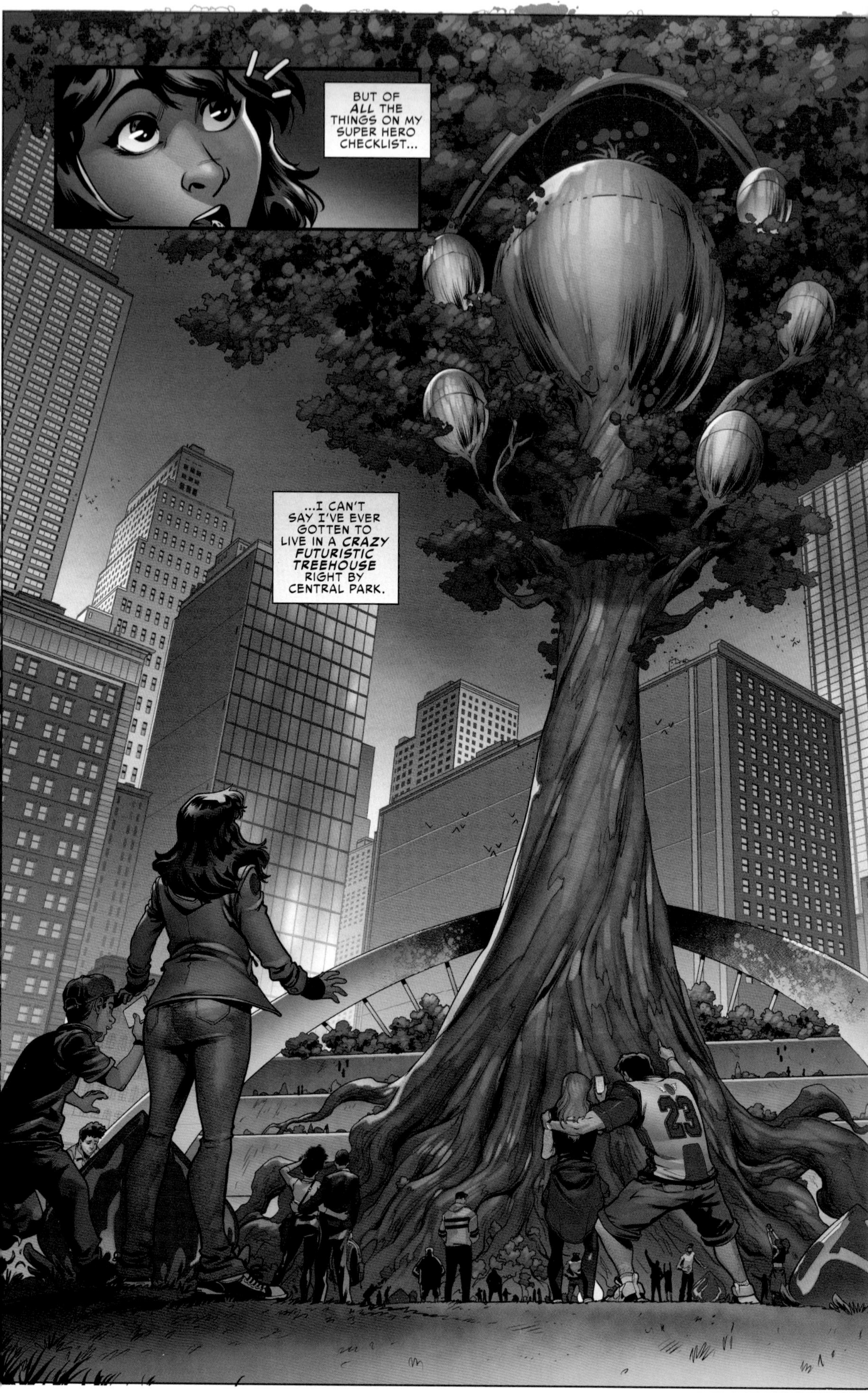
BUT OF ALL THE THINGS ON MY SUPER HERO CHECKLIST...
...I CAN'T SAY I'VE EVER GOTTEN TO LIVE IN A CRAZY FUTURISTIC TREEHOUSE RIGHT BY CENTRAL PARK.
23

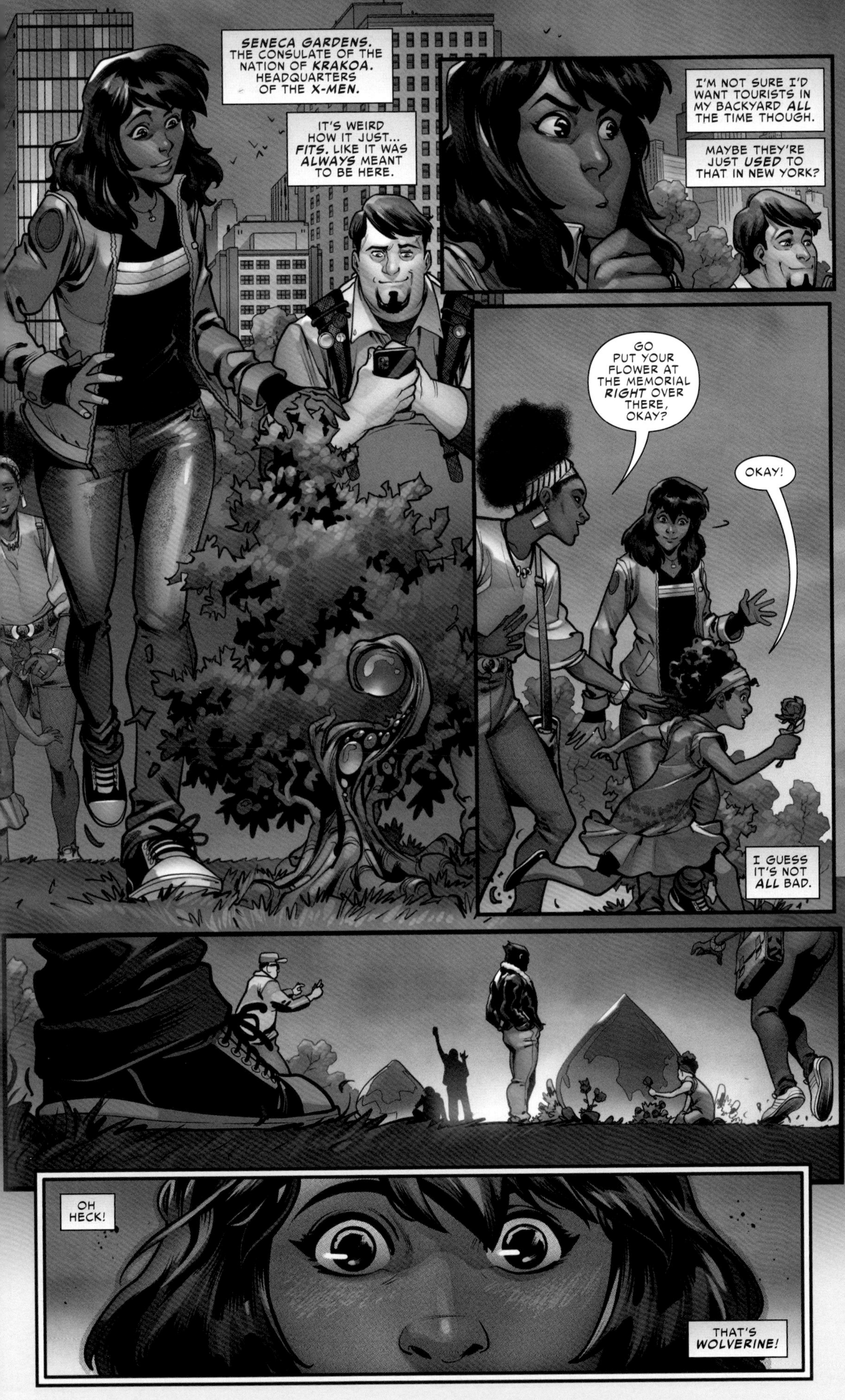
SENECA GARDENS. THE CONSULATE OF THE NATION OF KRAKOA. HEADQUARTERS OF THE X-MEN.
IT'S WEIRD HOW IT JUST... FITS. LIKE IT WAS ALWAYS MEANT TO BE HERE.
I'M NOT SURE I'D WANT TOURISTS IN MY BACKYARD ALL THE TIME THOUGH.
MAYBE THEY'RE JUST USED TO THAT IN NEW YORK?
GO PUT YOUR FLOWER AT THE MEMORIAL RIGHT OVER THERE, OKAY?
OKAY!
I GUESS IT'S NOT ALL BAD.
OH HECK!
THAT'S WOLVERINE!

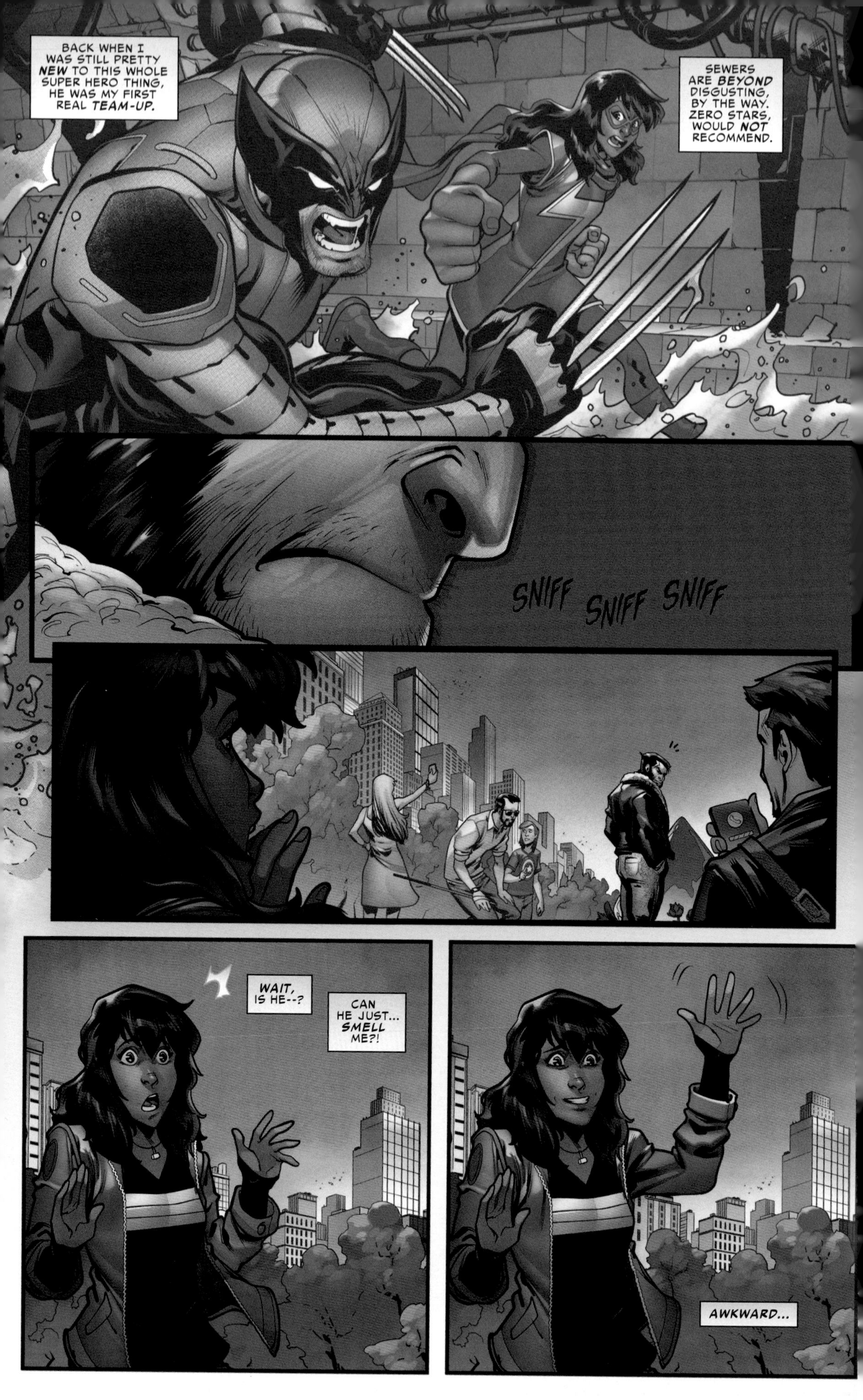
BACK WHEN I WAS STILL PRETTY NEW TO THIS WHOLE SUPER HERO THING, HE WAS MY FIRST REAL TEAM-UP.
SEWERS ARE BEYOND DISGUSTING, BY THE WAY. ZERO STARS, WOULD NOT RECOMMEND.
SNIFF SNIFF SNIFF
WAIT, IS HE--?
CAN HE JUST... SMELL ME?!
AWKWARD...

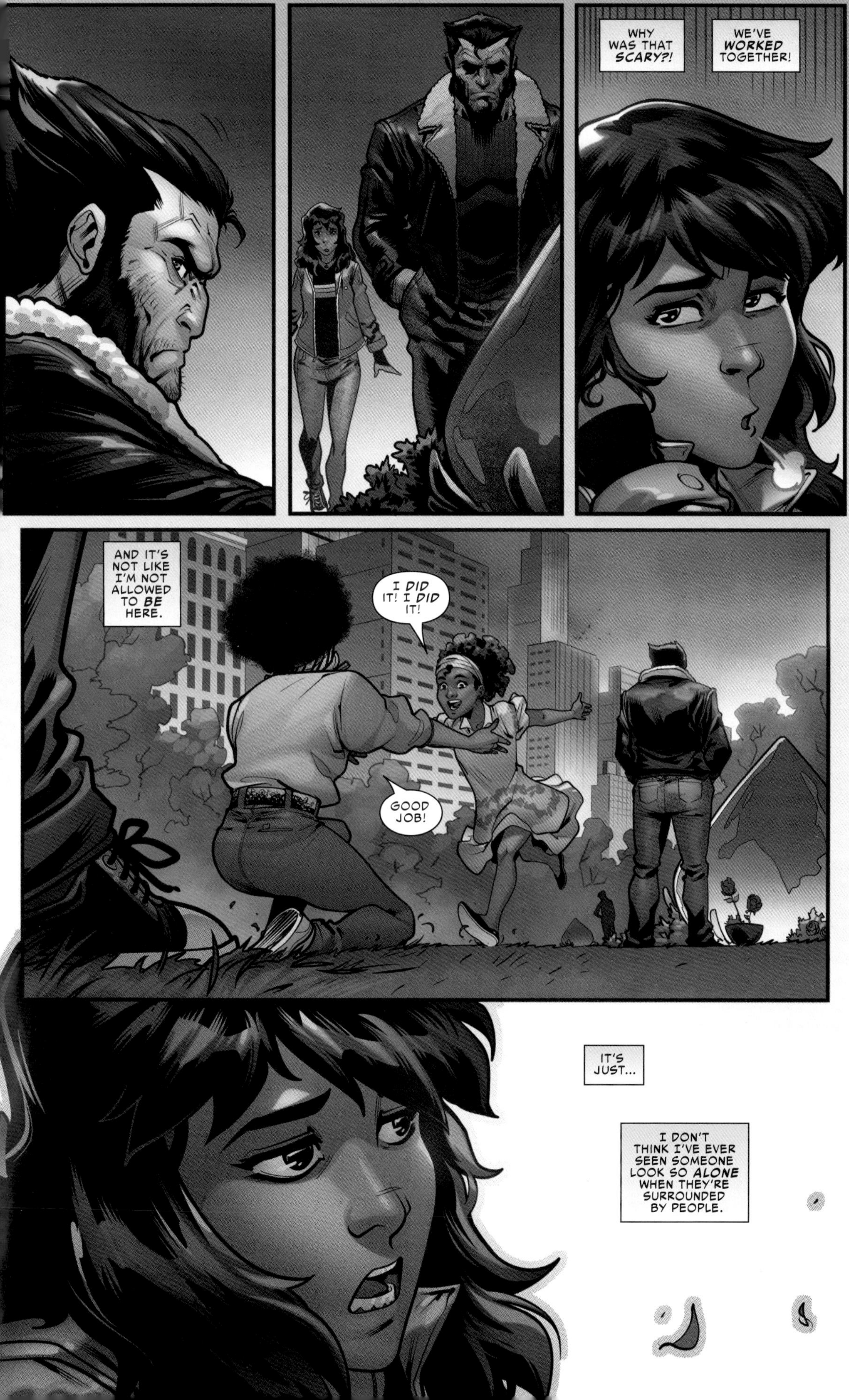
WHY WAS THAT SCARY?!
WE'VE WORKED TOGETHER!
AND IT'S NOT LIKE I'M NOT ALLOWED TO BE HERE.
I DID IT! I DID IT!
GOOD JOB!
IT'S JUST...
I DON'T THINK I'VE EVER SEEN SOMEONE LOOK SO ALONE WHEN THEY'RE SURROUNDED BY PEOPLE.

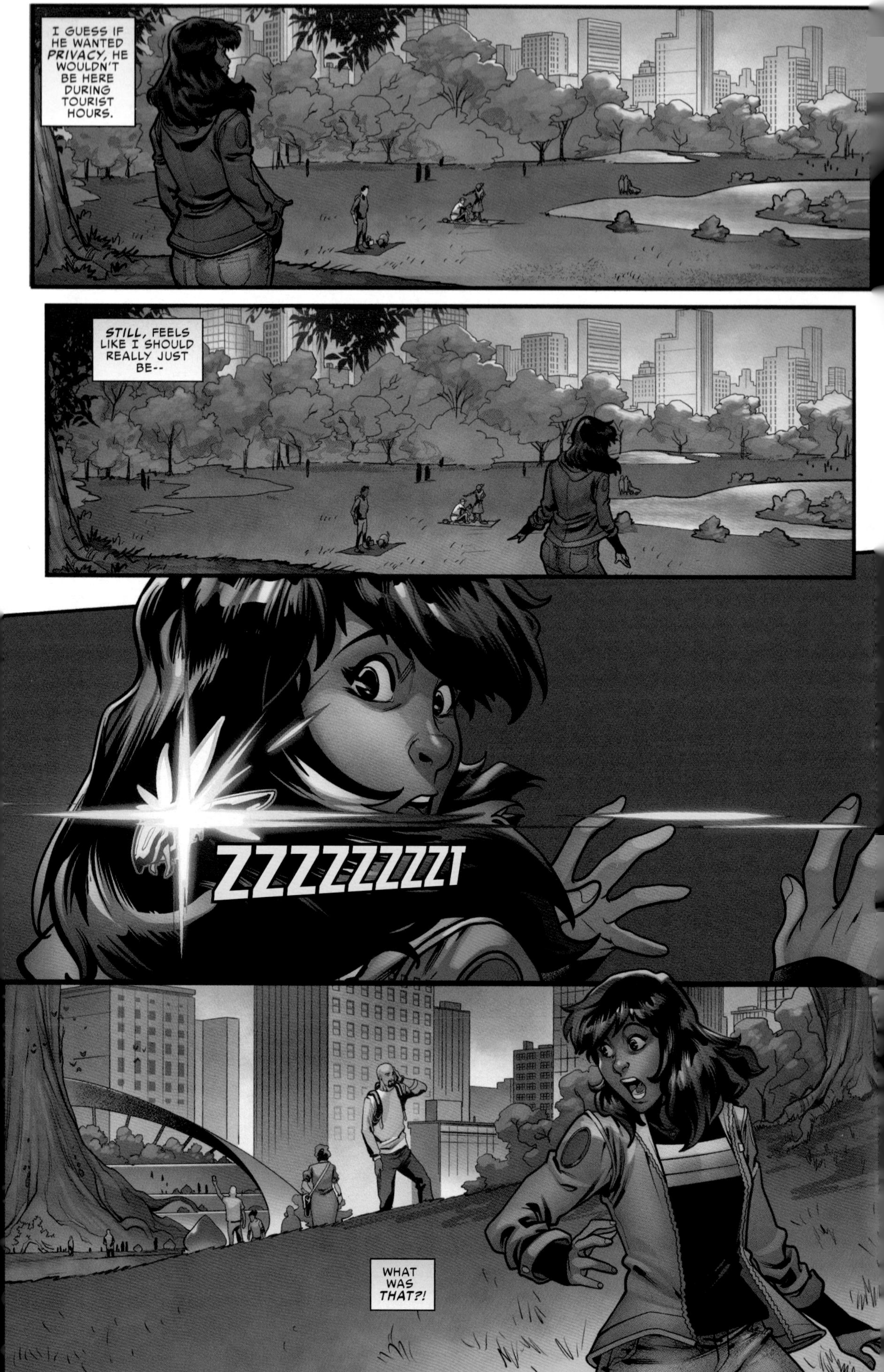
I GUESS IF HE WANTED PRIVACY, HE WOULDN'T BE HERE DURING TOURIST HOURS.
STILL, FEELS LIKE I SHOULD REALLY JUST BE--
ZZZZZZZZZT
WHAT WAS THAT?!

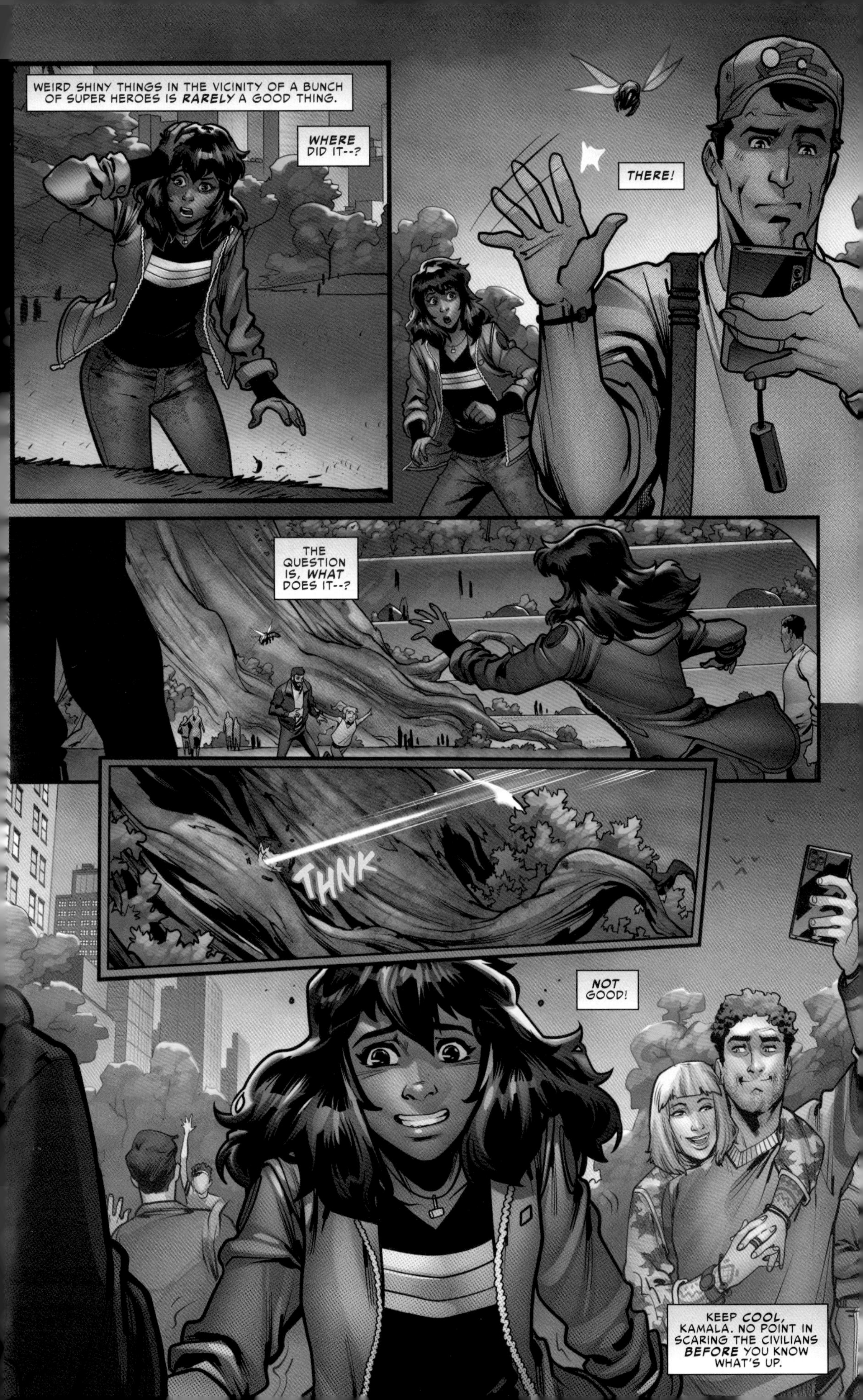
WEIRD SHINY THINGS IN THE VICINITY OF A BUNCH OF SUPER HEROES IS RARELY A GOOD THING.
WHERE DID IT--?
THERE!
THE QUESTION IS, WHAT DOES IT--?
THNK
NOT GOOD!
KEEP COOL, KAMALA. NO POINT IN SCARING THE CIVILIANS BEFORE YOU KNOW WHAT'S UP.

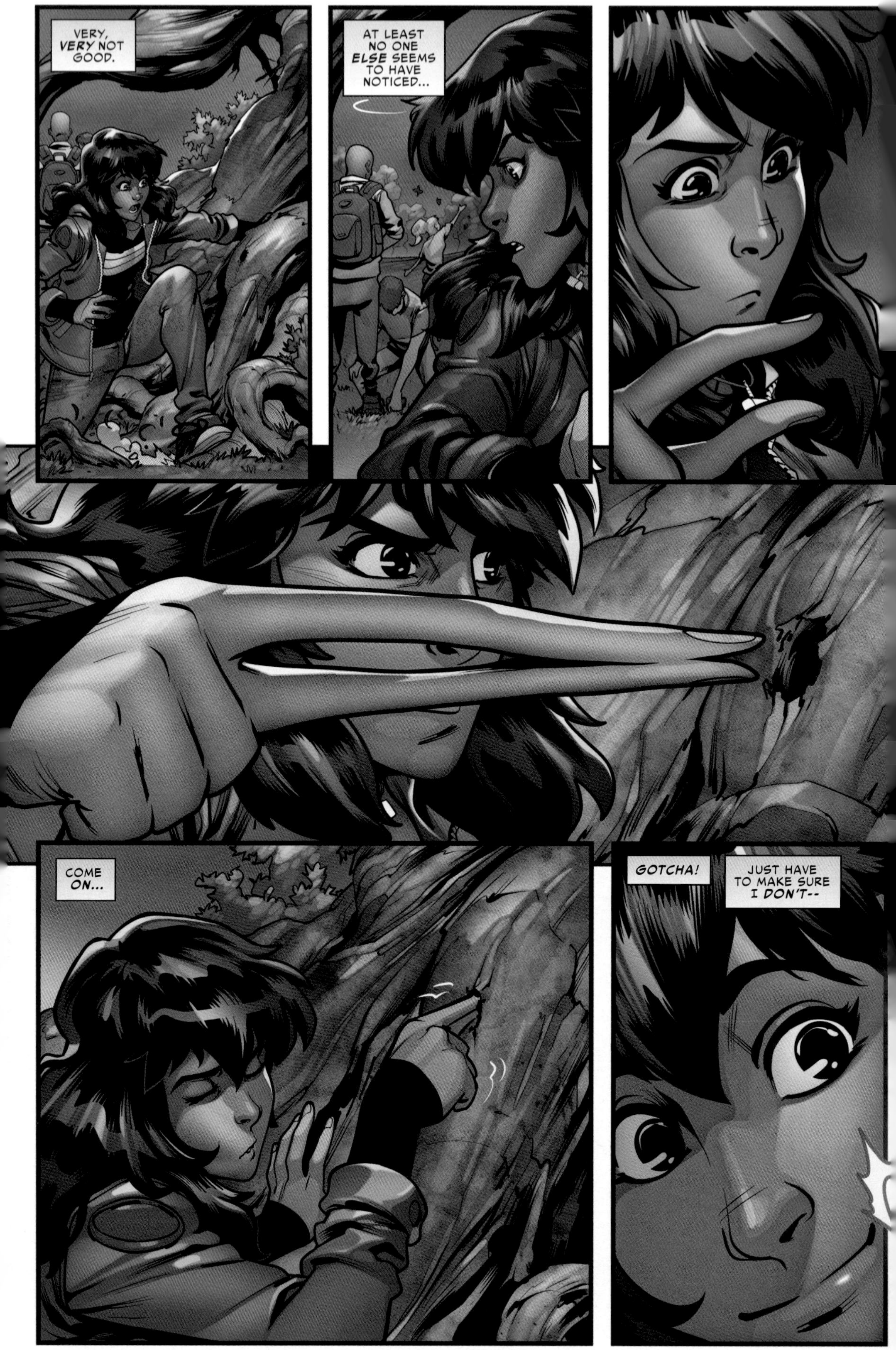
VERY, *VERY* NOT GOOD.
AT LEAST NO ONE *ELSE* SEEMS TO HAVE NOTICED...
COME *ON*...
GOTCHA!
JUST HAVE TO MAKE SURE I *DON'T*--

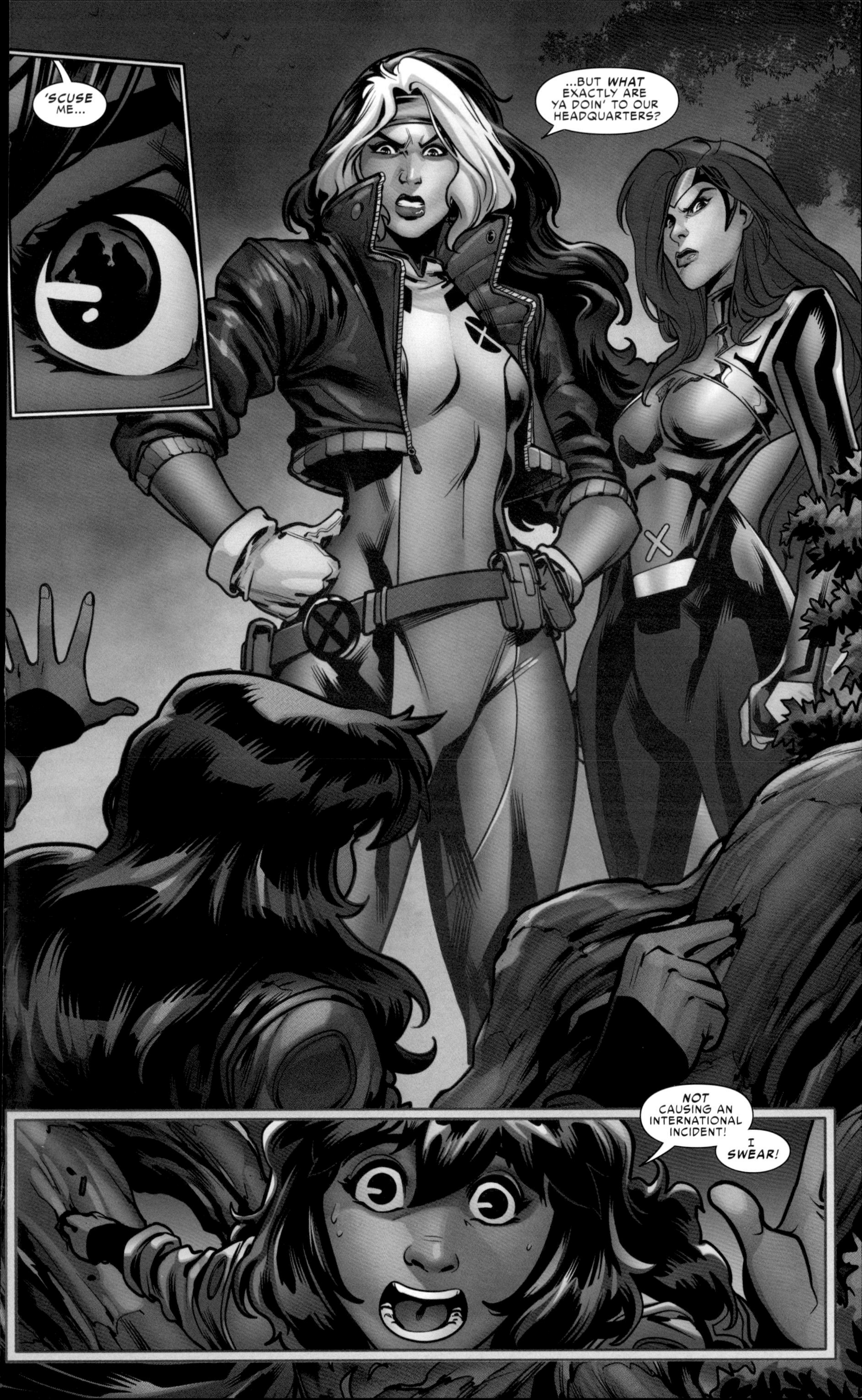
'SCUSE ME...
...BUT WHAT EXACTLY ARE YA DOIN' TO OUR HEADQUARTERS?
NOT CAUSING AN INTERNATIONAL INCIDENT!
I SWEAR!

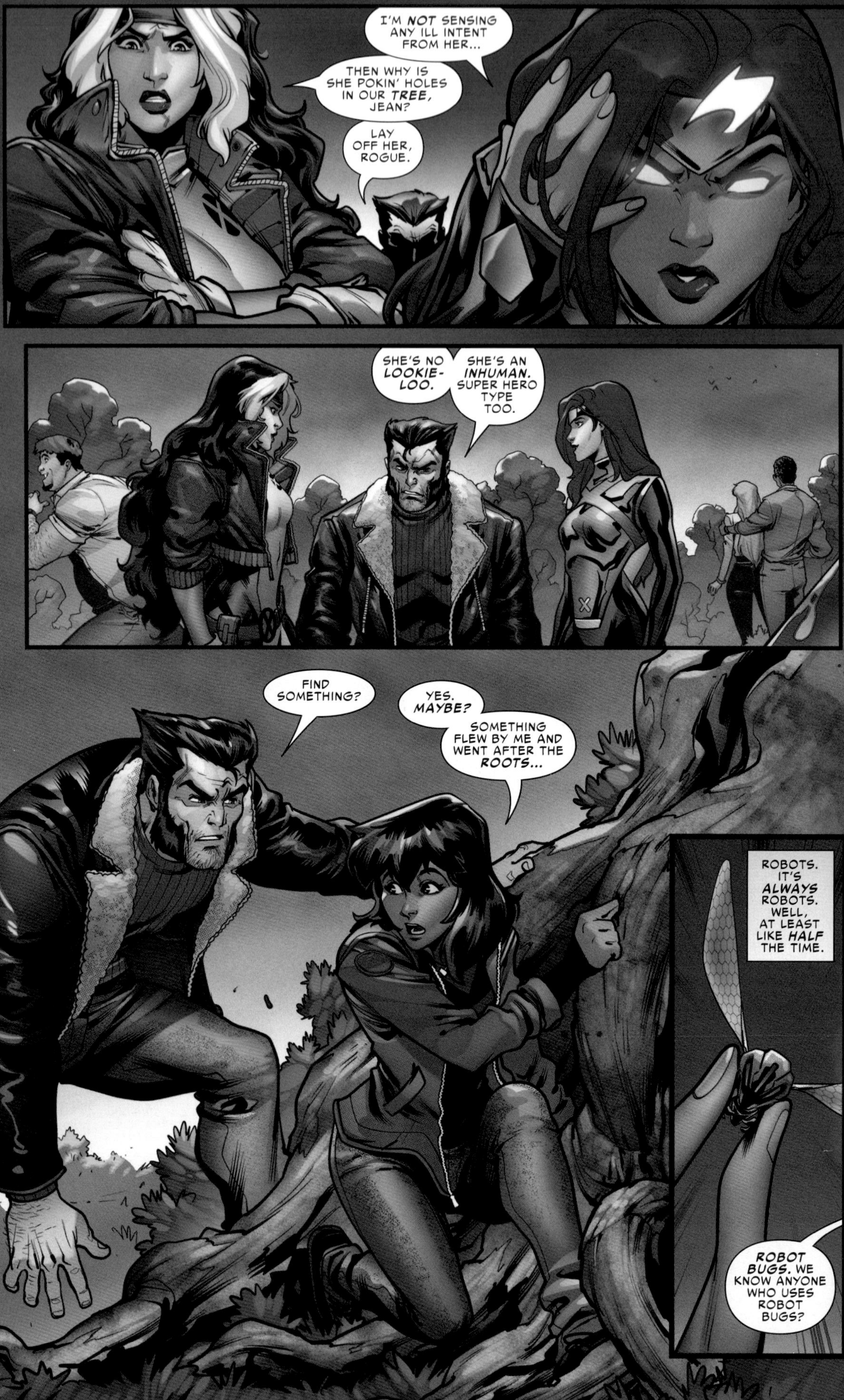
I'M NOT SENSING ANY ILL INTENT FROM HER...
THEN WHY IS SHE POKIN' HOLES IN OUR TREE, JEAN?
LAY OFF HER, ROGUE.
SHE'S NO LOOKIE-LOO.
SHE'S AN INHUMAN. SUPER HERO TYPE TOO.
FIND SOMETHING?
YES. MAYBE?
SOMETHING FLEW BY ME AND WENT AFTER THE ROOTS...
ROBOTS. IT'S ALWAYS ROBOTS. WELL, AT LEAST LIKE HALF THE TIME.
ROBOT BUGS. WE KNOW ANYONE WHO USES ROBOT BUGS?

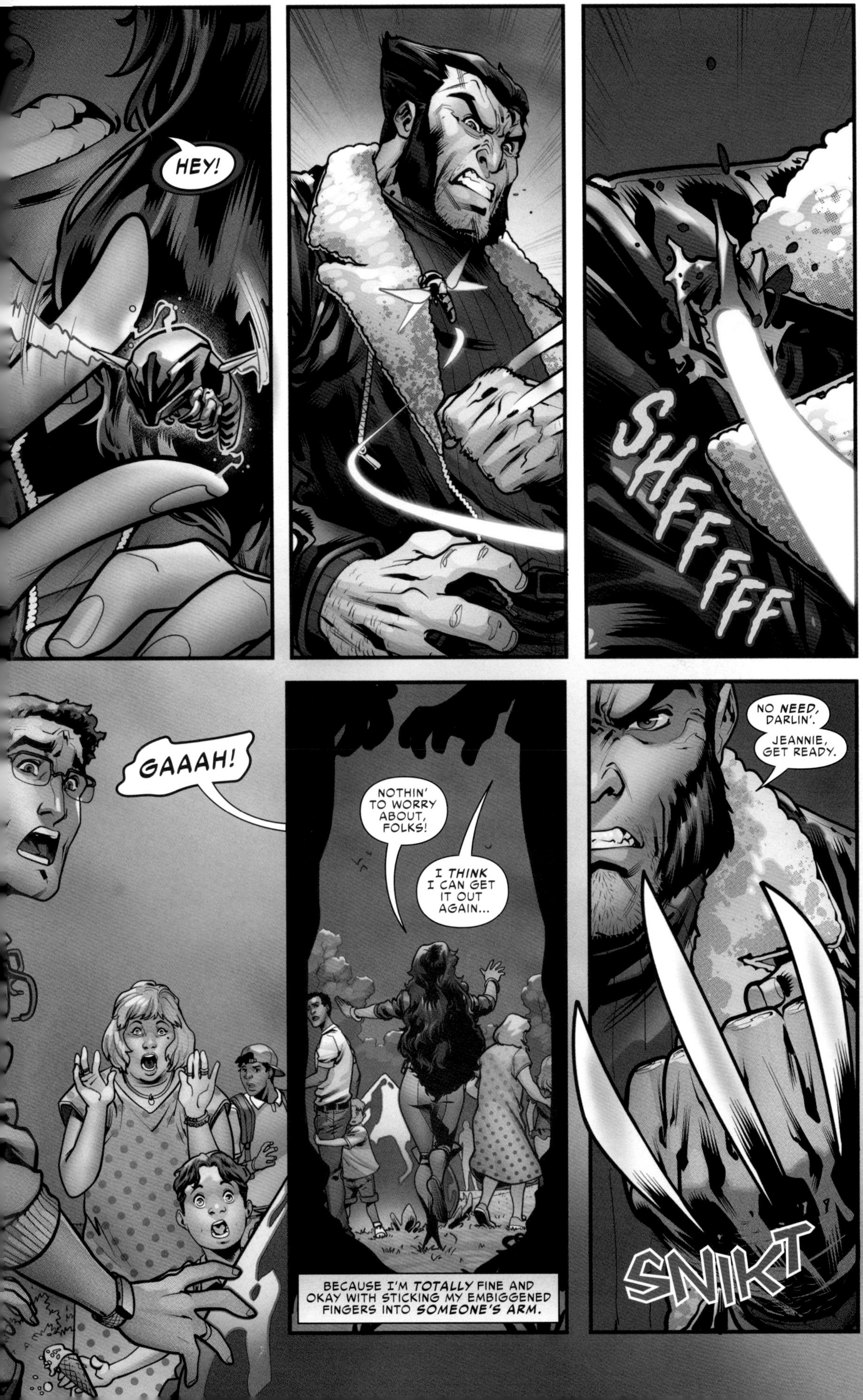
HEY!
SHFFFFFF
GAAAH!
NOTHIN' TO WORRY ABOUT, FOLKS!
I THINK I CAN GET IT OUT AGAIN...
BECAUSE I'M TOTALLY FINE AND OKAY WITH STICKING MY EMBIGGENED FINGERS INTO SOMEONE'S ARM.
NO NEED, DARLIN'.
JEANNIE, GET READY.
SNIKT

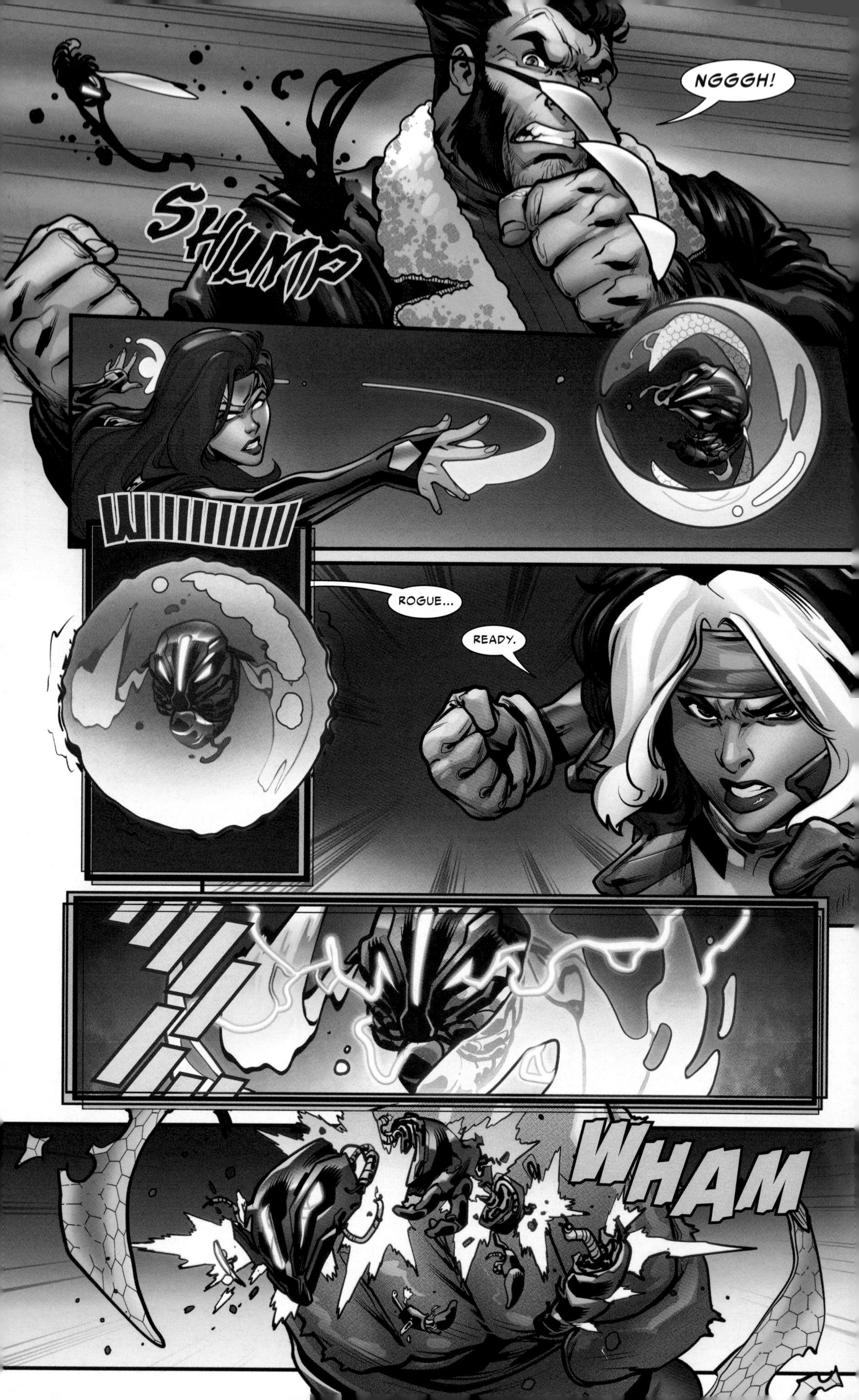
NGGGH!
SHLMP
WIIIIIIIIII
ROGUE...
READY.
WHAM

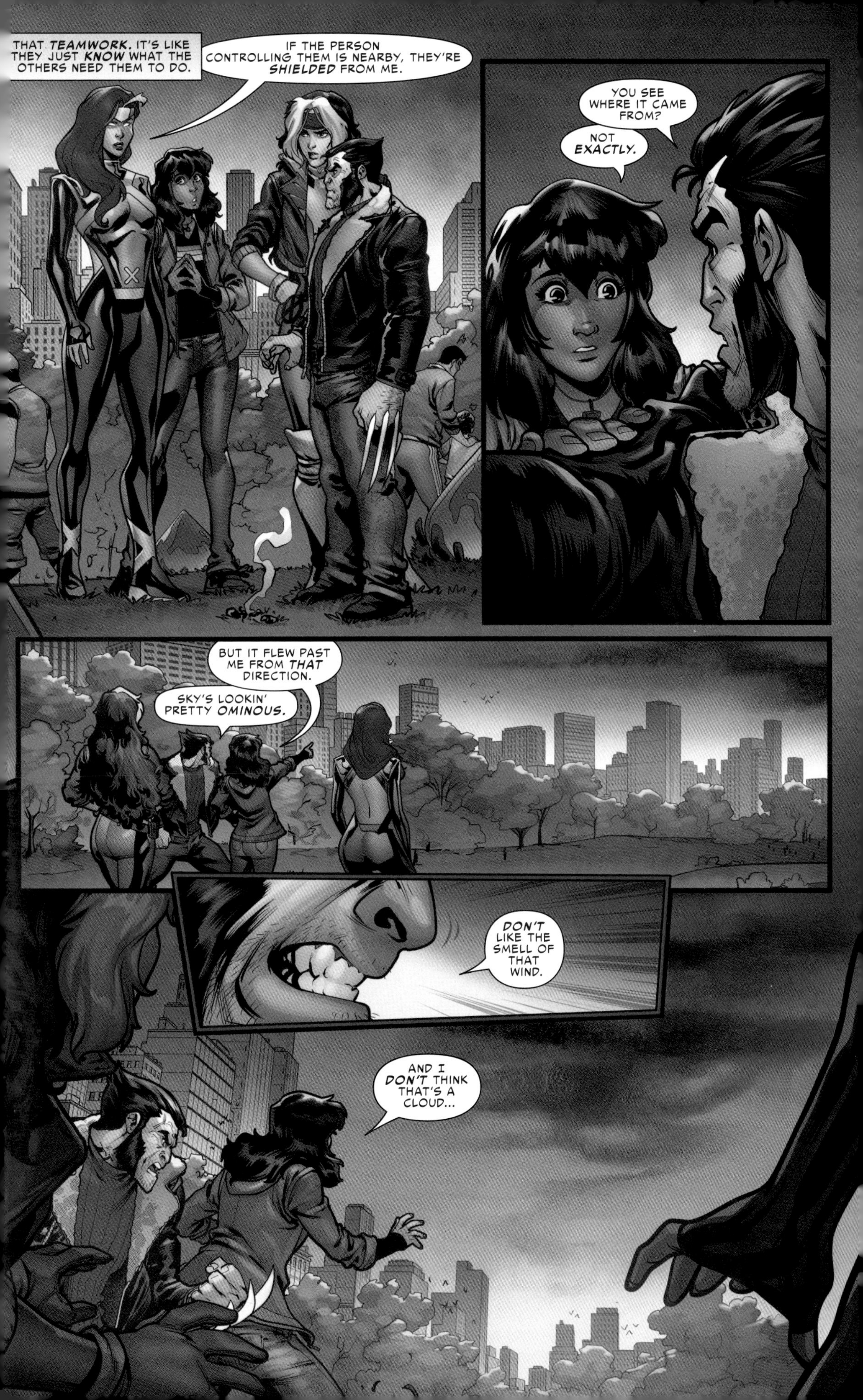
THAT TEAMWORK. IT'S LIKE THEY JUST KNOW WHAT THE OTHERS NEED THEM TO DO.
IF THE PERSON CONTROLLING THEM IS NEARBY, THEY'RE SHIELDED FROM ME.
YOU SEE WHERE IT CAME FROM?
NOT EXACTLY.
BUT IT FLEW PAST ME FROM THAT DIRECTION.
SKY'S LOOKIN' PRETTY OMINOUS.
DON'T LIKE THE SMELL OF THAT WIND.
AND I DON'T THINK THAT'S A CLOUD...

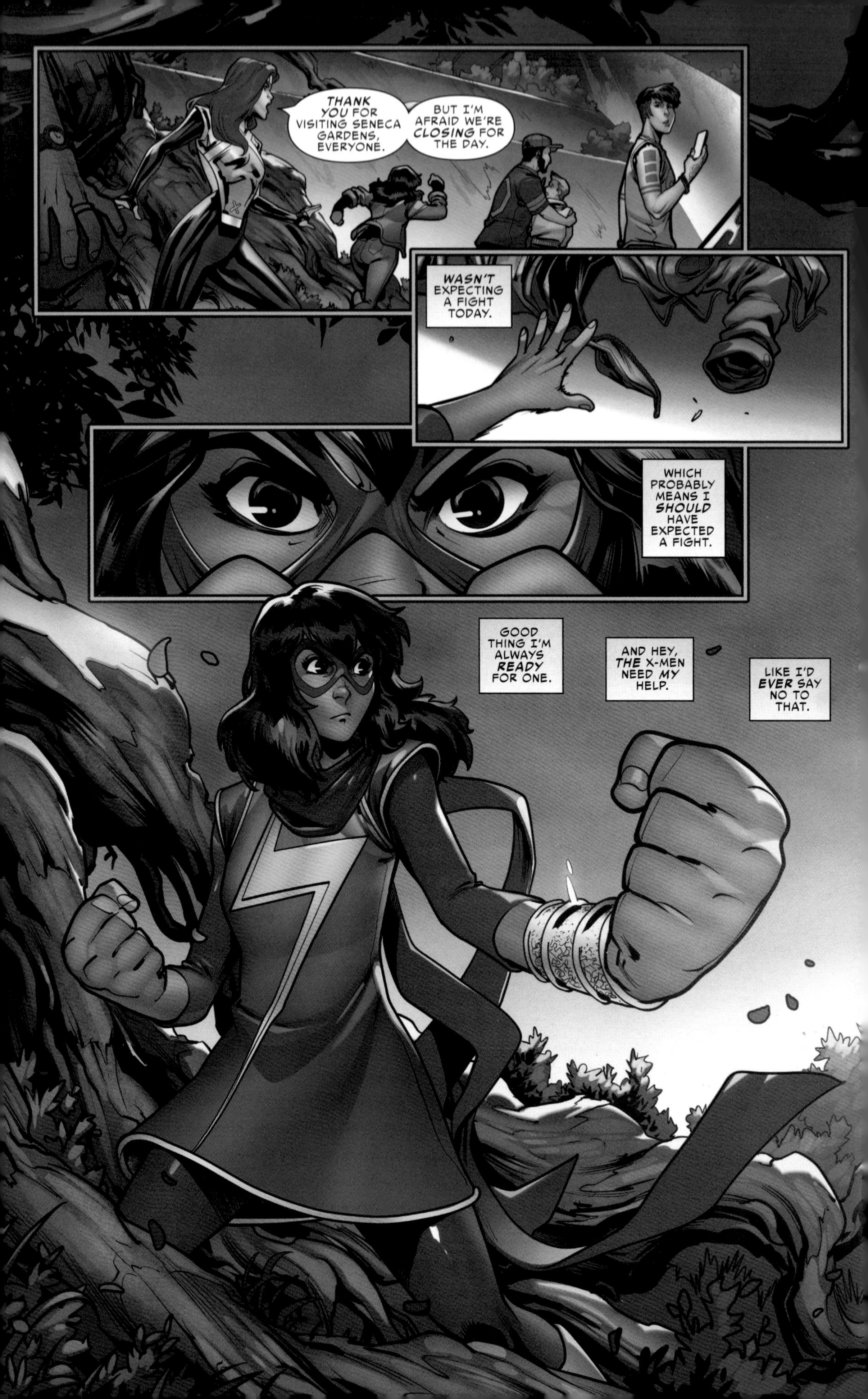

THANK YOU FOR VISITING SENECA GARDENS, EVERYONE.
BUT I'M AFRAID WE'RE CLOSING FOR THE DAY.
WASN'T EXPECTING A FIGHT TODAY.
WHICH PROBABLY MEANS I SHOULD HAVE EXPECTED A FIGHT.
GOOD THING I'M ALWAYS READY FOR ONE.
AND HEY, THE X-MEN NEED MY HELP.
LIKE I'D EVER SAY NO TO THAT.

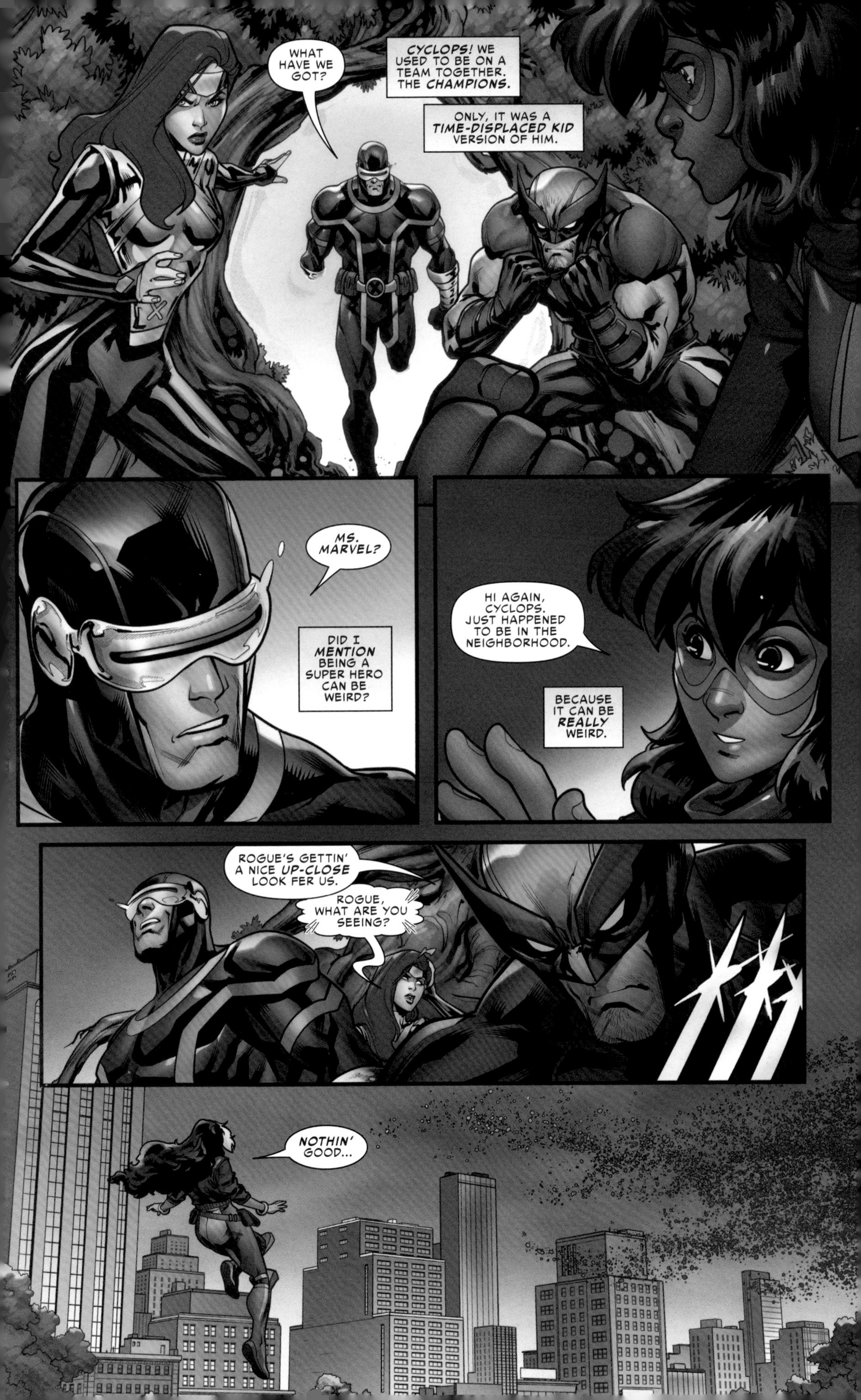

WHAT HAVE WE GOT?
CYCLOPS! WE USED TO BE ON A TEAM TOGETHER. THE CHAMPIONS.
ONLY, IT WAS A TIME-DISPLACED KID VERSION OF HIM.
MS. MARVEL?
DID I MENTION BEING A SUPER HERO CAN BE WEIRD?
HI AGAIN, CYCLOPS. JUST HAPPENED TO BE IN THE NEIGHBORHOOD.
BECAUSE IT CAN BE REALLY WEIRD.
ROGUE'S GETTIN' A NICE UP-CLOSE LOOK FER US.
ROGUE, WHAT ARE YOU SEEING?
NOTHIN' GOOD...

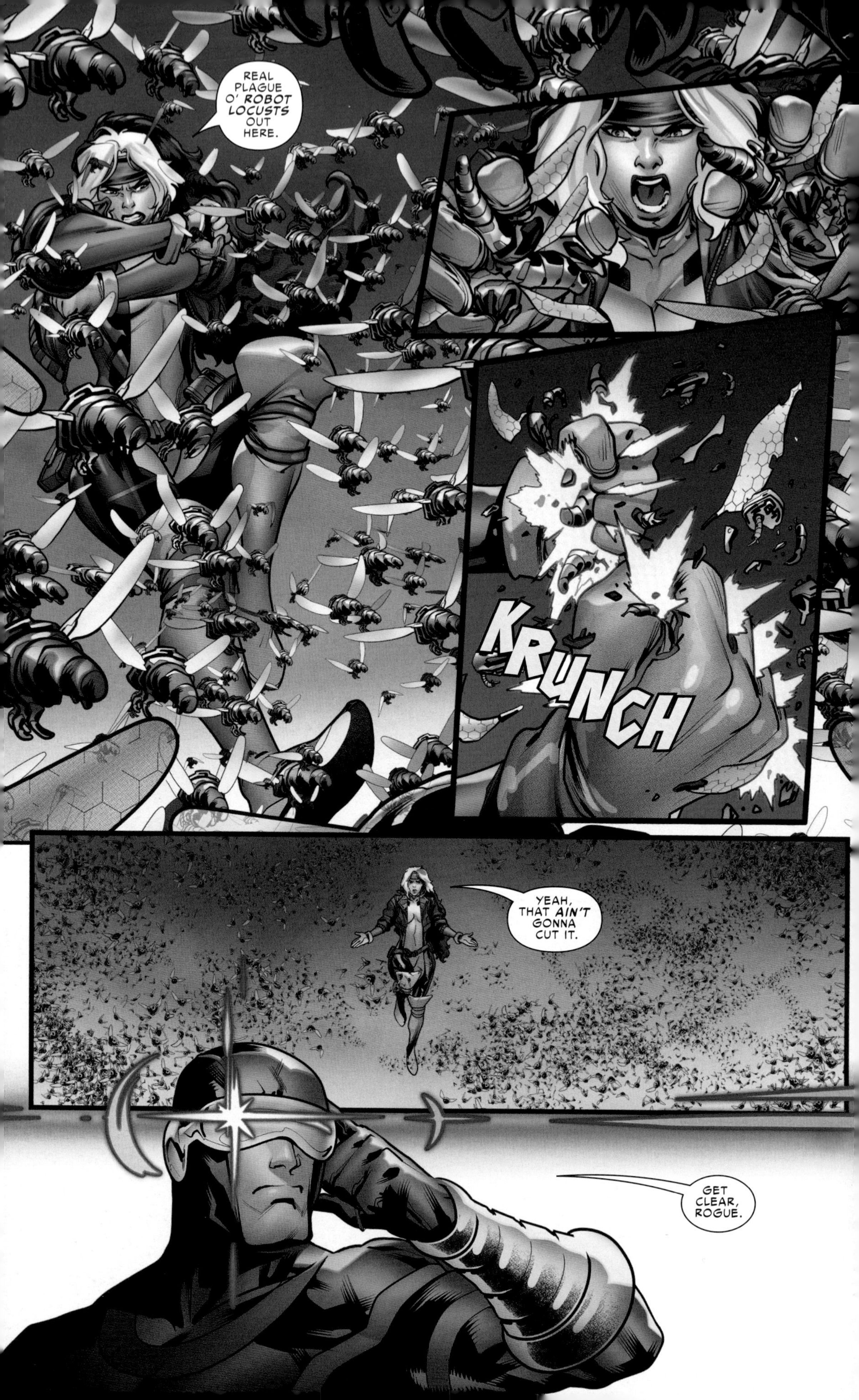
REAL PLAGUE O' ROBOT LOCUSTS OUT HERE.
KRUNCH
YEAH, THAT AIN'T GONNA CUT IT.
GET CLEAR, ROGUE.

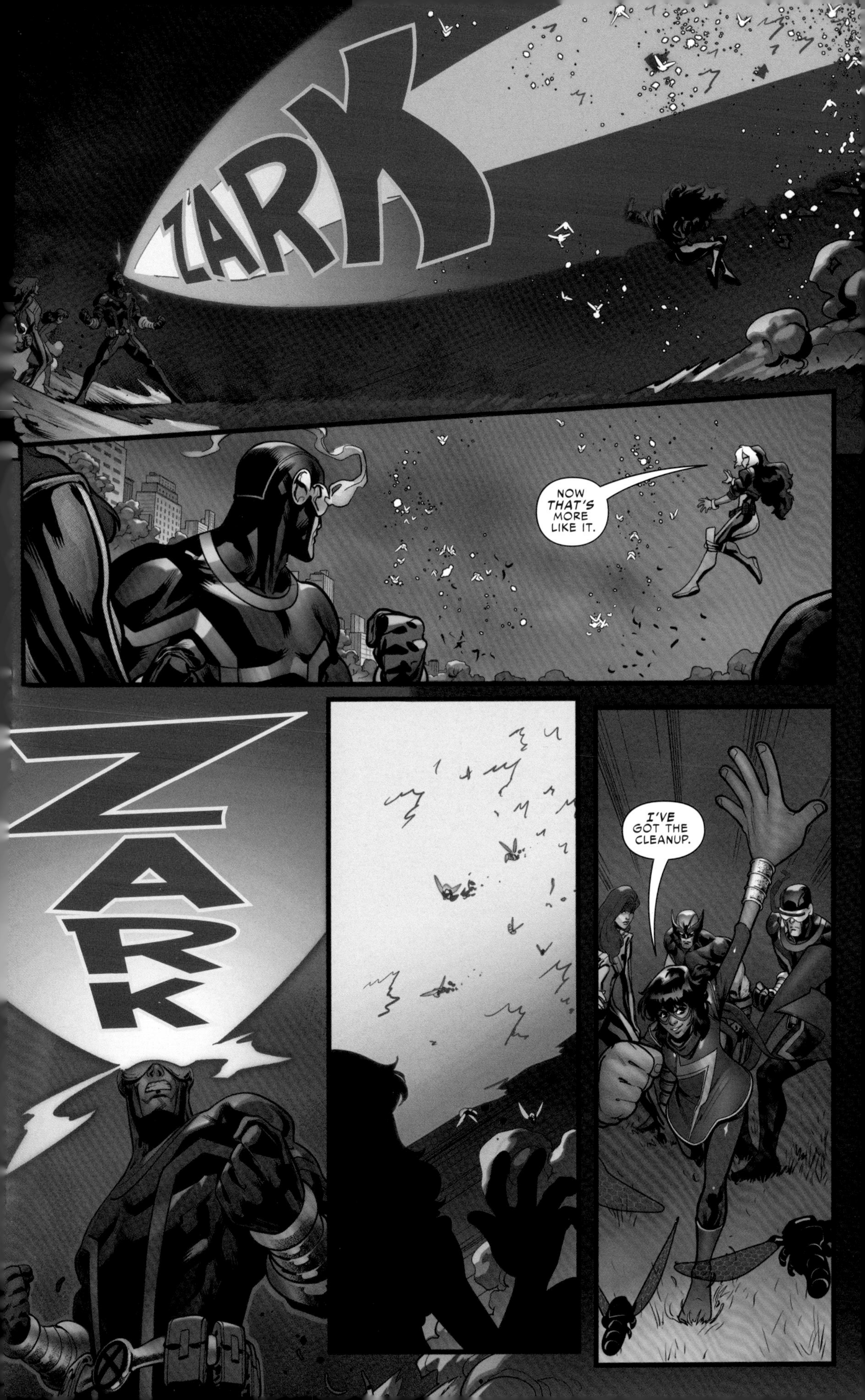
ZARK
NOW THAT'S MORE LIKE IT.
ZARK
I'VE GOT THE CLEANUP.

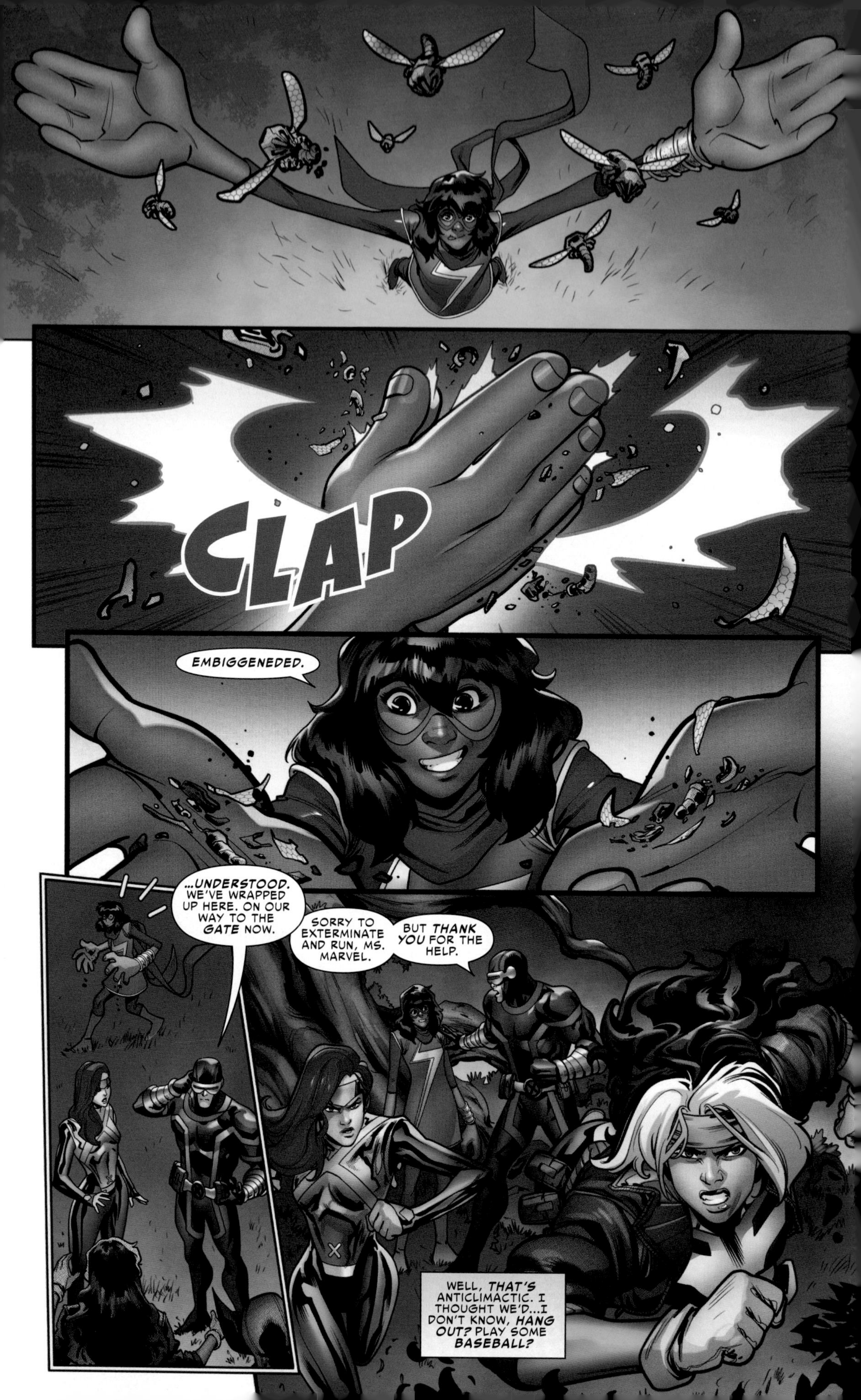

CLAP
EMBIGGENEDED.
...UNDERSTOOD. WE'VE WRAPPED UP HERE. ON OUR WAY TO THE GATE NOW.
SORRY TO EXTERMINATE AND RUN, MS. MARVEL.
BUT THANK YOU FOR THE HELP.
WELL, THAT'S ANTICLIMACTIC. I THOUGHT WE'D...I DON'T KNOW, HANG OUT? PLAY SOME BASEBALL?

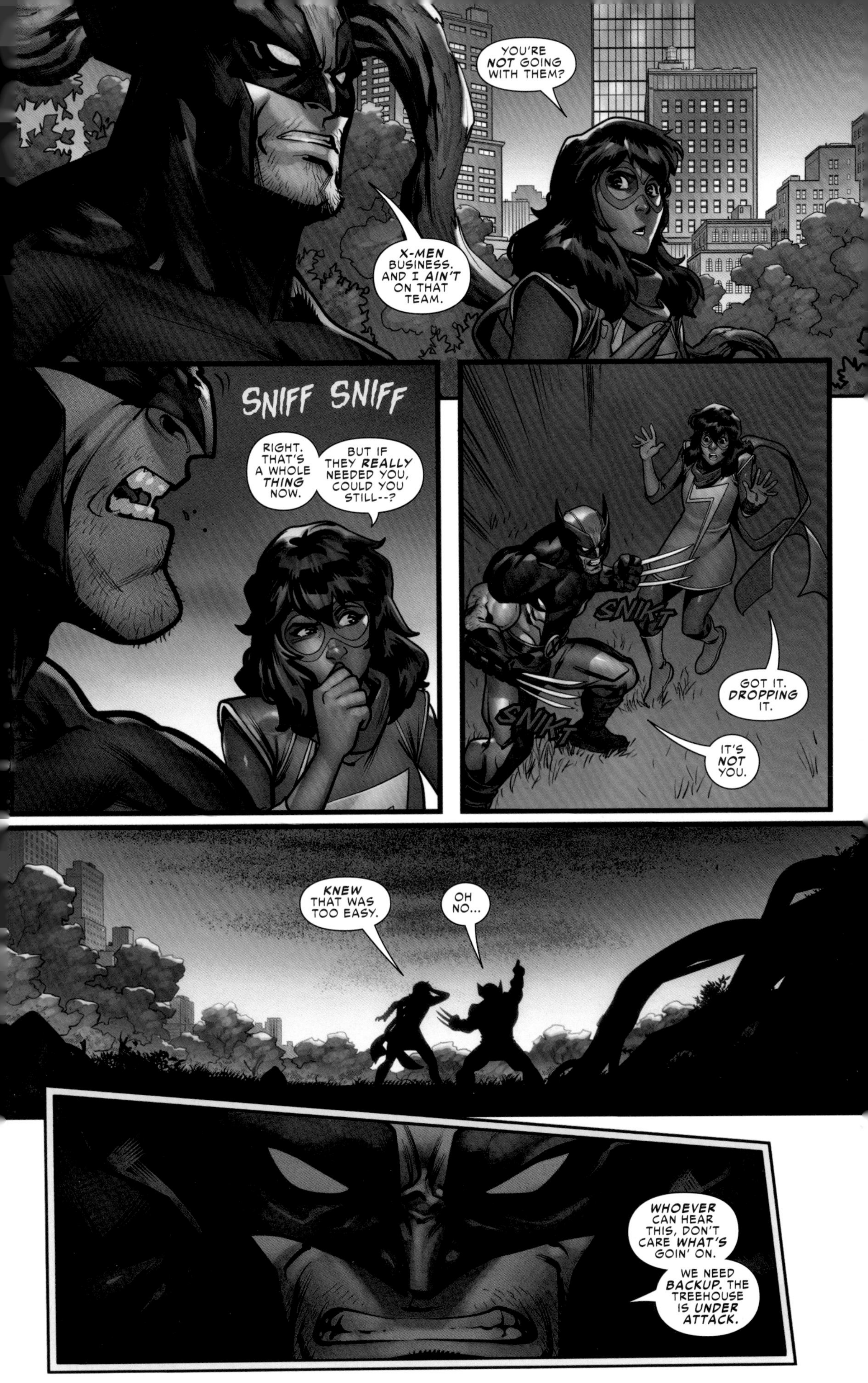
YOU'RE NOT GOING WITH THEM?
X-MEN BUSINESS. AND I AIN'T ON THAT TEAM.
SNIFF SNIFF
RIGHT. THAT'S A WHOLE THING NOW.
BUT IF THEY REALLY NEEDED YOU, COULD YOU STILL--?
SNIKT
SNIKT
GOT IT. DROPPING IT.
IT'S NOT YOU.
KNEW THAT WAS TOO EASY.
OH NO...
WHOEVER CAN HEAR THIS, DON'T CARE WHAT'S GOIN' ON.
WE NEED BACKUP. THE TREEHOUSE IS UNDER ATTACK.

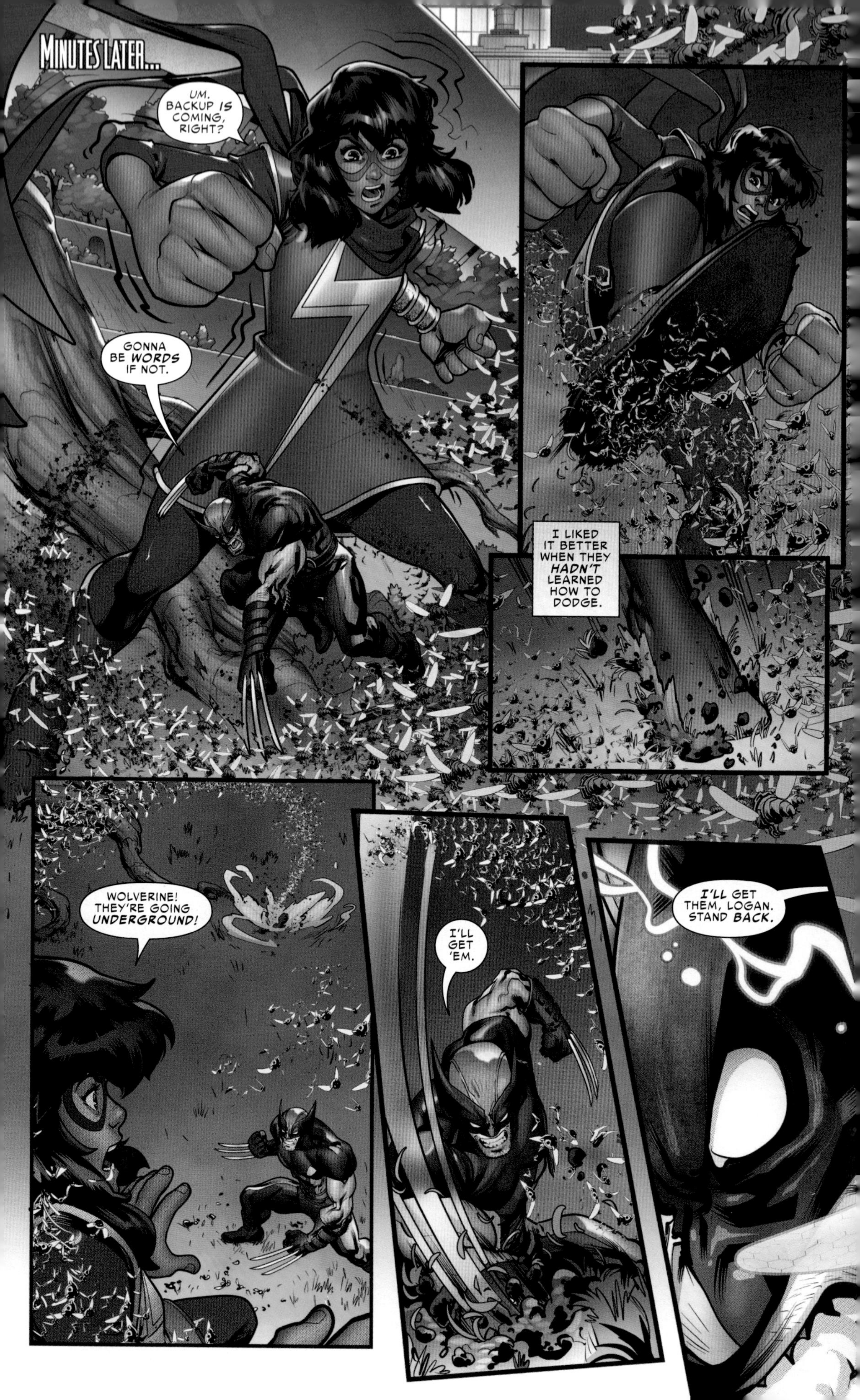
MINUTES LATER...
UM. BACKUP IS COMING, RIGHT?
GONNA BE WORDS IF NOT.
I LIKED IT BETTER WHEN THEY HADN'T LEARNED HOW TO DODGE.
WOLVERINE! THEY'RE GOING UNDERGROUND!
I'LL GET 'EM.
I'LL GET THEM, LOGAN. STAND BACK.

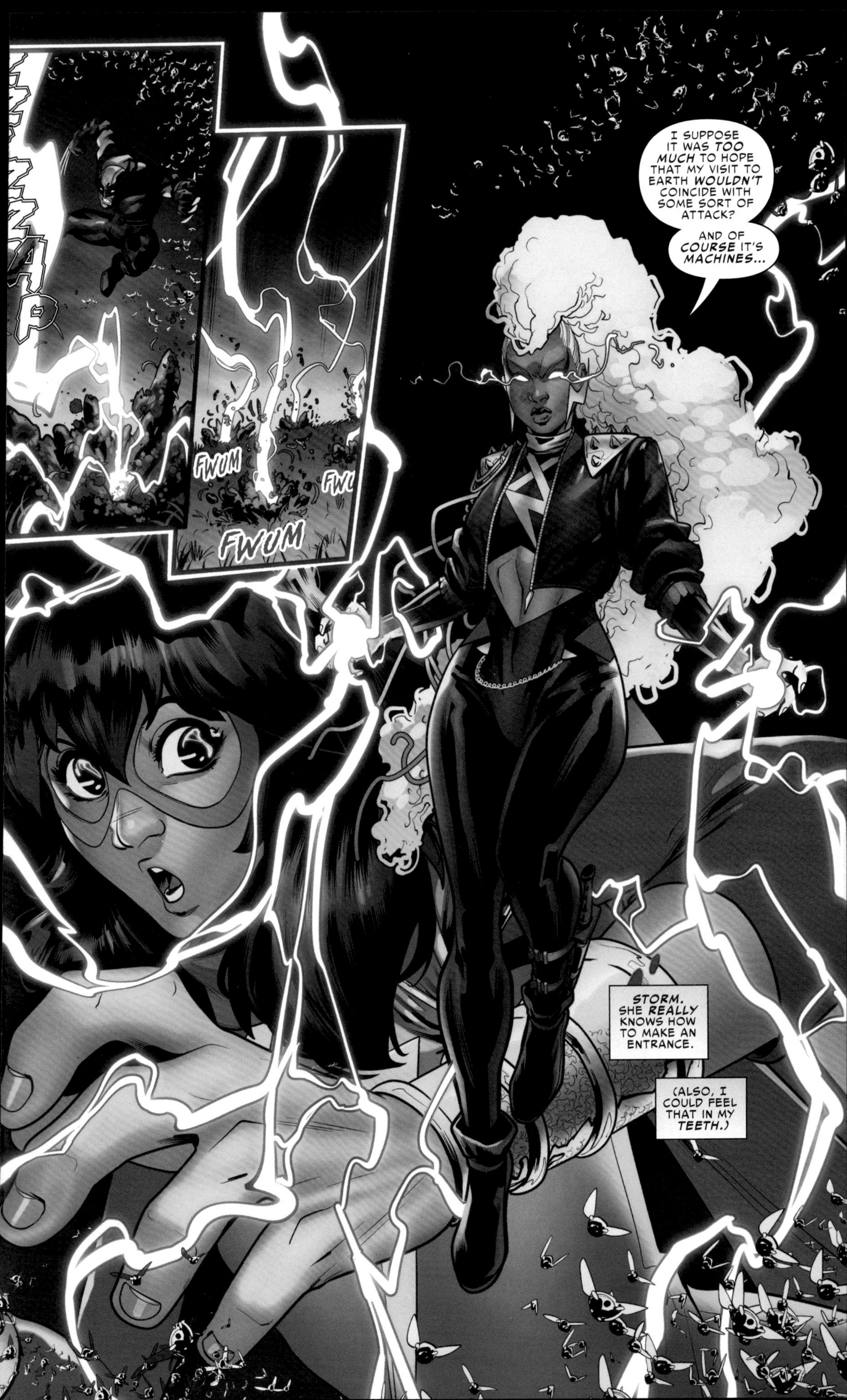
FWUM
FWUM
I SUPPOSE IT WAS TOO MUCH TO HOPE THAT MY VISIT TO EARTH WOULDN'T COINCIDE WITH SOME SORT OF ATTACK?
AND OF COURSE IT'S MACHINES...
STORM. SHE REALLY KNOWS HOW TO MAKE AN ENTRANCE.
(ALSO, I COULD FEEL THAT IN MY TEETH.)

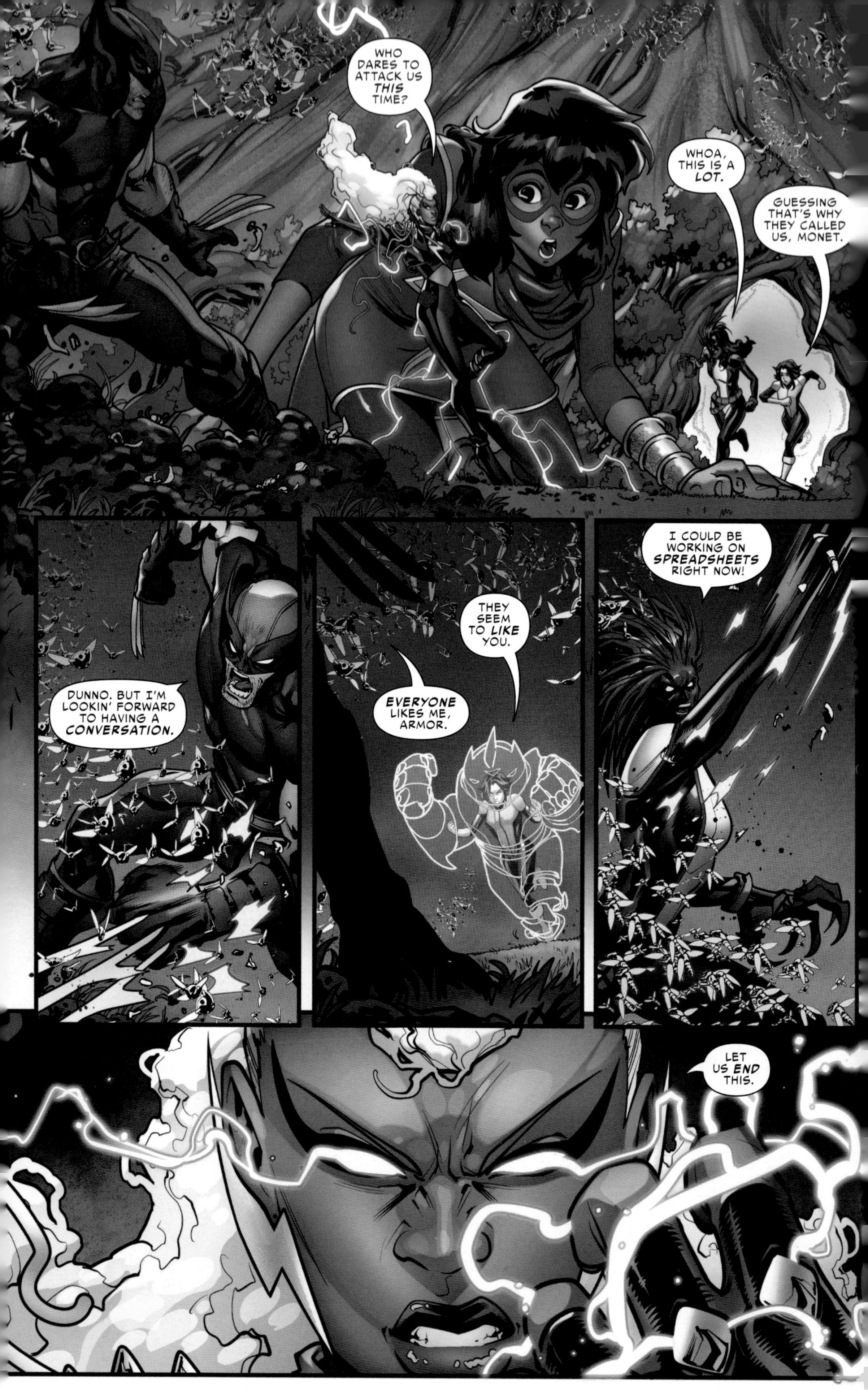
WHO DARES TO ATTACK US THIS TIME?
WHOA, THIS IS A LOT.
GUESSING THAT'S WHY THEY CALLED US, MONET.
DUNNO. BUT I'M LOOKIN' FORWARD TO HAVING A CONVERSATION.
THEY SEEM TO LIKE YOU.
EVERYONE LIKES ME, ARMOR.
I COULD BE WORKING ON SPREADSHEETS RIGHT NOW!
LET US END THIS.

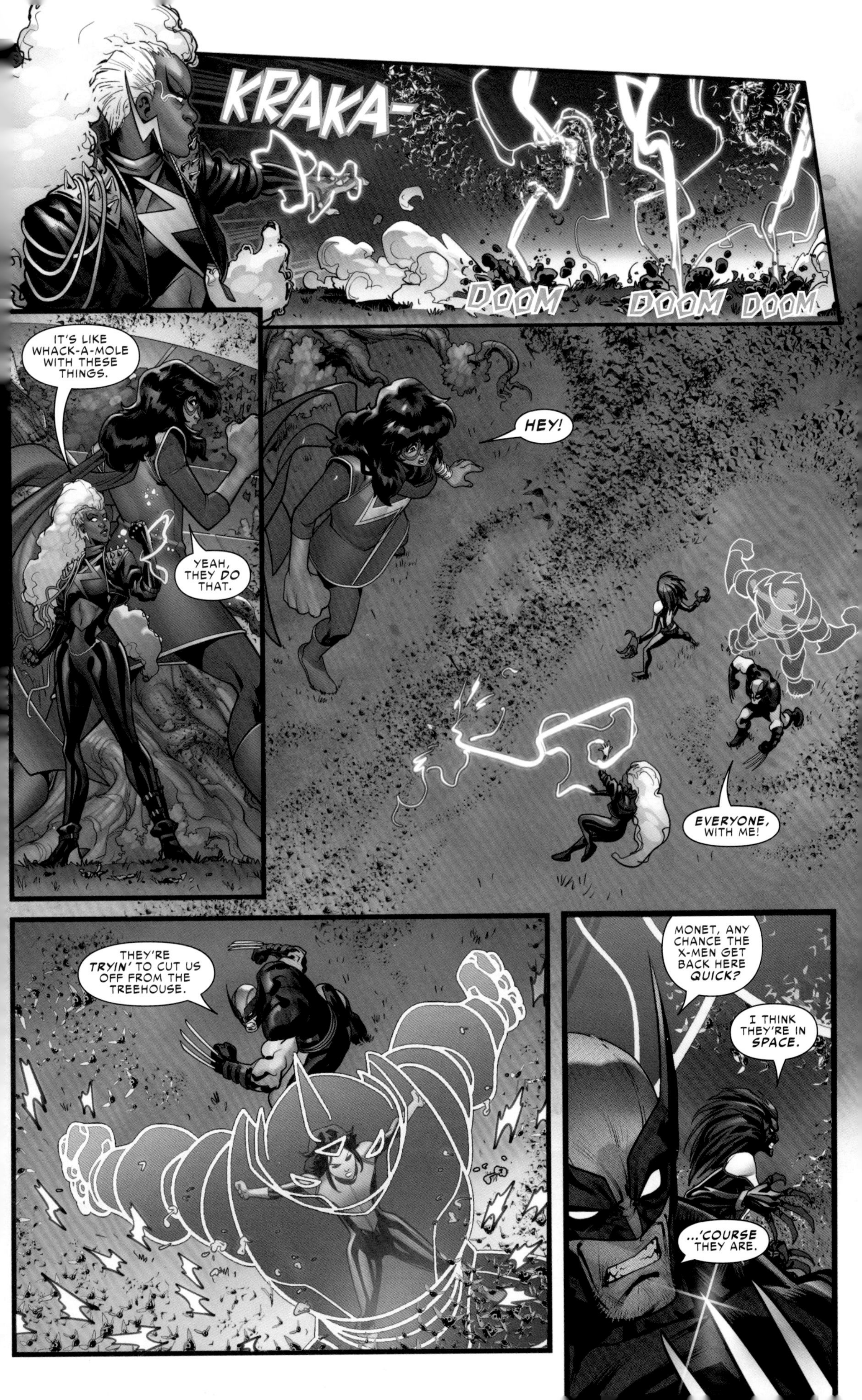
KRAKA-
DOOM
DOOM
DOOM
IT'S LIKE WHACK-A-MOLE WITH THESE THINGS.
YEAH, THEY DO THAT.
HEY!
EVERYONE, WITH ME!
THEY'RE TRYIN' TO CUT US OFF FROM THE TREEHOUSE.
MONET, ANY CHANCE THE X-MEN GET BACK HERE QUICK?
I THINK THEY'RE IN SPACE.
...'COURSE THEY ARE.

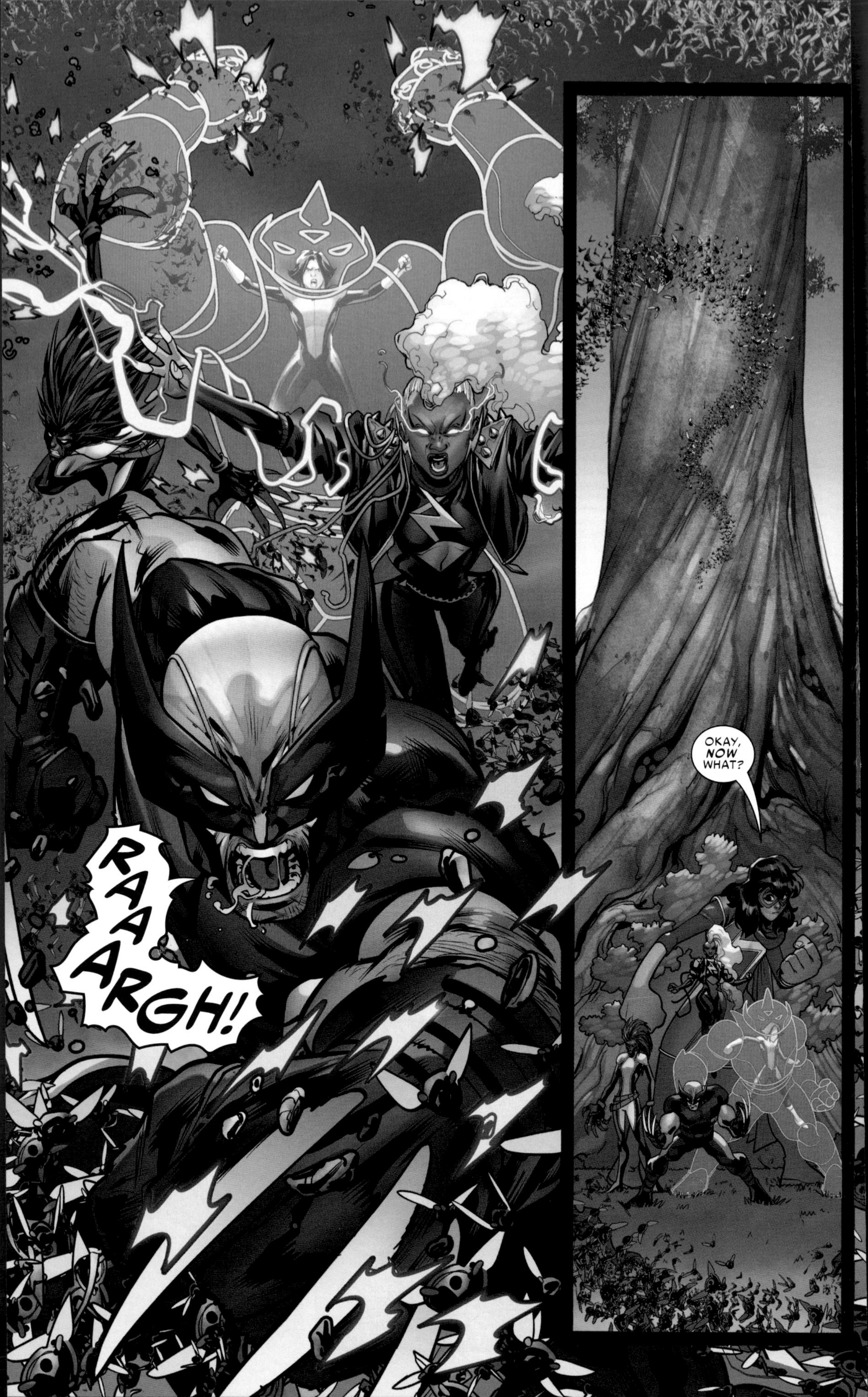
RAAAARGH!
OKAY, NOW WHAT?

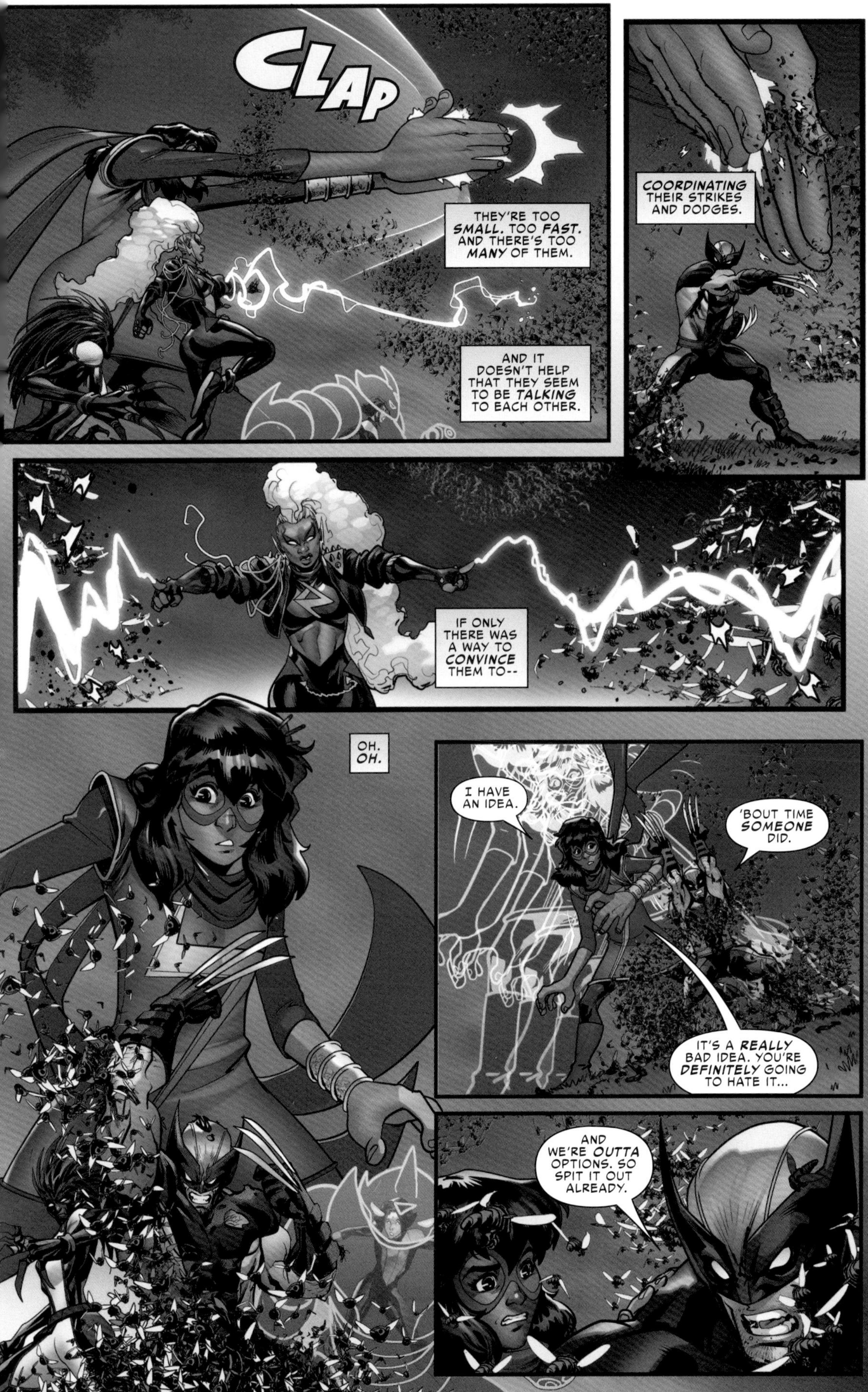
CLAP
THEY'RE TOO SMALL. TOO FAST. AND THERE'S TOO MANY OF THEM.
AND IT DOESN'T HELP THAT THEY SEEM TO BE TALKING TO EACH OTHER.
COORDINATING THEIR STRIKES AND DODGES.
IF ONLY THERE WAS A WAY TO CONVINCE THEM TO--
OH. OH.
I HAVE AN IDEA.
'BOUT TIME SOMEONE DID.
IT'S A REALLY BAD IDEA. YOU'RE DEFINITELY GOING TO HATE IT...
AND WE'RE OUTTA OPTIONS. SO SPIT IT OUT ALREADY.

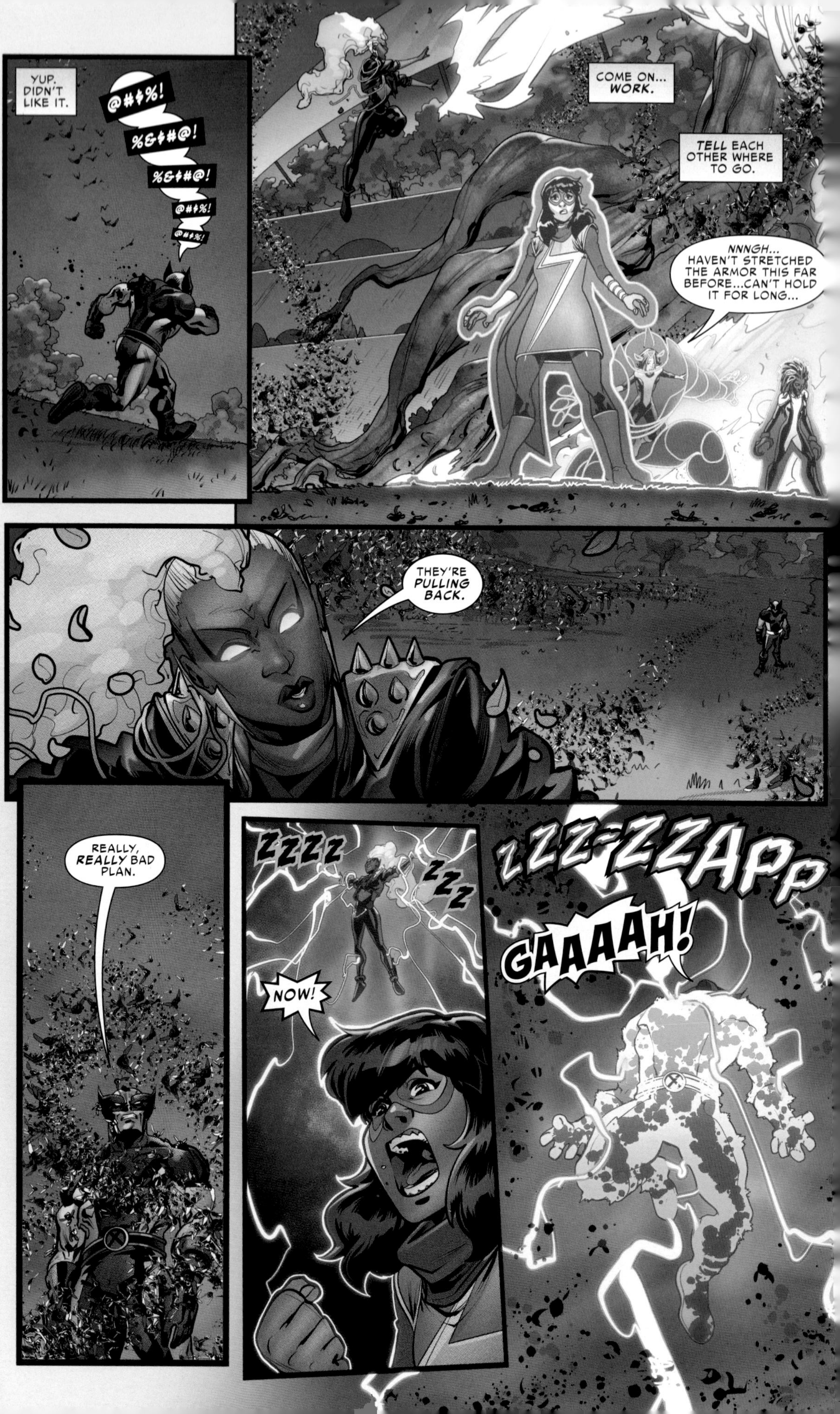
YUP. DIDN'T LIKE IT.
@#$%! %&$#@! %&$#@! @#$%! @#$%!
COME ON... WORK.
TELL EACH OTHER WHERE TO GO.
NNNGH... HAVEN'T STRETCHED THE ARMOR THIS FAR BEFORE...CAN'T HOLD IT FOR LONG...
THEY'RE PULLING BACK.
REALLY, REALLY BAD PLAN.
ZZZZ
ZZZ
NOW!
ZZZ-ZZZAPP
GAAAAH!

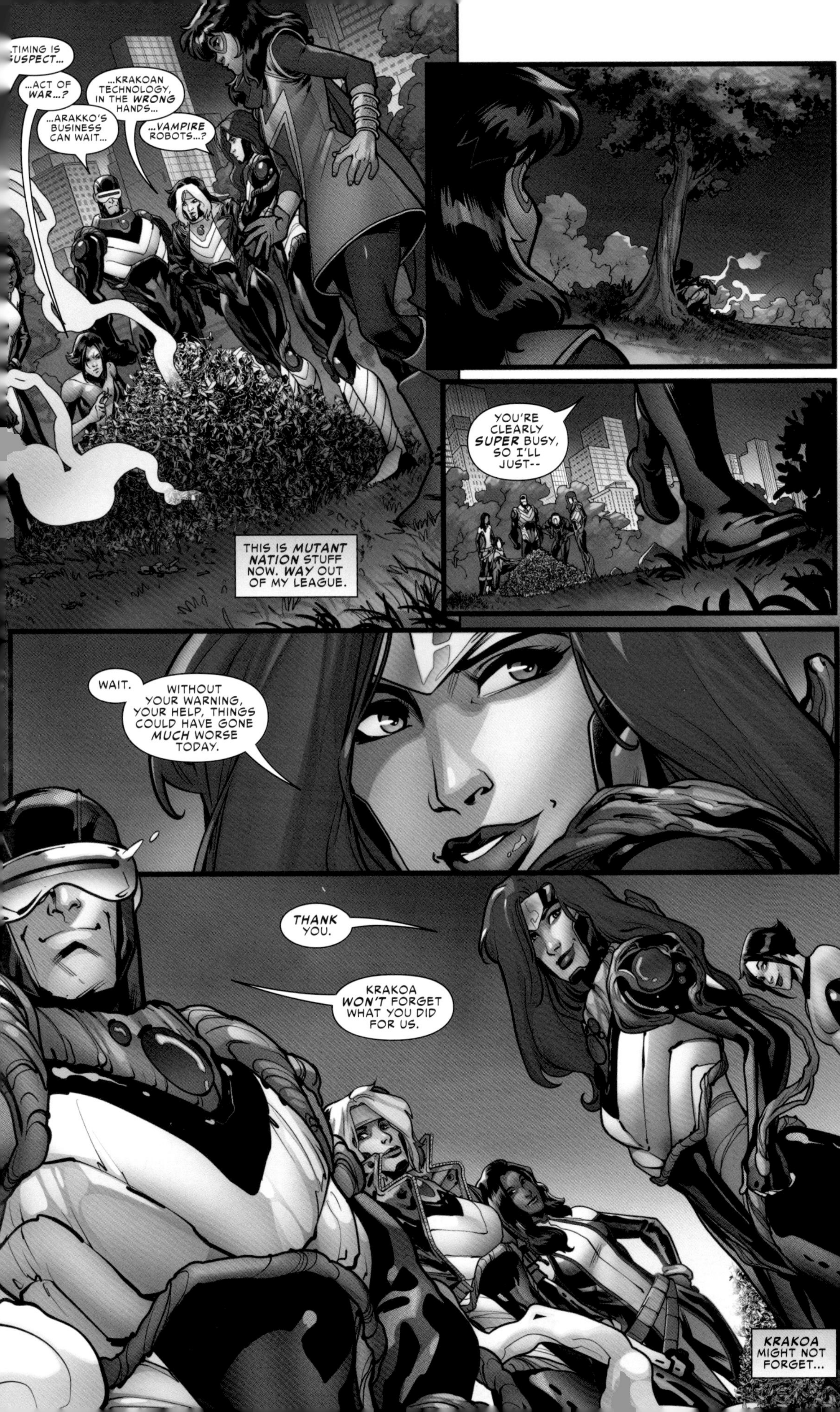
TIMING IS SUSPECT...
...ACT OF WAR...?
...KRAKOAN TECHNOLOGY, IN THE WRONG HANDS...
...ARAKKO'S BUSINESS CAN WAIT...
...VAMPIRE ROBOTS...?
THIS IS MUTANT NATION STUFF NOW. WAY OUT OF MY LEAGUE.
YOU'RE CLEARLY SUPER BUSY, SO I'LL JUST--
WAIT.
WITHOUT YOUR WARNING, YOUR HELP, THINGS COULD HAVE GONE MUCH WORSE TODAY.
THANK YOU.
KRAKOA WON'T FORGET WHAT YOU DID FOR US.
KRAKOA MIGHT NOT FORGET...

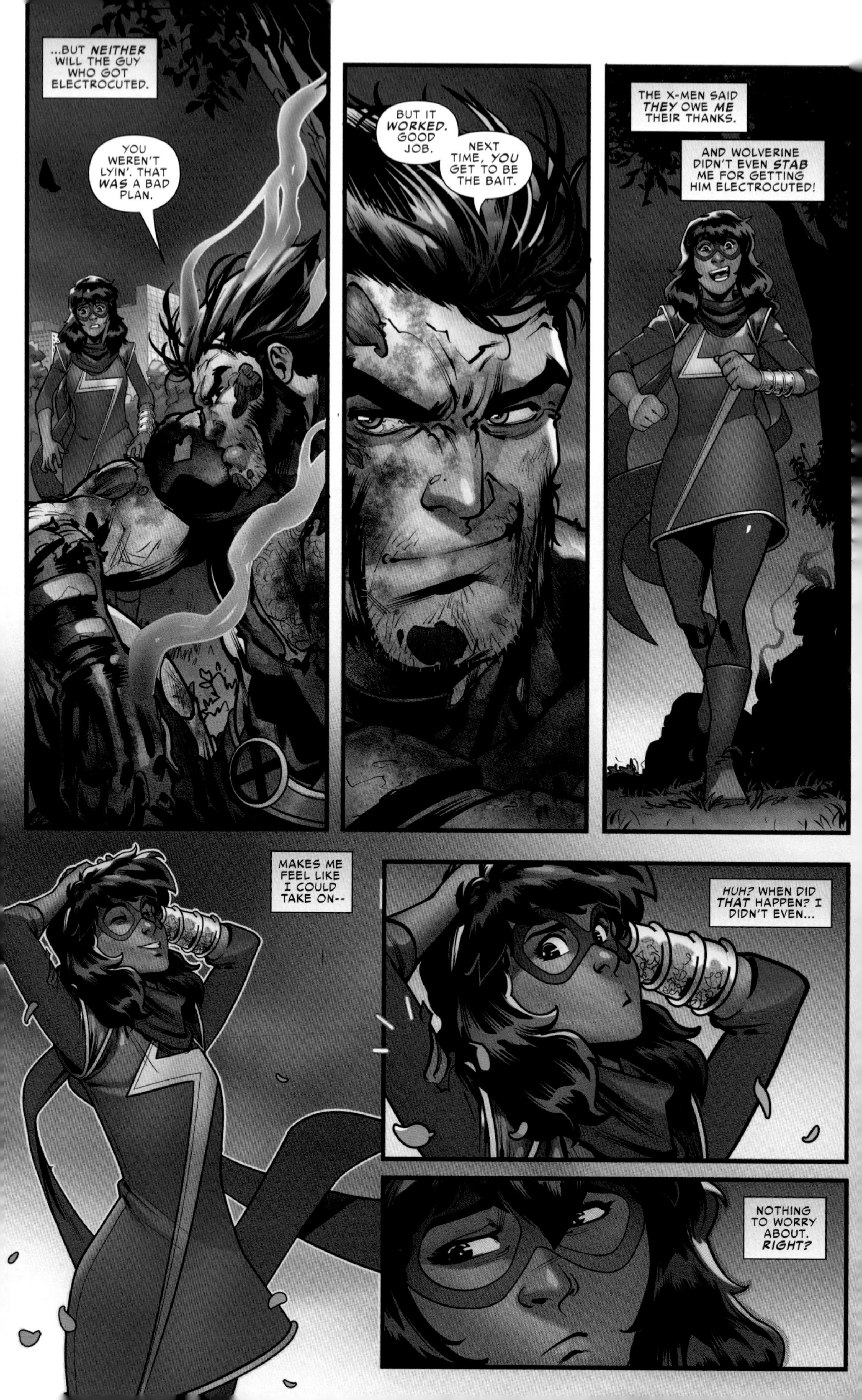

...BUT NEITHER WILL THE GUY WHO GOT ELECTROCUTED.
YOU WEREN'T LYIN'. THAT WAS A BAD PLAN.
BUT IT WORKED. GOOD JOB.
NEXT TIME, YOU GET TO BE THE BAIT.
THE X-MEN SAID THEY OWE ME THEIR THANKS.
AND WOLVERINE DIDN'T EVEN STAB ME FOR GETTING HIM ELECTROCUTED!
MAKES ME FEEL LIKE I COULD TAKE ON--
HUH? WHEN DID THAT HAPPEN? I DIDN'T EVEN...
NOTHING TO WORRY ABOUT. RIGHT?

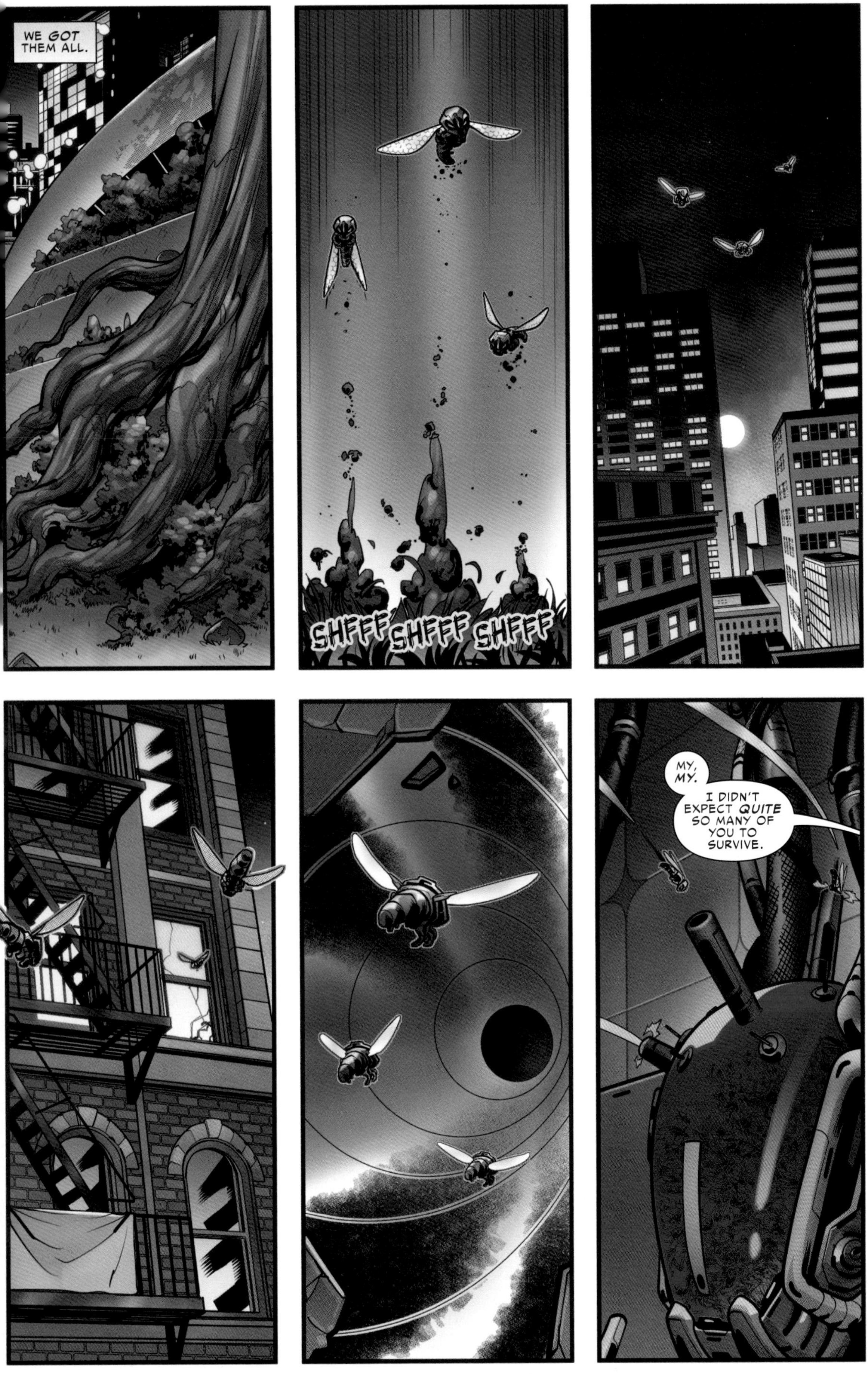
WE GOT THEM ALL.
SHFFF SHFFF SHFFF
MY, MY.
I DIDN'T EXPECT QUITE SO MANY OF YOU TO SURVIVE.

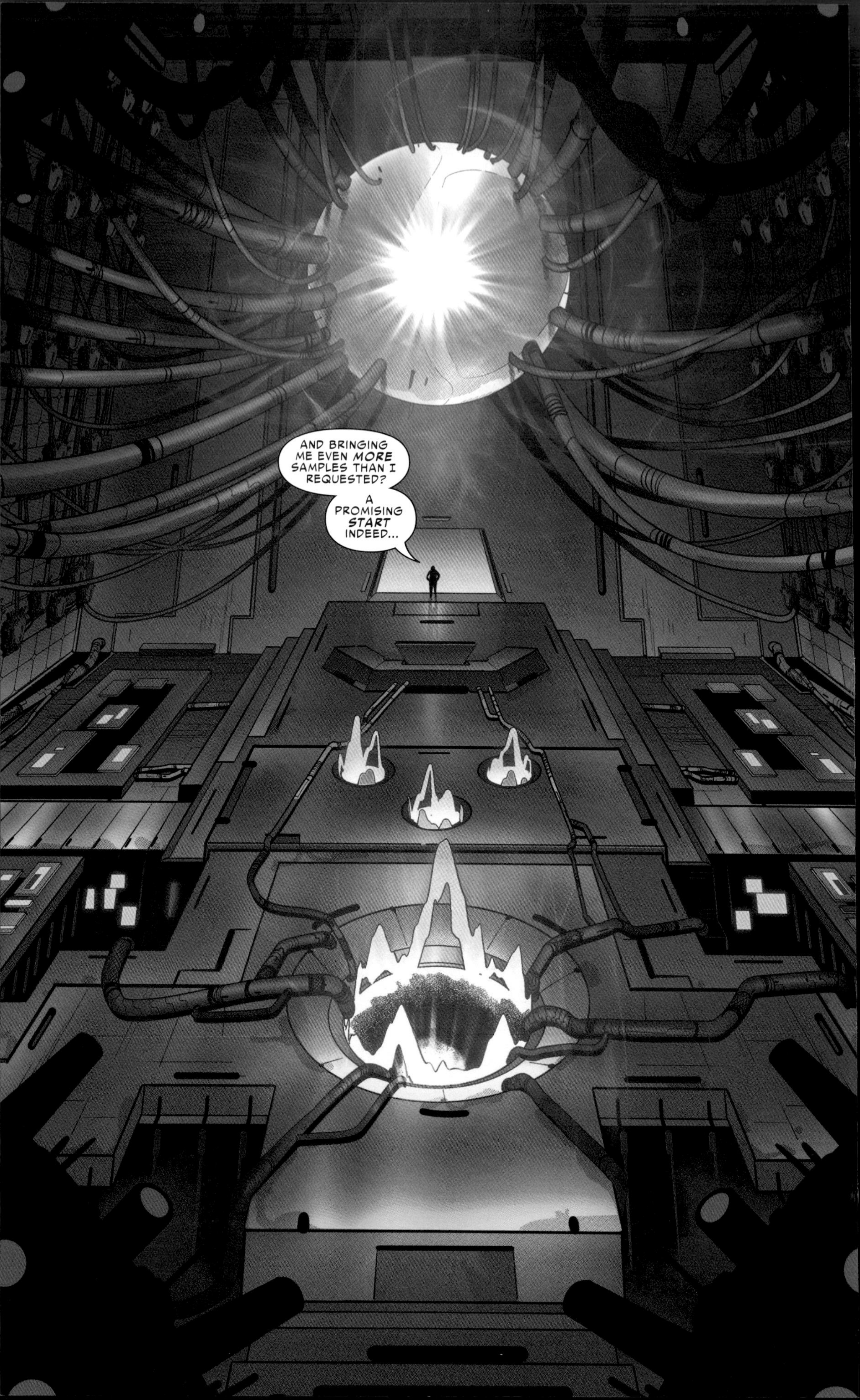
AND BRINGING ME EVEN MORE SAMPLES THAN I REQUESTED?
A PROMISING START INDEED...

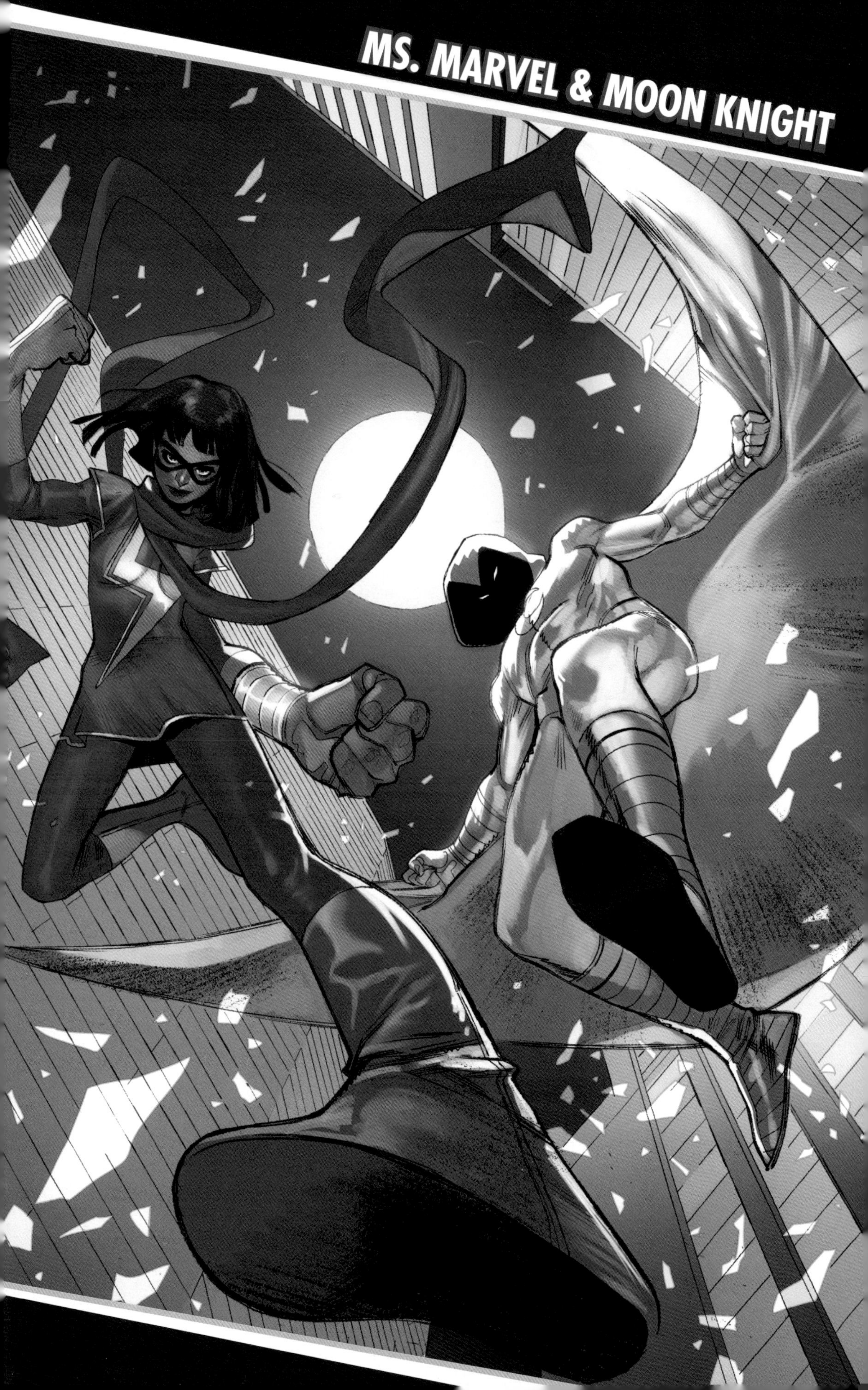
MS. MARVEL & MOON KNIGHT

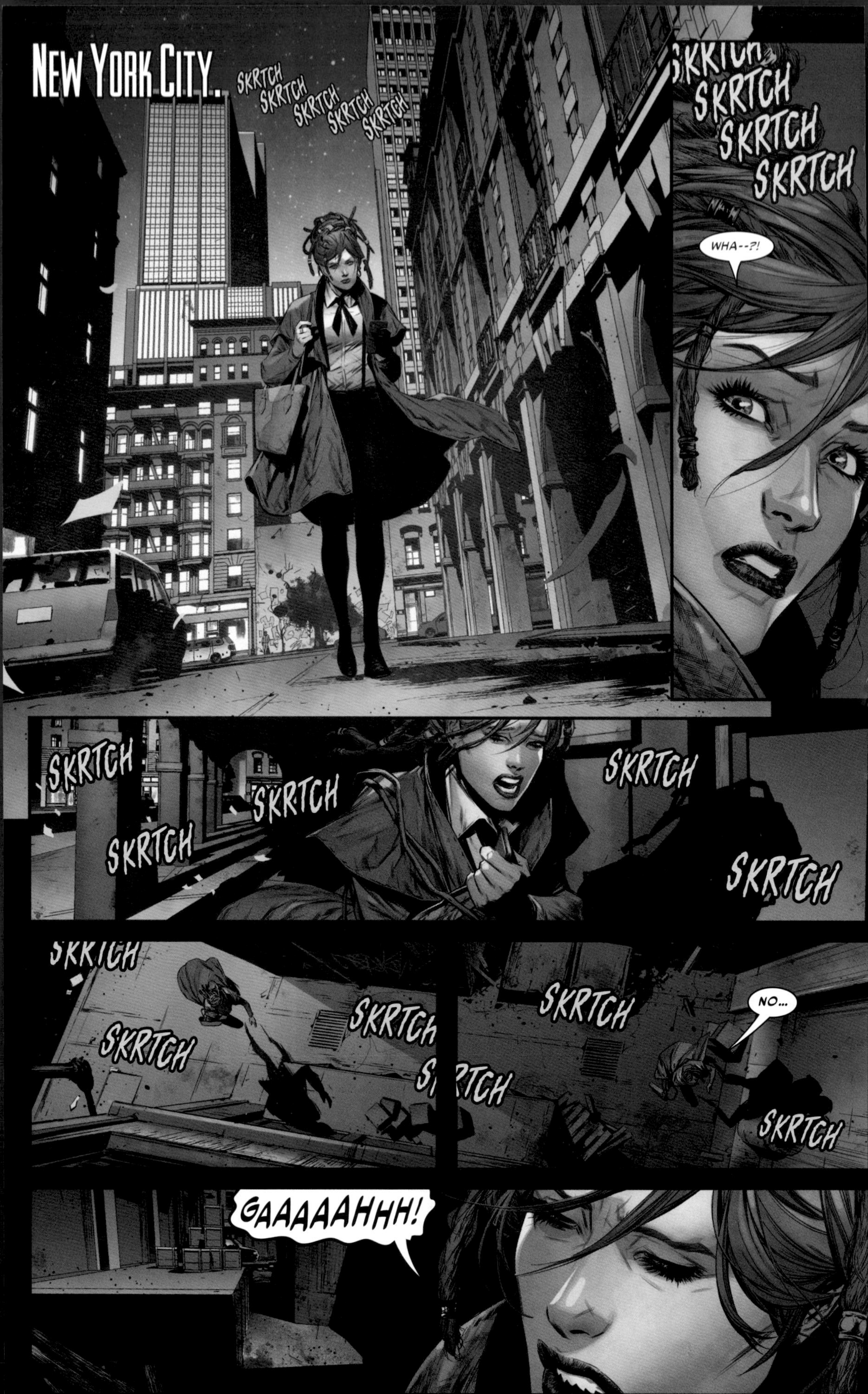
NEW YORK CITY..
SKRTCH
SKRTCH
SKRTCH
SKRTCH
SKRTCH
SKRTCH
SKRTCH
SKRTCH
SKRTCH
WHA--?!
SKRTCH
SKRTCH
SKRTCH
SKRTCH
SKRTCH
SKRTCH
SKRTCH
SKRTCH
SKRTCH
SKRTCH
NO...
SKRTCH
GAAAAAHHH!

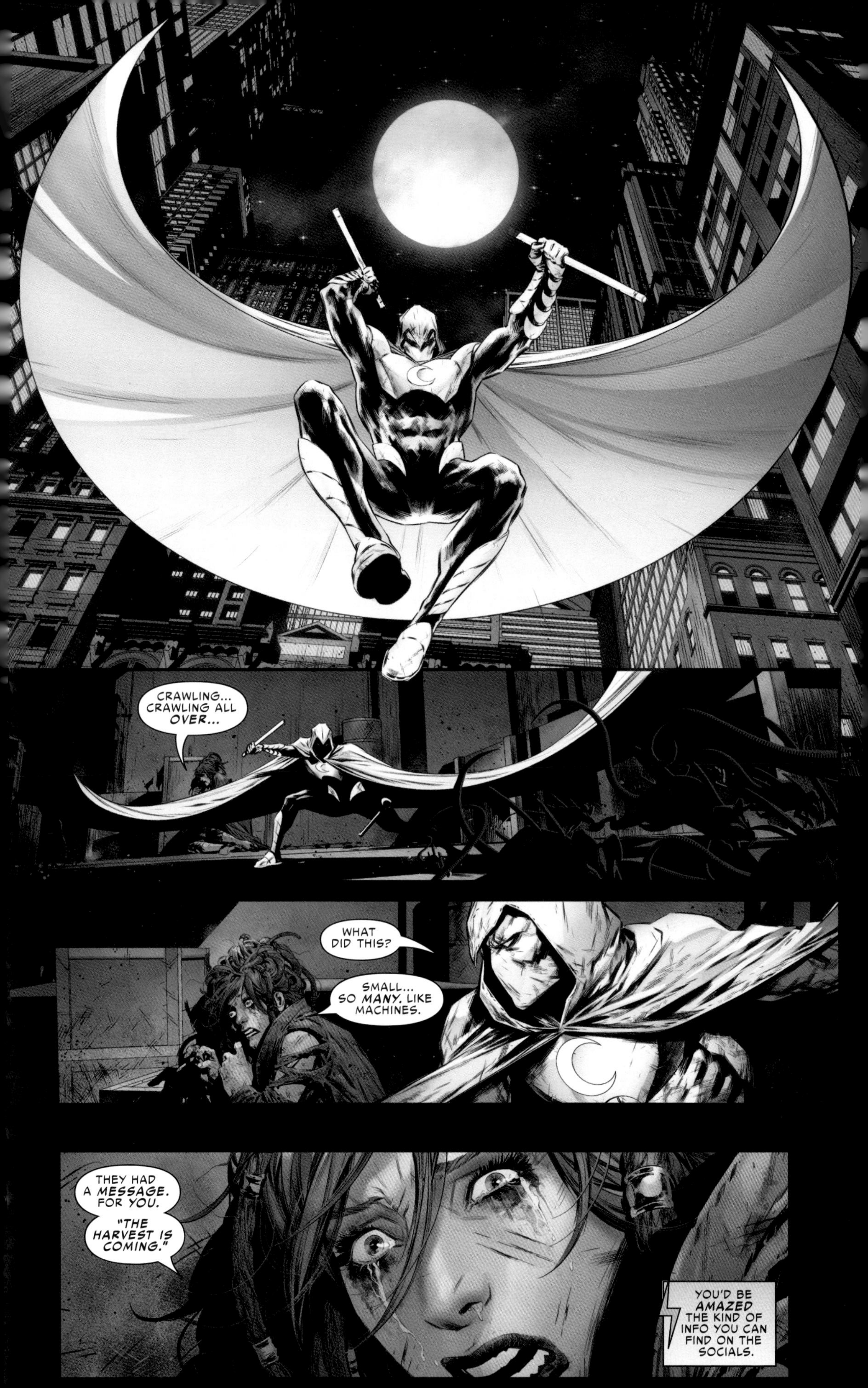
CRAWLING... CRAWLING ALL OVER...
WHAT DID THIS?
SMALL... SO MANY. LIKE MACHINES.
THEY HAD A MESSAGE. FOR YOU.
"THE HARVEST IS COMING."
YOU'D BE AMAZED THE KIND OF INFO YOU CAN FIND ON THE SOCIALS.

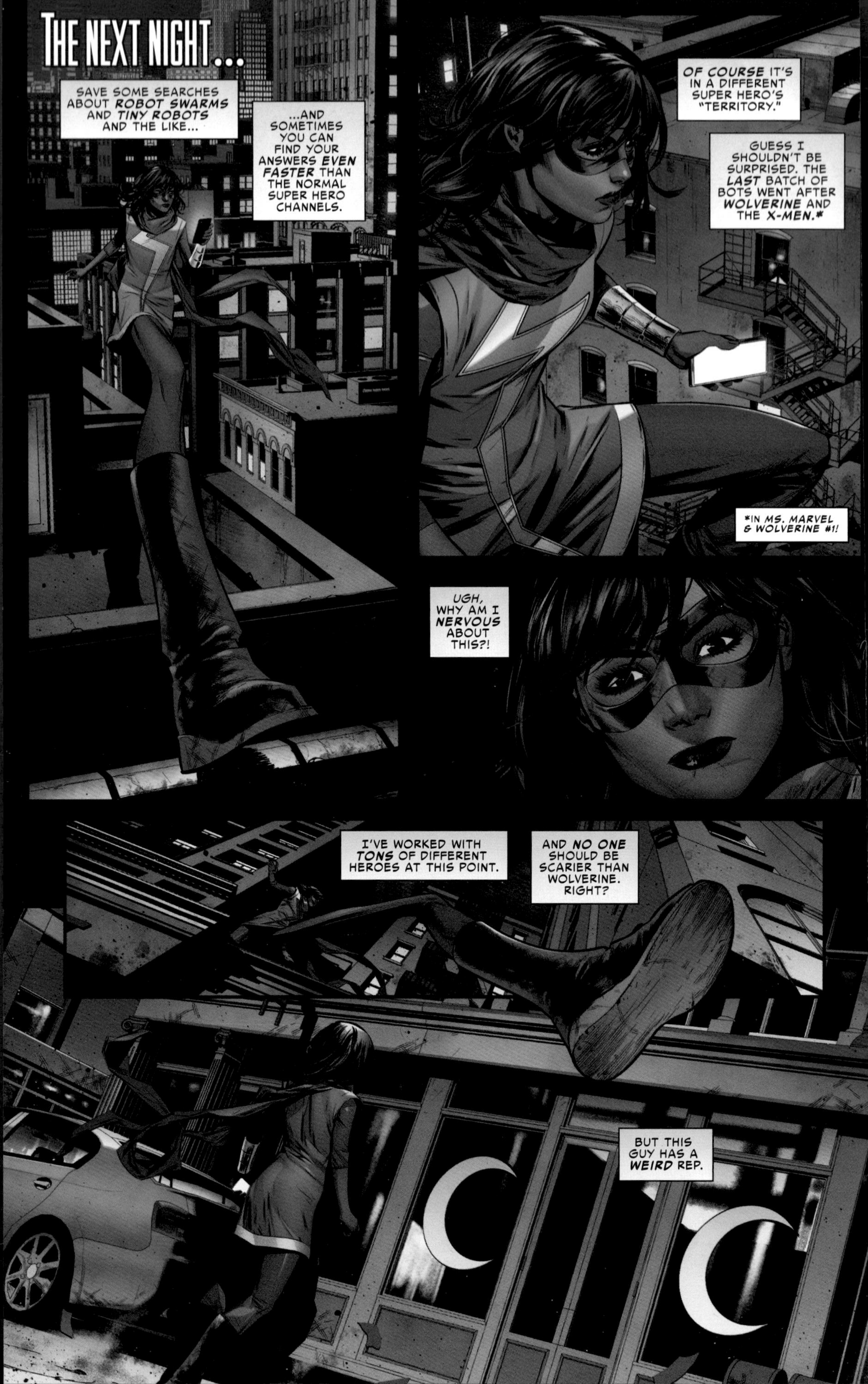
THE NEXT NIGHT...
SAVE SOME SEARCHES ABOUT ROBOT SWARMS AND TINY ROBOTS AND THE LIKE...
...AND SOMETIMES YOU CAN FIND YOUR ANSWERS EVEN FASTER THAN THE NORMAL SUPER HERO CHANNELS.
OF COURSE IT'S IN A DIFFERENT SUPER HERO'S "TERRITORY."
GUESS I SHOULDN'T BE SURPRISED. THE LAST BATCH OF BOTS WENT AFTER WOLVERINE AND THE X-MEN.*
*IN MS. MARVEL & WOLVERINE #1!
UGH, WHY AM I NERVOUS ABOUT THIS?!
I'VE WORKED WITH TONS OF DIFFERENT HEROES AT THIS POINT.
AND NO ONE SHOULD BE SCARIER THAN WOLVERINE. RIGHT?
BUT THIS GUY HAS A WEIRD REP.

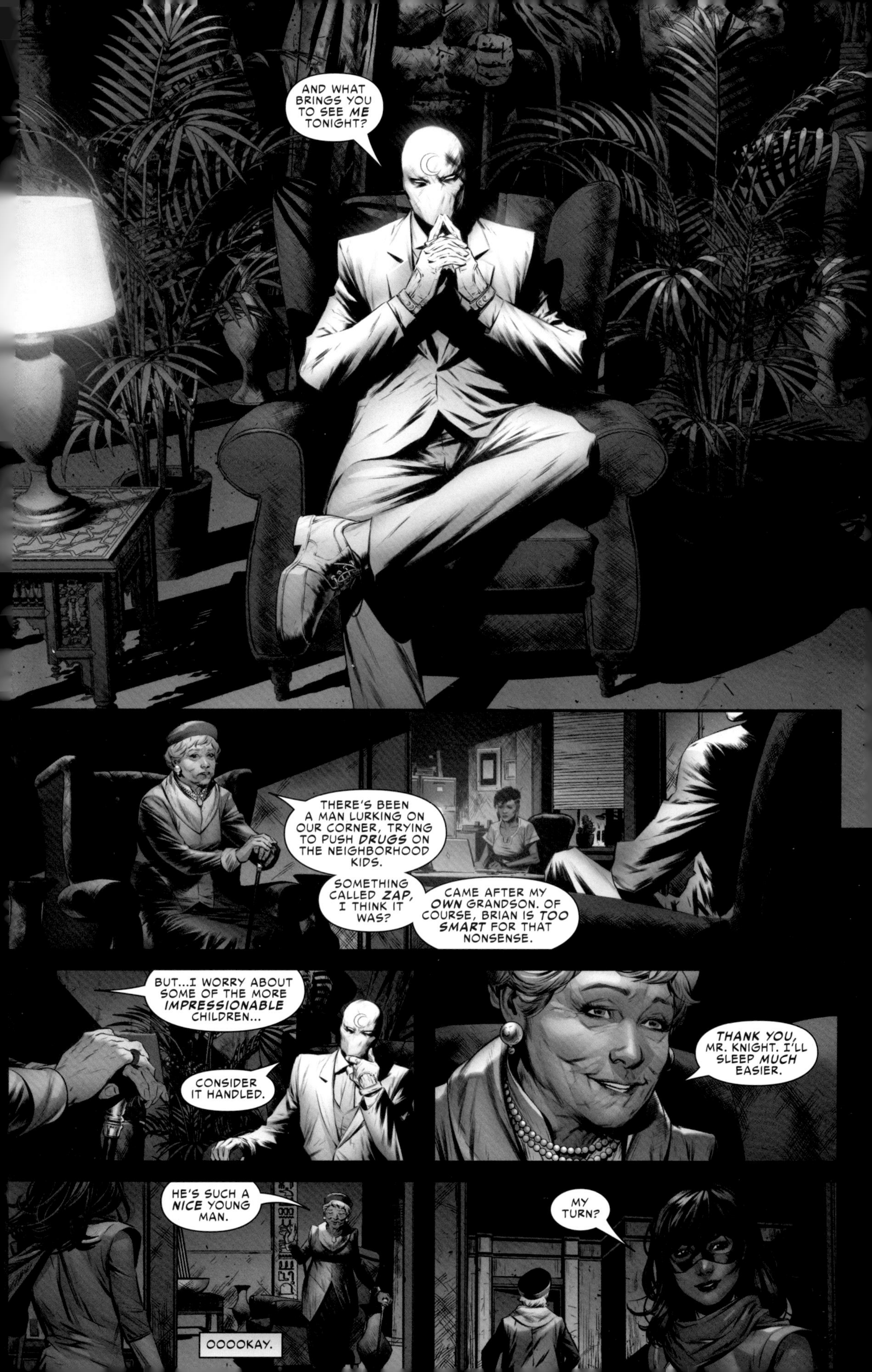
AND WHAT BRINGS YOU TO SEE *ME* TONIGHT?
THERE'S BEEN A MAN LURKING ON OUR CORNER, TRYING TO PUSH *DRUGS* ON THE NEIGHBORHOOD KIDS.
SOMETHING CALLED *ZAP*, I THINK IT WAS?
CAME AFTER MY *OWN* GRANDSON. OF COURSE, BRIAN IS *TOO SMART* FOR THAT NONSENSE.
BUT...I WORRY ABOUT SOME OF THE MORE *IMPRESSIONABLE* CHILDREN...
CONSIDER IT HANDLED.
THANK YOU, MR. KNIGHT. I'LL SLEEP *MUCH* EASIER.
HE'S SUCH A *NICE* YOUNG MAN.
OOOOKAY.
MY TURN?

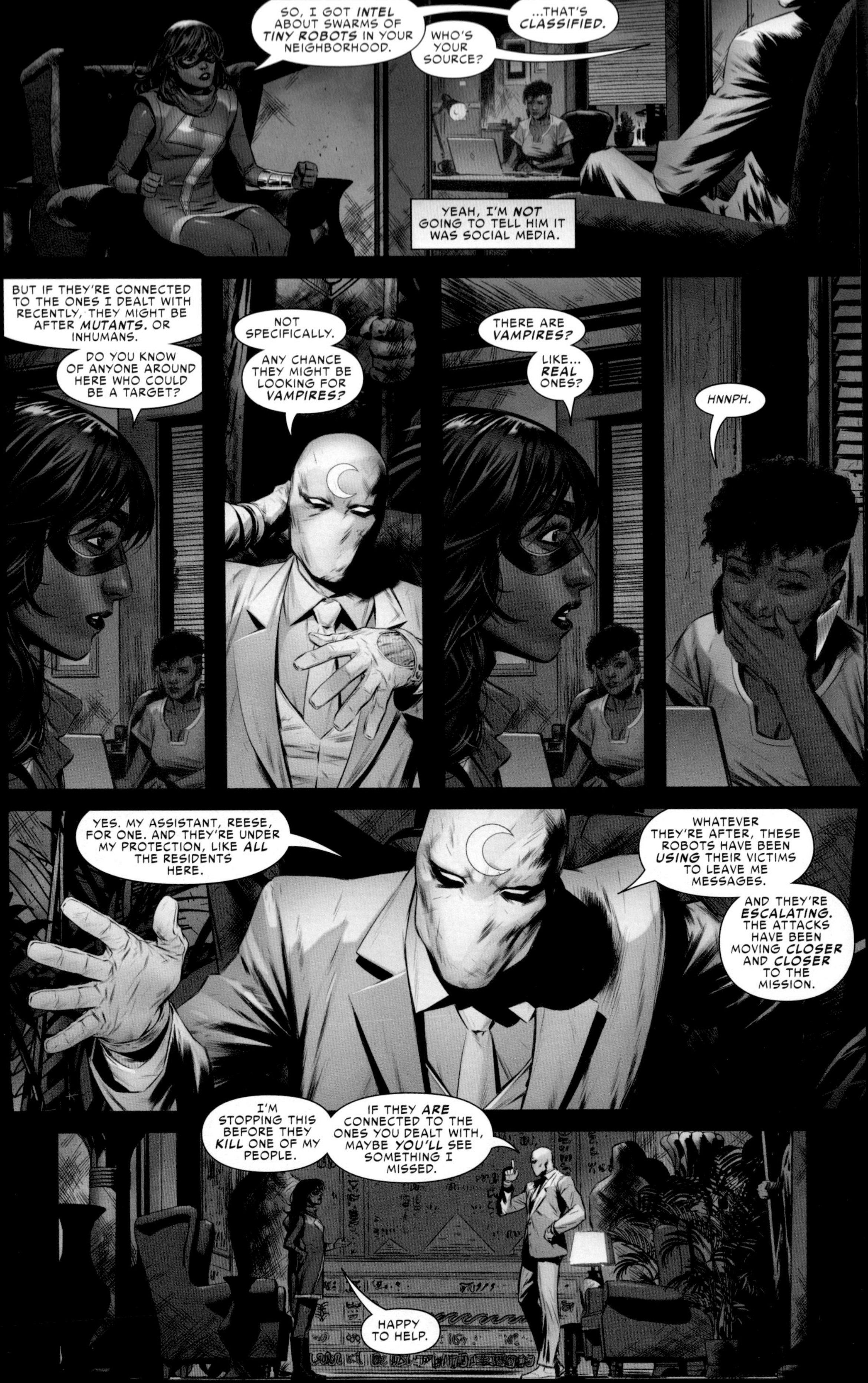

SO, I GOT INTEL ABOUT SWARMS OF TINY ROBOTS IN YOUR NEIGHBORHOOD.
...THAT'S CLASSIFIED.
WHO'S YOUR SOURCE?
YEAH, I'M NOT GOING TO TELL HIM IT WAS SOCIAL MEDIA.
BUT IF THEY'RE CONNECTED TO THE ONES I DEALT WITH RECENTLY, THEY MIGHT BE AFTER MUTANTS. OR INHUMANS.
DO YOU KNOW OF ANYONE AROUND HERE WHO COULD BE A TARGET?
NOT SPECIFICALLY.
ANY CHANCE THEY MIGHT BE LOOKING FOR VAMPIRES?
THERE ARE VAMPIRES?
LIKE... REAL ONES?
HNNPH.
YES. MY ASSISTANT, REESE, FOR ONE. AND THEY'RE UNDER MY PROTECTION, LIKE ALL THE RESIDENTS HERE.
WHATEVER THEY'RE AFTER, THESE ROBOTS HAVE BEEN USING THEIR VICTIMS TO LEAVE ME MESSAGES.
AND THEY'RE ESCALATING. THE ATTACKS HAVE BEEN MOVING CLOSER AND CLOSER TO THE MISSION.
I'M STOPPING THIS BEFORE THEY KILL ONE OF MY PEOPLE.
IF THEY ARE CONNECTED TO THE ONES YOU DEALT WITH, MAYBE YOU'LL SEE SOMETHING I MISSED.
HAPPY TO HELP.

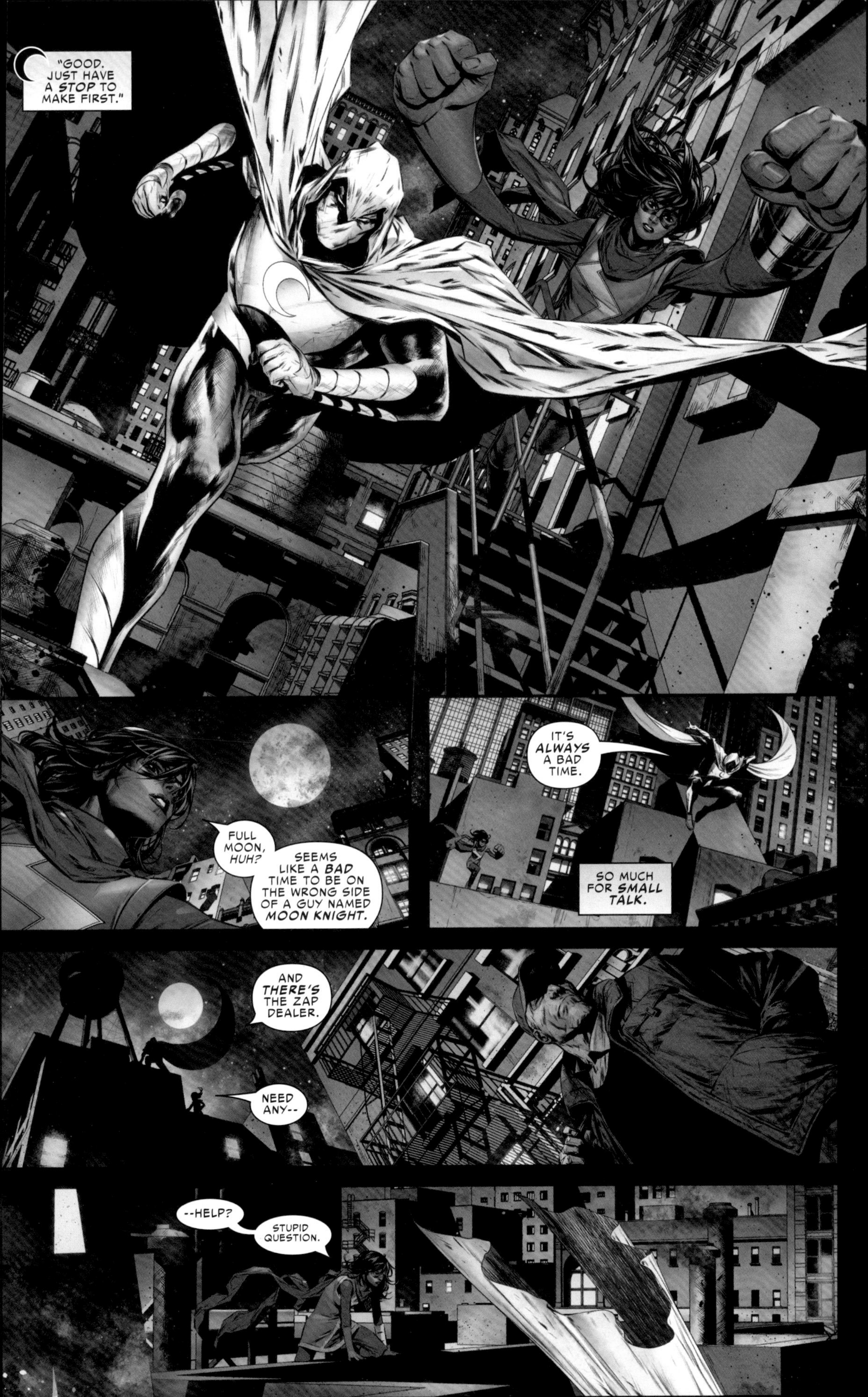
"GOOD. JUST HAVE A STOP TO MAKE FIRST."
FULL MOON, HUH?
SEEMS LIKE A BAD TIME TO BE ON THE WRONG SIDE OF A GUY NAMED MOON KNIGHT.
IT'S ALWAYS A BAD TIME.
SO MUCH FOR SMALL TALK.
AND THERE'S THE ZAP DEALER.
NEED ANY--
--HELP?
STUPID QUESTION.

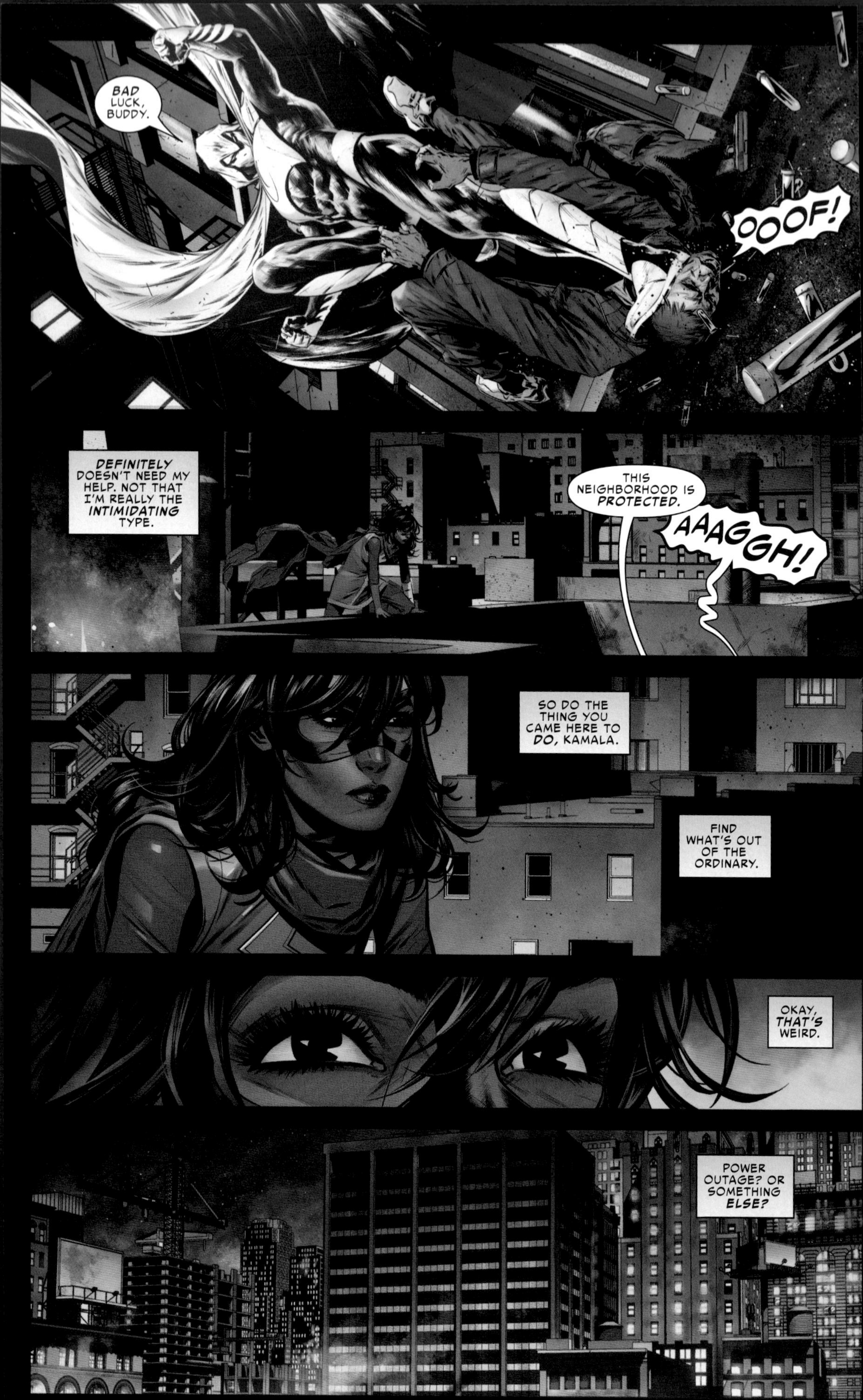
BAD LUCK, BUDDY.
OOOF!
DEFINITELY DOESN'T NEED MY HELP. NOT THAT I'M REALLY THE INTIMIDATING TYPE.
THIS NEIGHBORHOOD IS PROTECTED.
AAAGGH!
SO DO THE THING YOU CAME HERE TO DO, KAMALA.
FIND WHAT'S OUT OF THE ORDINARY.
OKAY, THAT'S WEIRD.
POWER OUTAGE? OR SOMETHING ELSE?

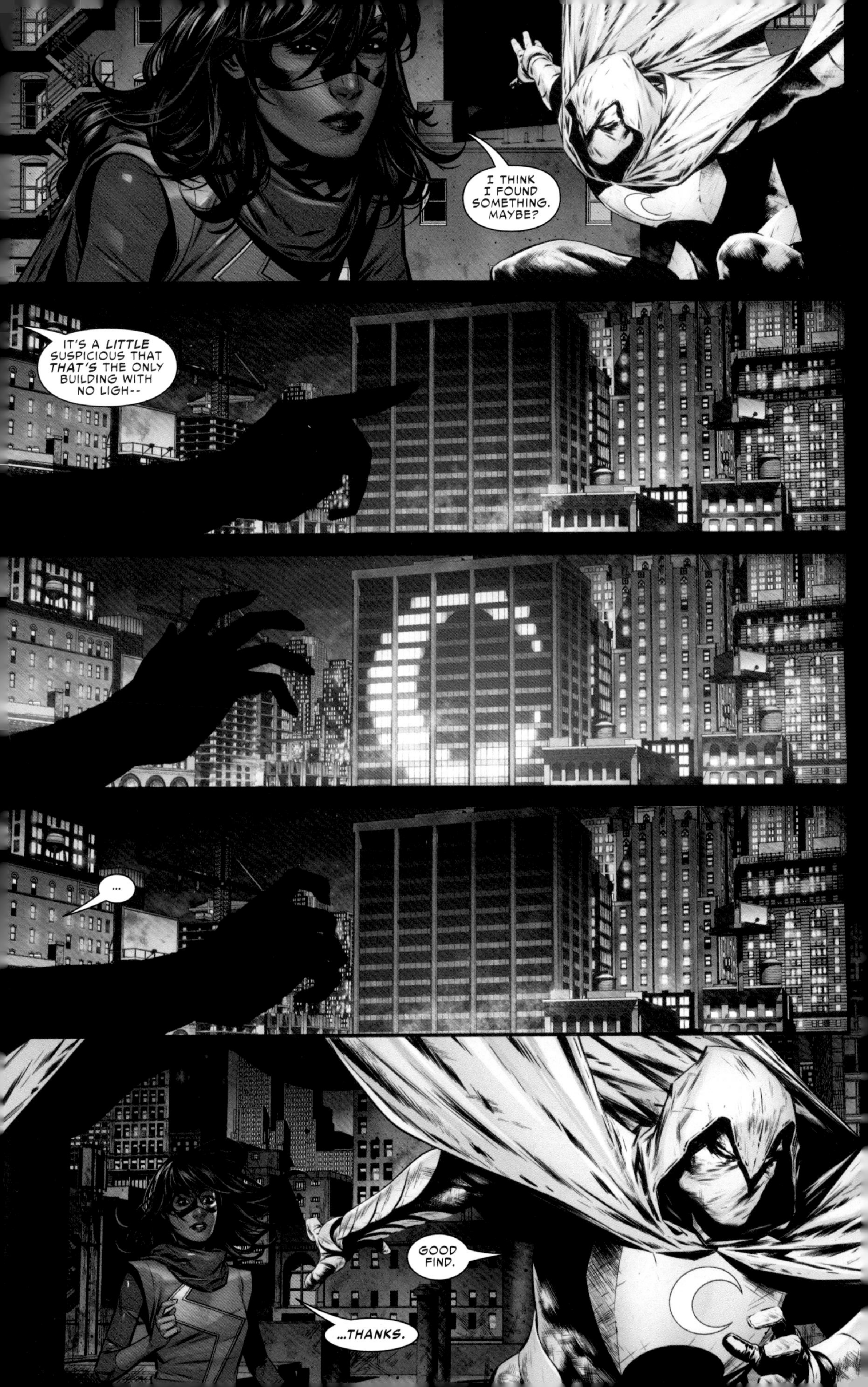
I THINK I FOUND SOMETHING. MAYBE?
IT'S A *LITTLE* SUSPICIOUS THAT *THAT'S* THE ONLY BUILDING WITH NO LIGH--
...
GOOD FIND.
...THANKS.

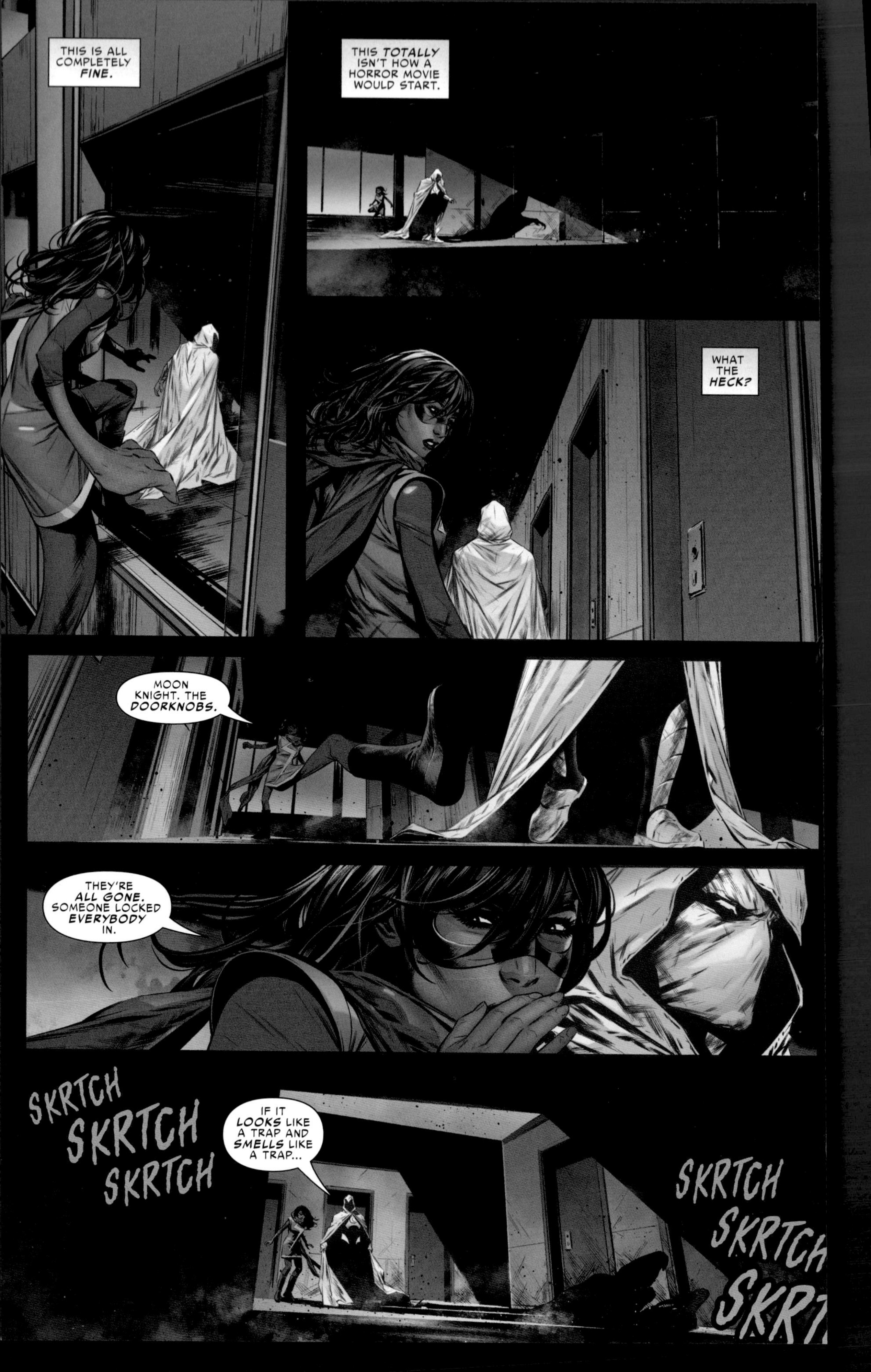
THIS IS ALL COMPLETELY FINE.
THIS TOTALLY ISN'T HOW A HORROR MOVIE WOULD START.
WHAT THE HECK?
MOON KNIGHT. THE DOORKNOBS.
THEY'RE ALL GONE. SOMEONE LOCKED EVERYBODY IN.
SKRTCH SKRTCH SKRTCH
IF IT LOOKS LIKE A TRAP AND SMELLS LIKE A TRAP...
SKRTCH SKRTCH SKRT

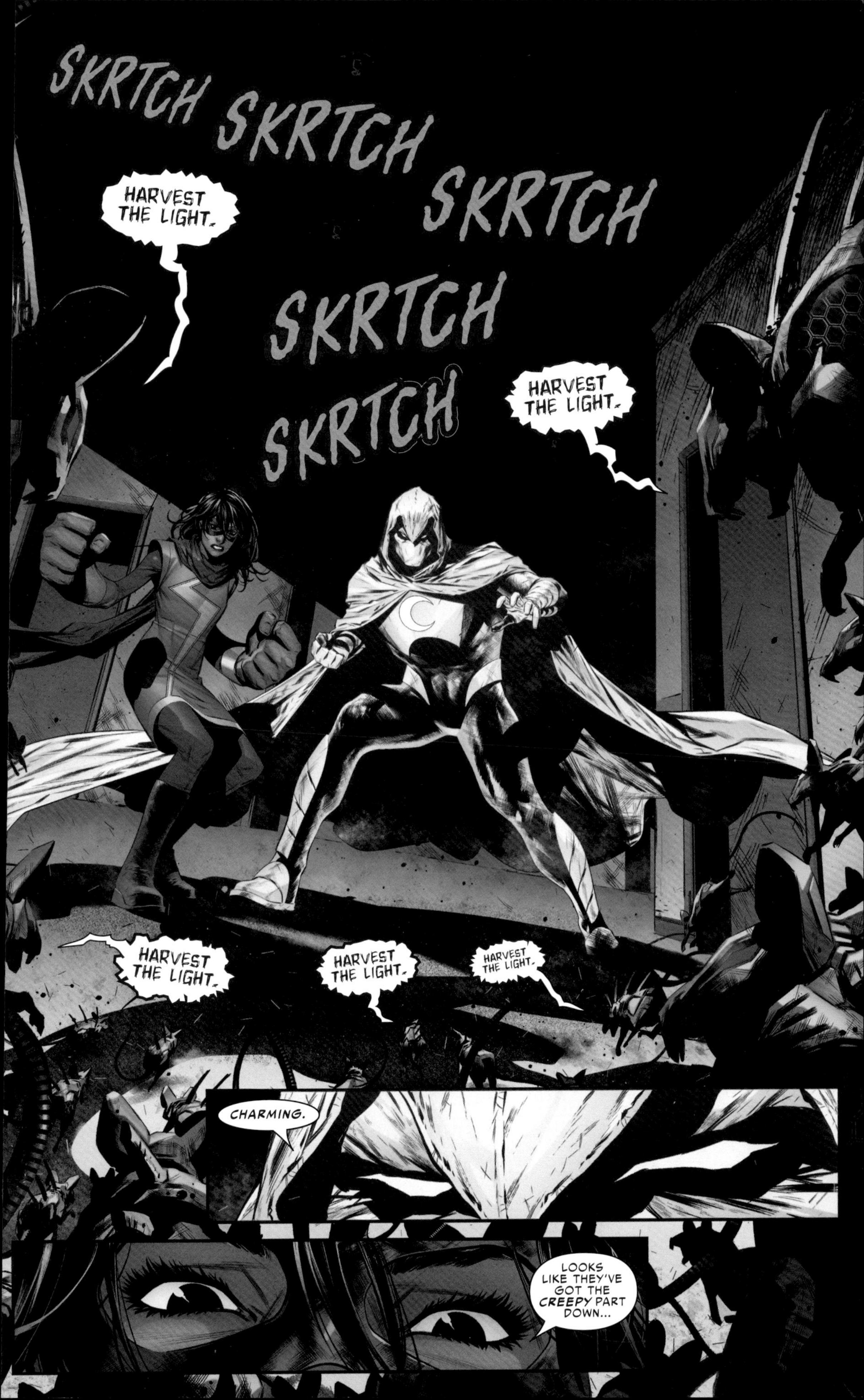
SKRTCH SKRTCH
HARVEST THE LIGHT.
SKRTCH
SKRTCH
SKRTCH
HARVEST THE LIGHT.
HARVEST THE LIGHT.
HARVEST THE LIGHT.
HARVEST THE LIGHT.
CHARMING.
LOOKS LIKE THEY'VE GOT THE CREEPY PART DOWN...

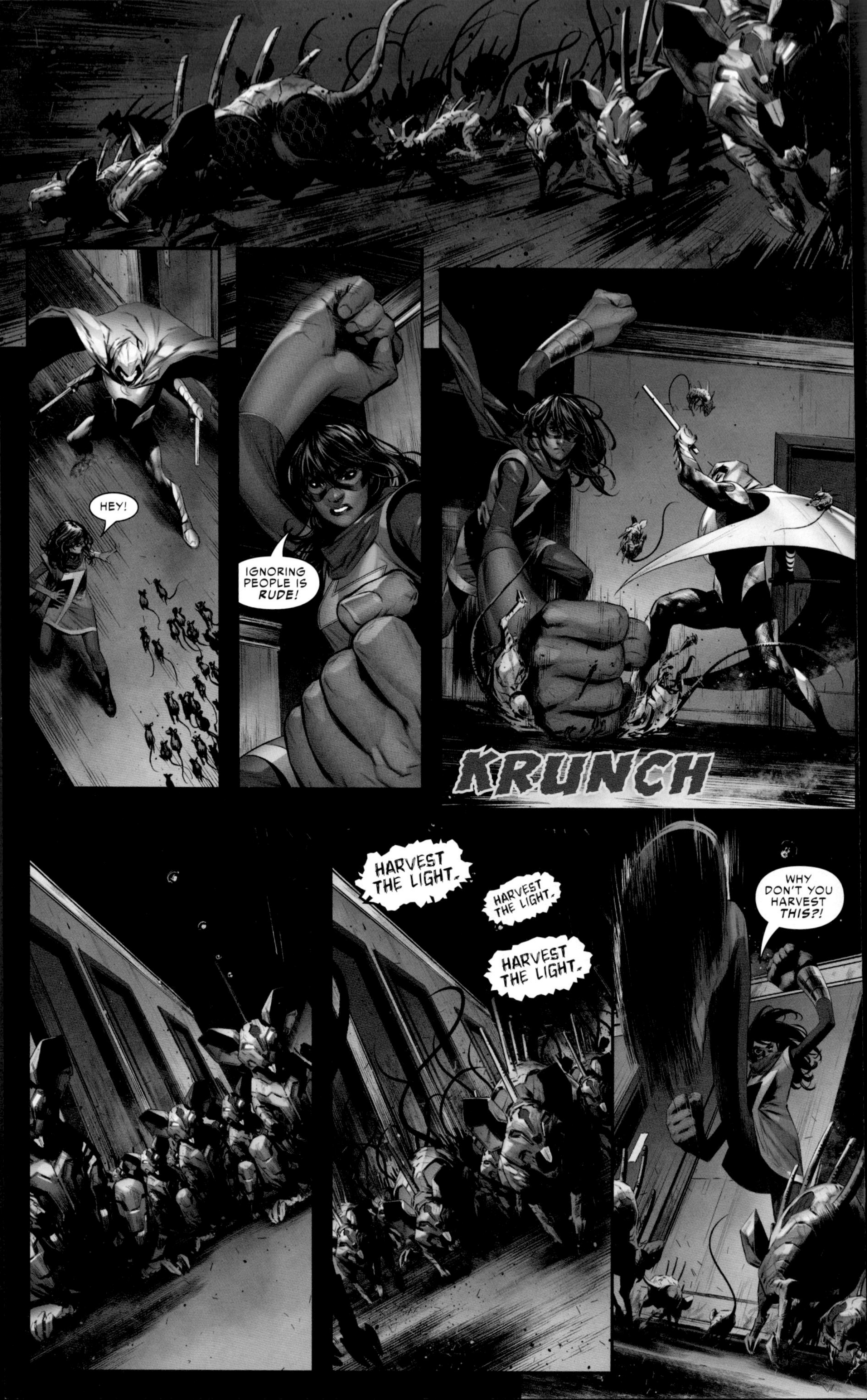
HEY!
IGNORING PEOPLE IS RUDE!
KRUNCH
HARVEST THE LIGHT.
HARVEST THE LIGHT.
HARVEST THE LIGHT.
WHY DON'T YOU HARVEST THIS?!

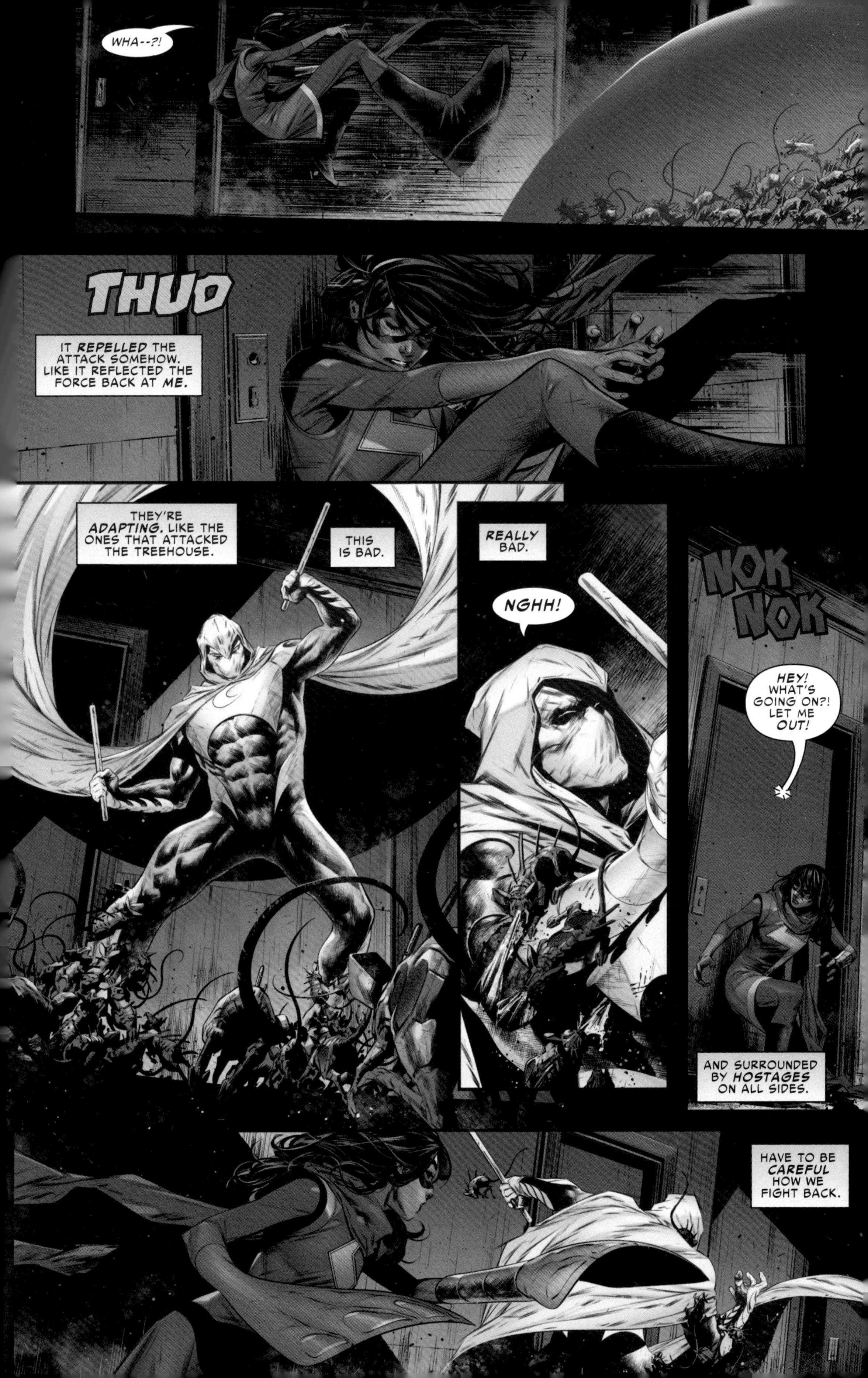
WHA--?!
THUD
IT REPELLED THE ATTACK SOMEHOW. LIKE IT REFLECTED THE FORCE BACK AT ME.
THEY'RE ADAPTING. LIKE THE ONES THAT ATTACKED THE TREEHOUSE.
THIS IS BAD.
REALLY BAD.
NGHH!
NOK NOK
HEY! WHAT'S GOING ON?! LET ME OUT!
AND SURROUNDED BY HOSTAGES ON ALL SIDES.
HAVE TO BE CAREFUL HOW WE FIGHT BACK.

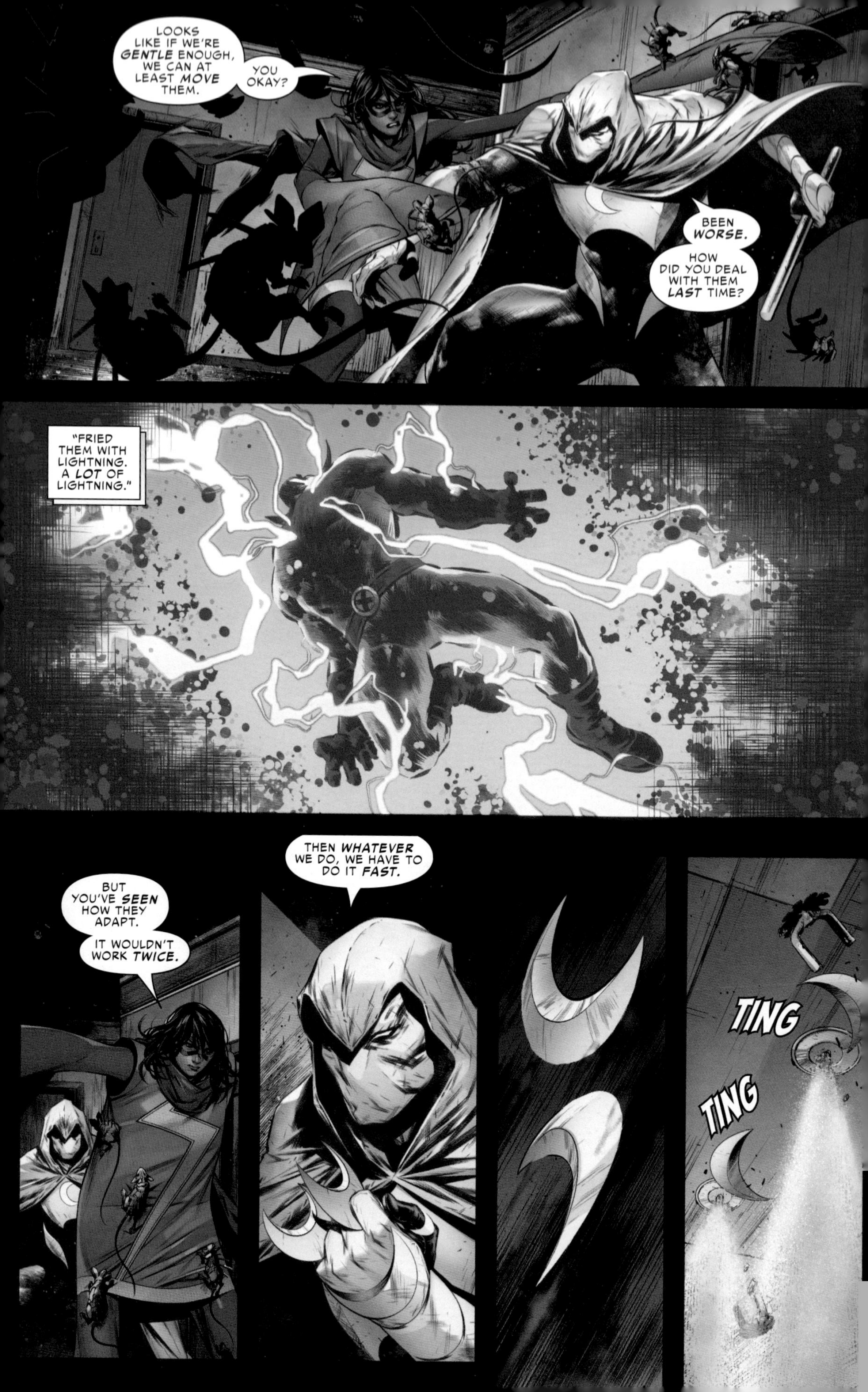

LOOKS LIKE IF WE'RE *GENTLE* ENOUGH, WE CAN AT LEAST *MOVE* THEM.
YOU OKAY?
BEEN *WORSE*.
HOW DID YOU DEAL WITH THEM *LAST* TIME?
"FRIED THEM WITH LIGHTNING. A *LOT* OF LIGHTNING."
BUT YOU'VE *SEEN* HOW THEY ADAPT.
IT WOULDN'T WORK *TWICE*.
THEN *WHATEVER* WE DO, WE HAVE TO DO IT *FAST*.
TING
TING

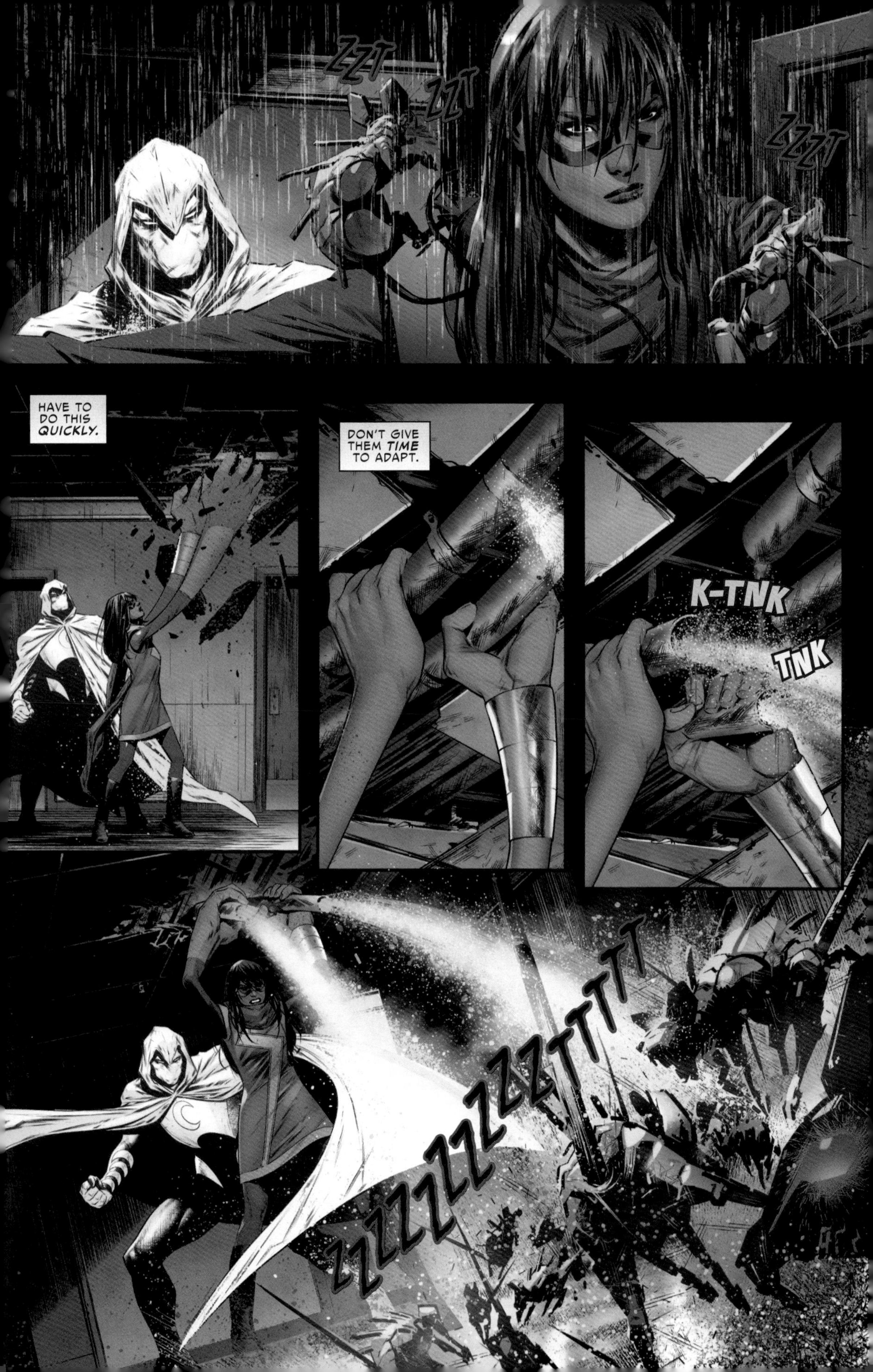

ZZT
ZZT
ZZZT
HAVE TO DO THIS *QUICKLY*.
DON'T GIVE THEM *TIME* TO ADAPT.
K-TNK
TNK
ZZZZZZZZZZTTTTTT

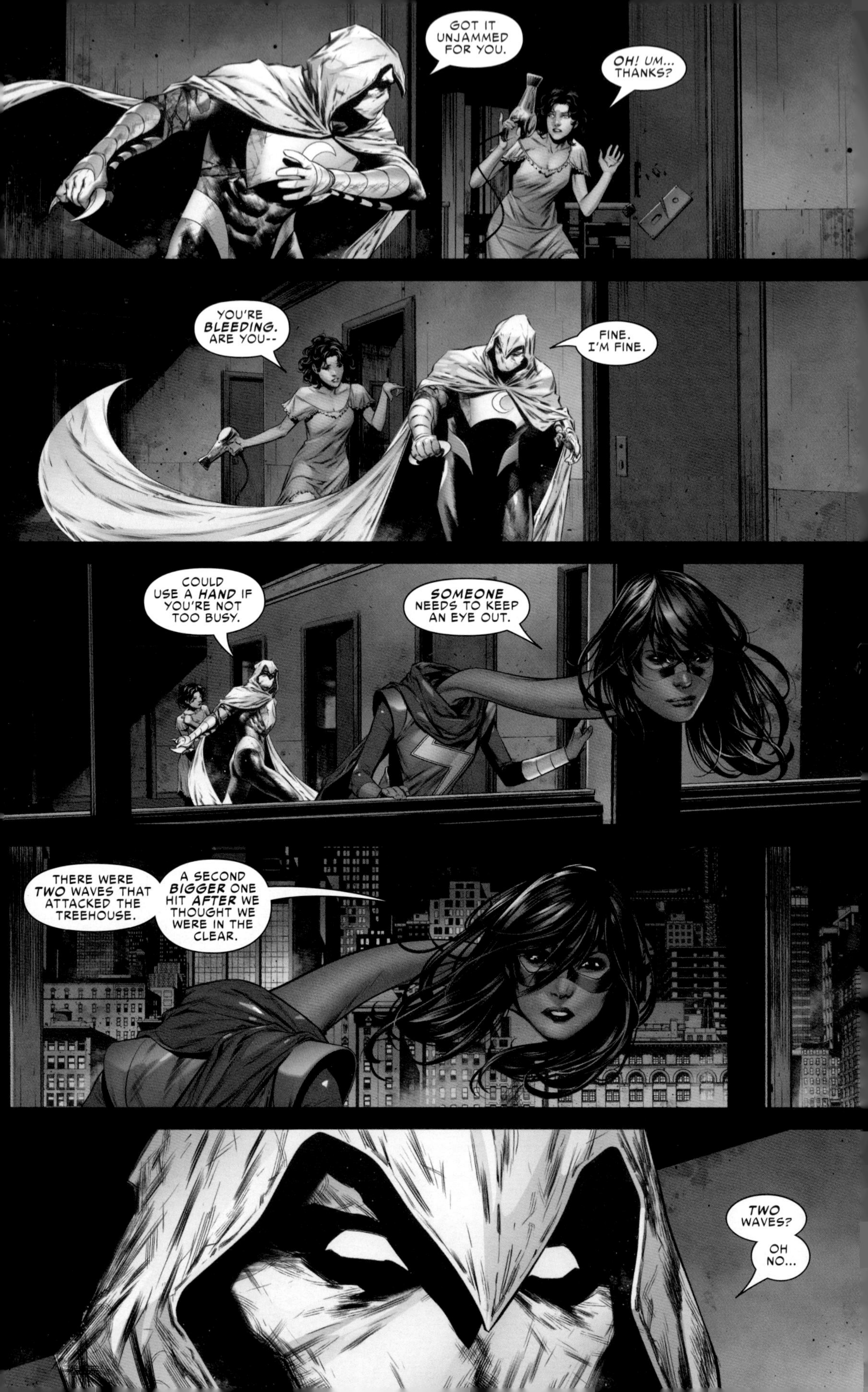
GOT IT UNJAMMED FOR YOU.
OH! UM... THANKS?
YOU'RE BLEEDING. ARE YOU--
FINE. I'M FINE.
COULD USE A HAND IF YOU'RE NOT TOO BUSY.
SOMEONE NEEDS TO KEEP AN EYE OUT.
THERE WERE TWO WAVES THAT ATTACKED THE TREEHOUSE.
A SECOND BIGGER ONE HIT AFTER WE THOUGHT WE WERE IN THE CLEAR.
TWO WAVES?
OH NO...

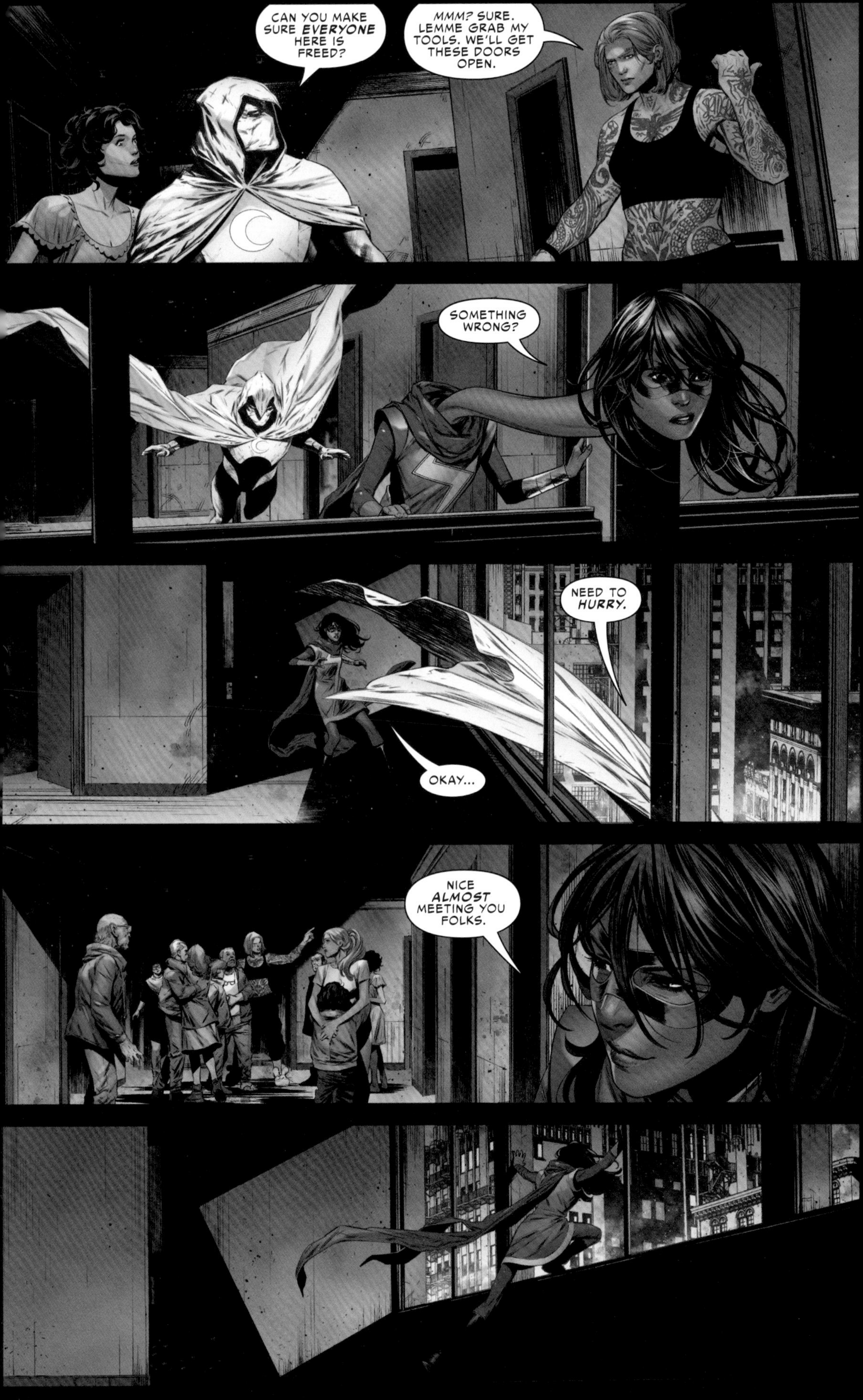
CAN YOU MAKE SURE *EVERYONE* HERE IS FREED?
MMM? SURE. LEMME GRAB MY TOOLS. WE'LL GET THESE DOORS OPEN.
SOMETHING WRONG?
NEED TO *HURRY.*
OKAY...
NICE *ALMOST* MEETING YOU FOLKS.

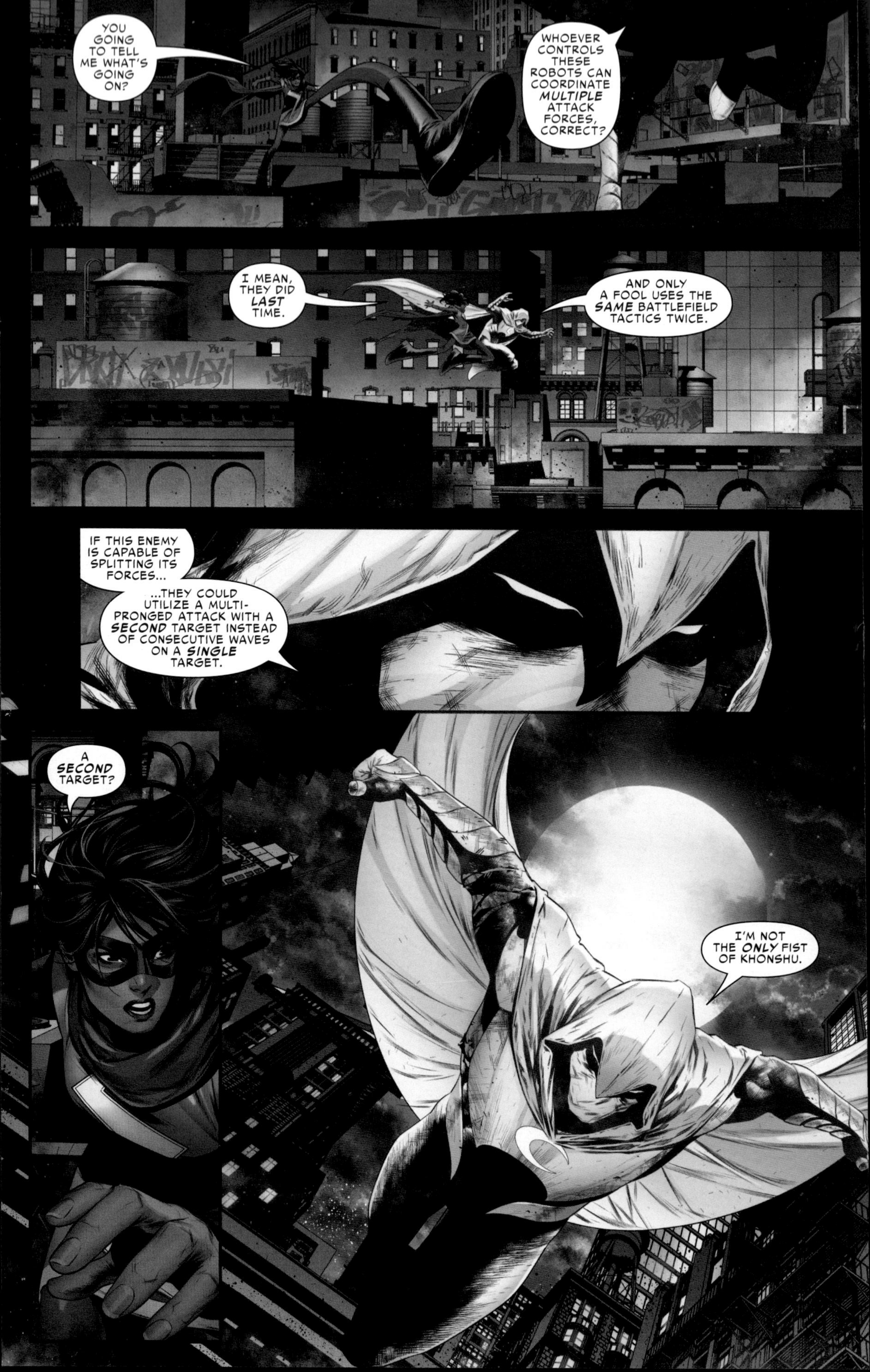
YOU GOING TO TELL ME WHAT'S GOING ON?
WHOEVER CONTROLS THESE ROBOTS CAN COORDINATE MULTIPLE ATTACK FORCES, CORRECT?
I MEAN, THEY DID LAST TIME.
AND ONLY A FOOL USES THE SAME BATTLEFIELD TACTICS TWICE.
IF THIS ENEMY IS CAPABLE OF SPLITTING ITS FORCES...
...THEY COULD UTILIZE A MULTI-PRONGED ATTACK WITH A SECOND TARGET INSTEAD OF CONSECUTIVE WAVES ON A SINGLE TARGET.
A SECOND TARGET?
I'M NOT THE ONLY FIST OF KHONSHU.

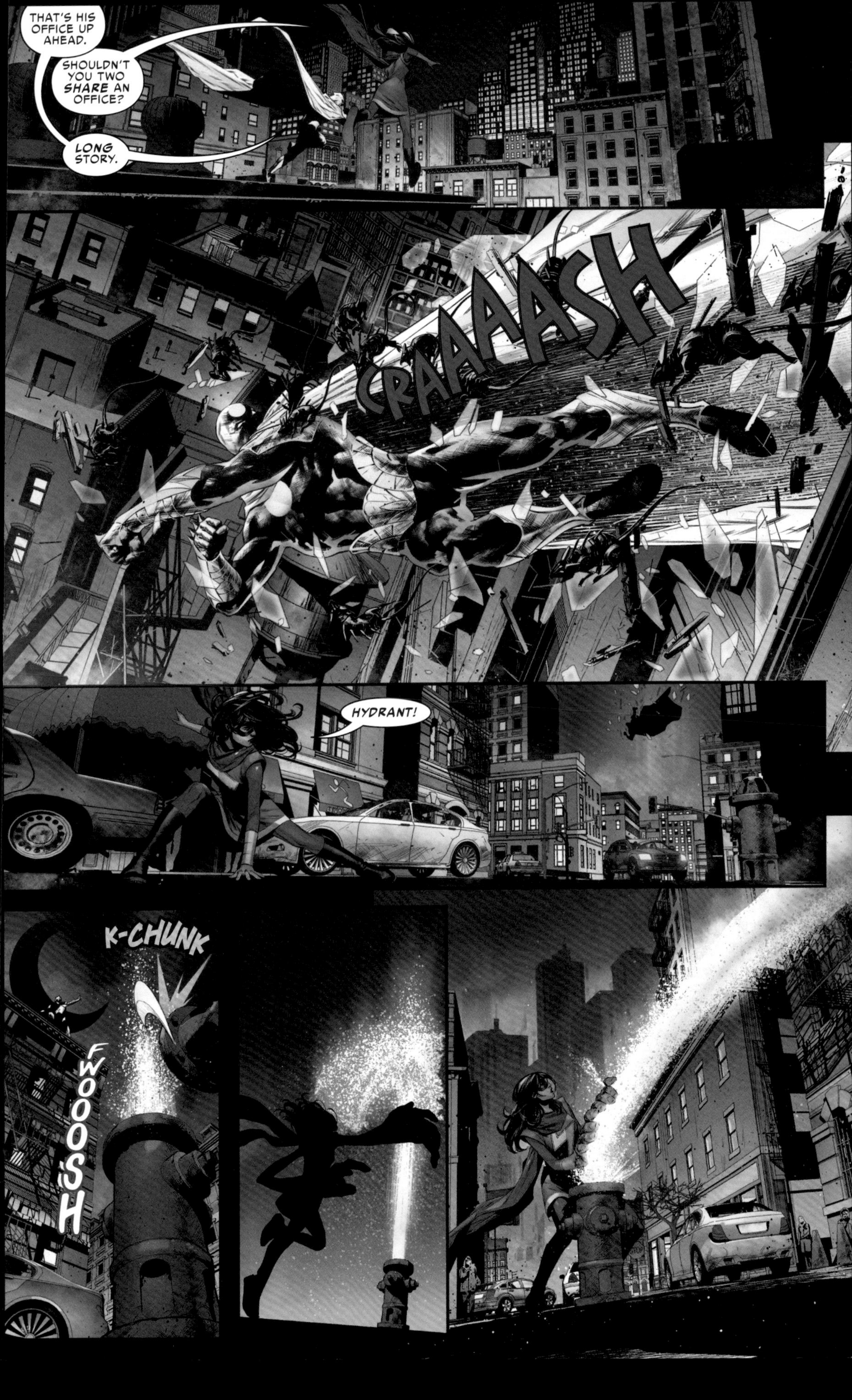
THAT'S HIS OFFICE UP AHEAD.
SHOULDN'T YOU TWO SHARE AN OFFICE?
LONG STORY.
CRAAAASH
HYDRANT!
K-CHUNK
FWOOOSH

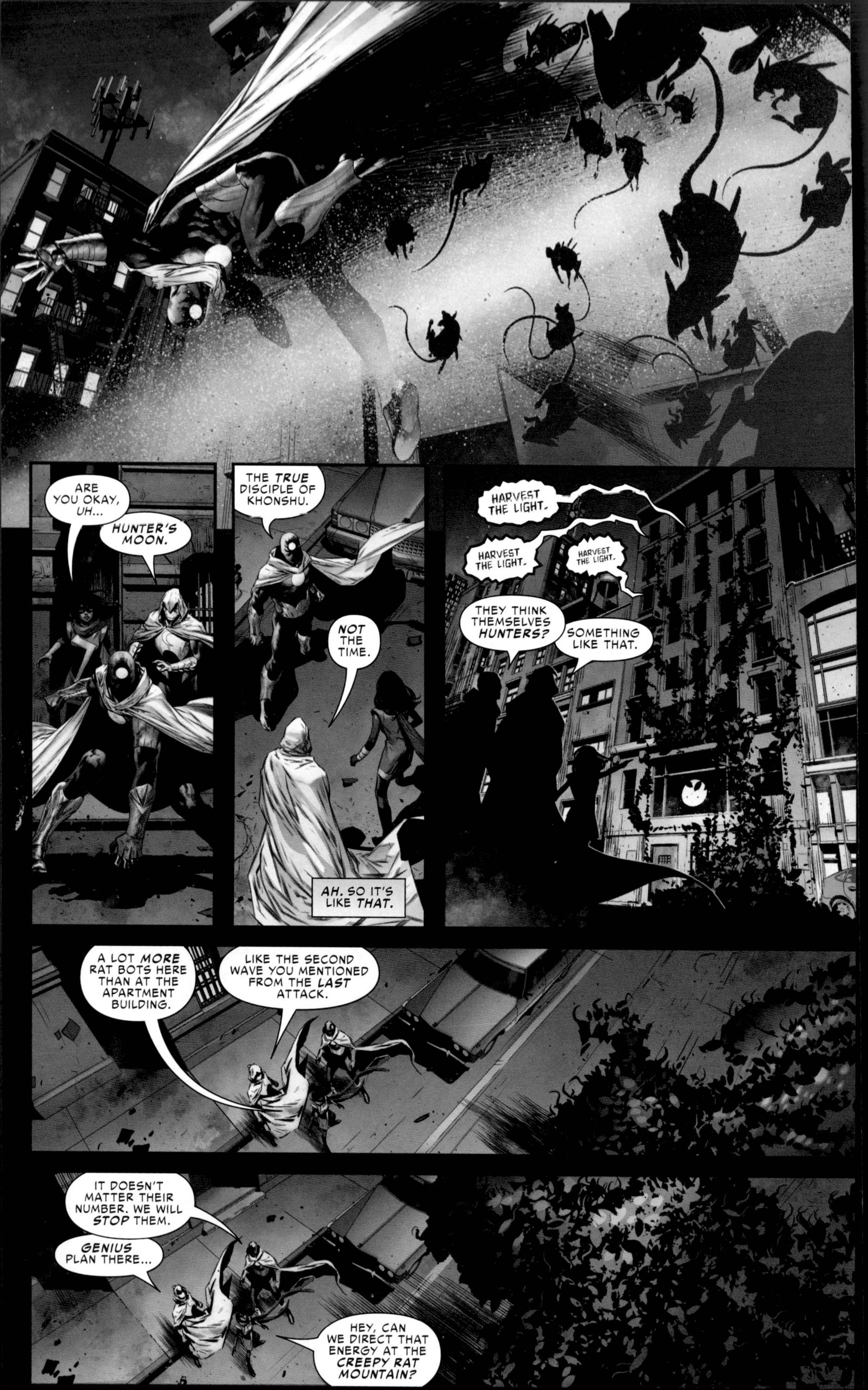

ARE YOU OKAY, UH...
HUNTER'S MOON.
THE TRUE DISCIPLE OF KHONSHU.
NOT THE TIME.
AH. SO IT'S LIKE THAT.
HARVEST THE LIGHT.
HARVEST THE LIGHT.
HARVEST THE LIGHT.
THEY THINK THEMSELVES HUNTERS?
SOMETHING LIKE THAT.
A LOT MORE RAT BOTS HERE THAN AT THE APARTMENT BUILDING.
LIKE THE SECOND WAVE YOU MENTIONED FROM THE LAST ATTACK.
IT DOESN'T MATTER THEIR NUMBER. WE WILL STOP THEM.
GENIUS PLAN THERE...
HEY, CAN WE DIRECT THAT ENERGY AT THE CREEPY RAT MOUNTAIN?

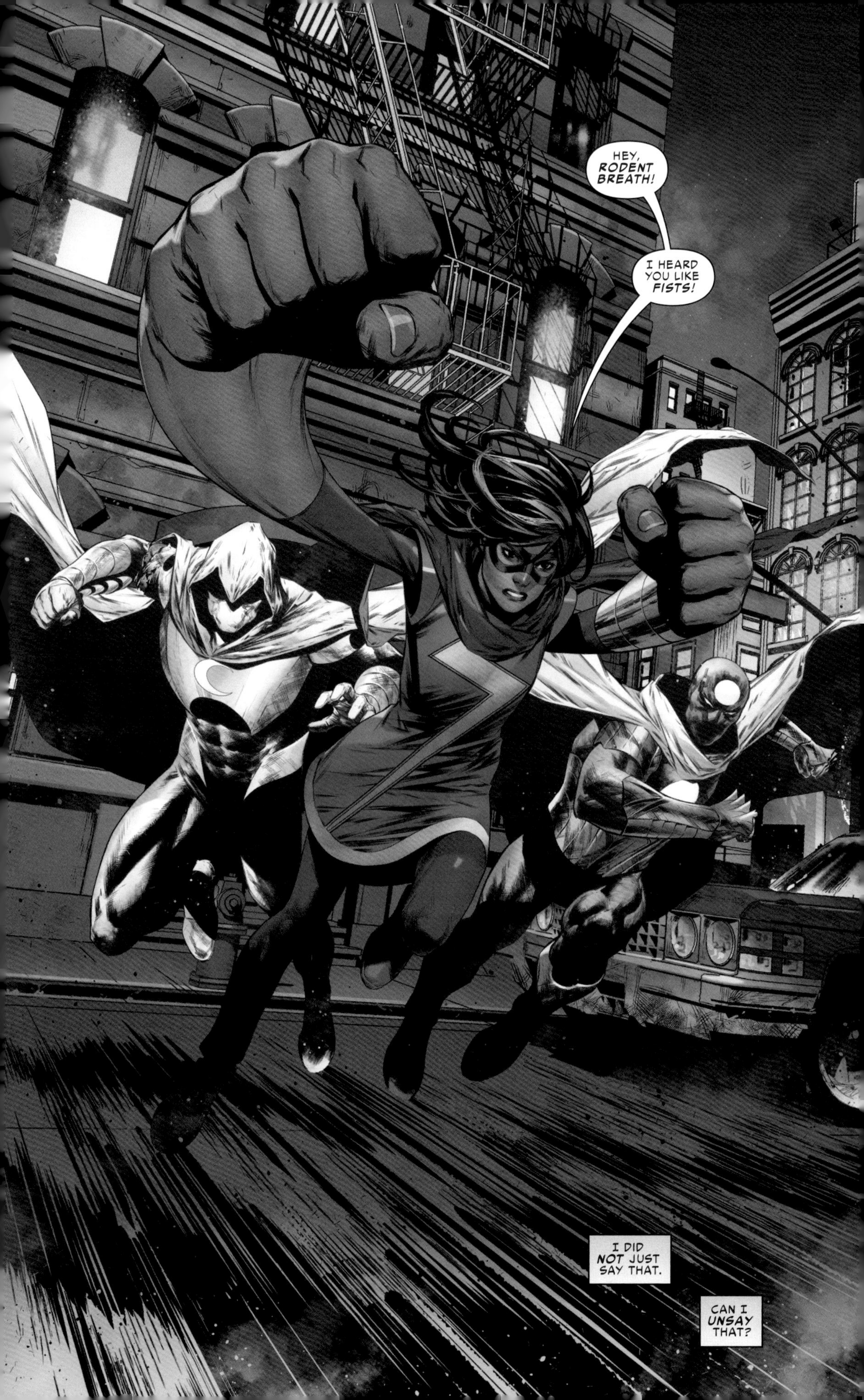
HEY, RODENT BREATH!
I HEARD YOU LIKE FISTS!
I DID NOT JUST SAY THAT.
CAN I UNSAY THAT?

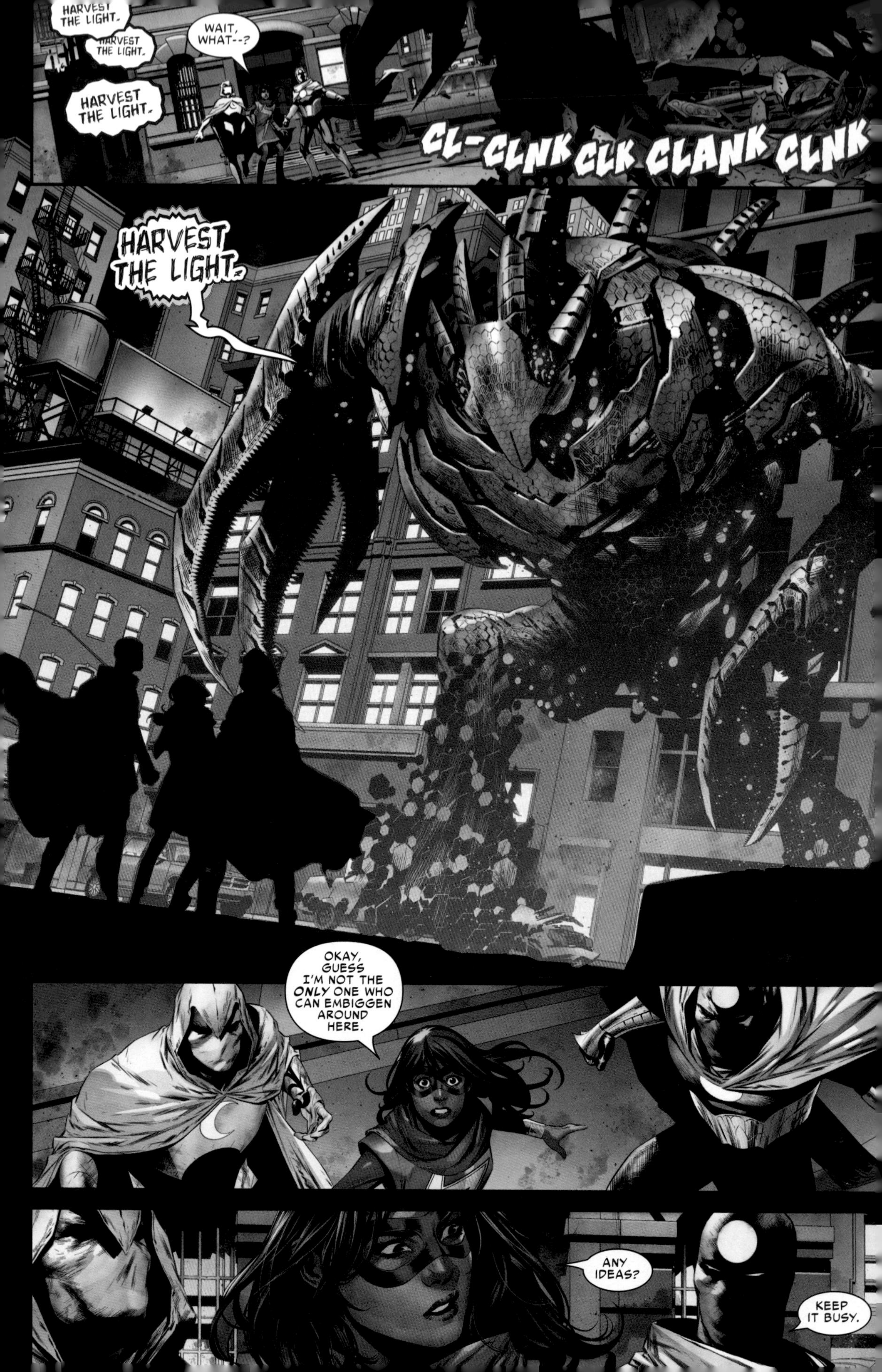
HARVEST THE LIGHT.
HARVEST THE LIGHT.
WAIT, WHAT--?
HARVEST THE LIGHT.
CL-CLNK CLK CLANK CLNK
HARVEST THE LIGHT.
OKAY, GUESS I'M NOT THE *ONLY* ONE WHO CAN EMBIGGEN AROUND HERE.
ANY IDEAS?
KEEP IT BUSY.

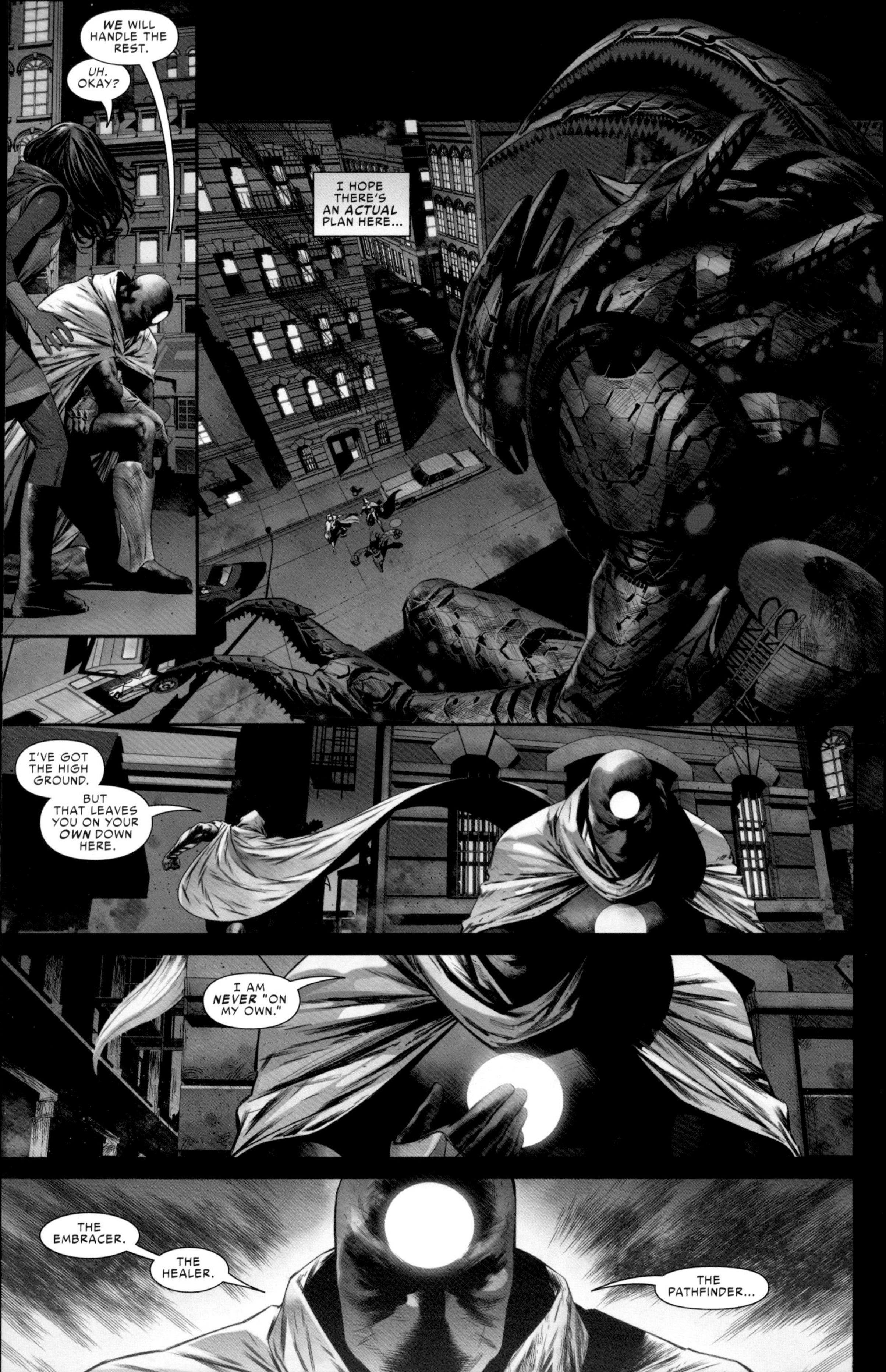
WE WILL HANDLE THE REST.
UH. OKAY?
I HOPE THERE'S AN ACTUAL PLAN HERE...
I'VE GOT THE HIGH GROUND.
BUT THAT LEAVES YOU ON YOUR OWN DOWN HERE.
I AM NEVER "ON MY OWN."
THE EMBRACER.
THE HEALER.
THE PATHFINDER...

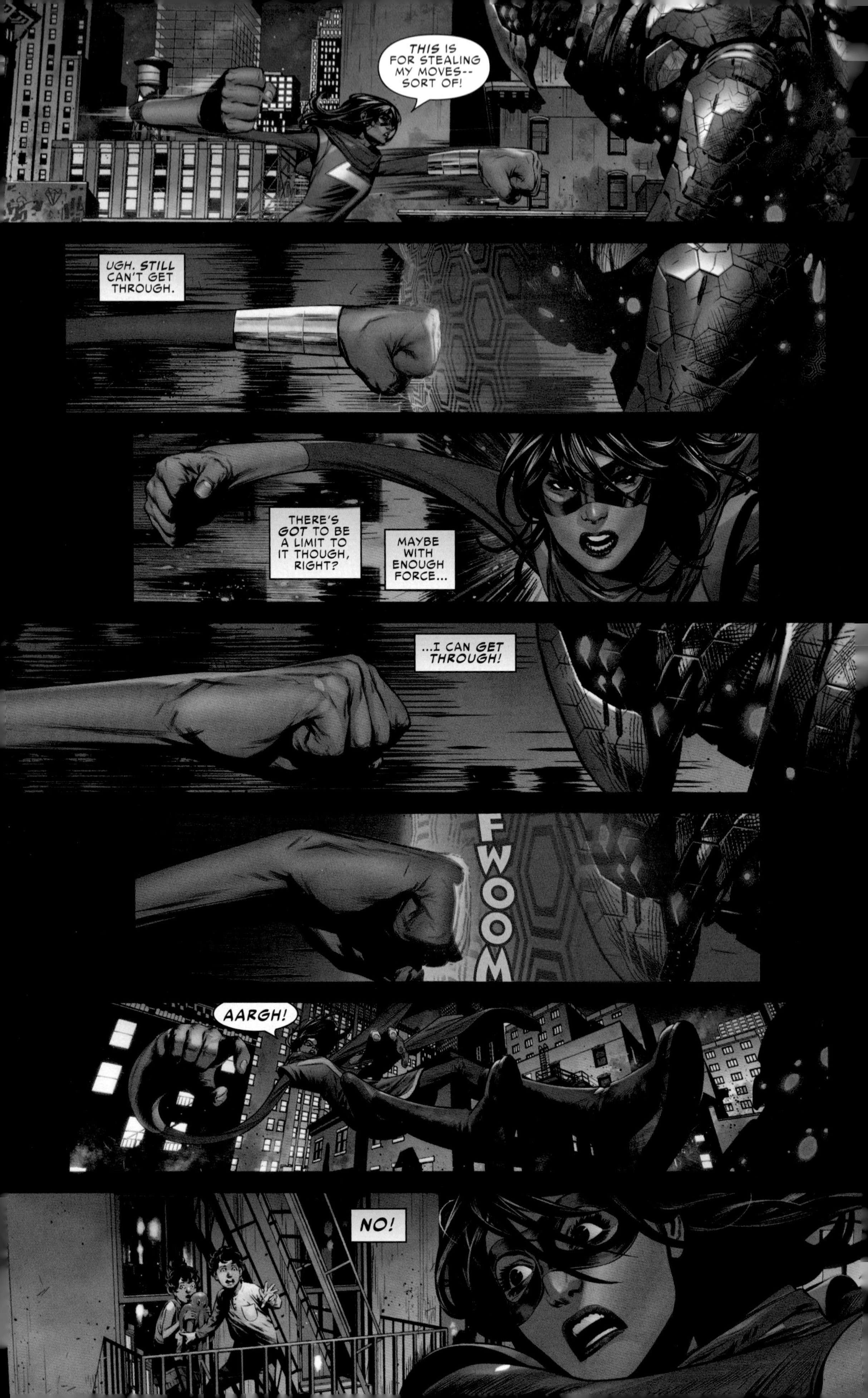
THIS IS FOR STEALING MY MOVES-- SORT OF!
UGH. STILL CAN'T GET THROUGH.
THERE'S GOT TO BE A LIMIT TO IT THOUGH, RIGHT?
MAYBE WITH ENOUGH FORCE...
...I CAN GET THROUGH!
FWOOM
AARGH!
NO!

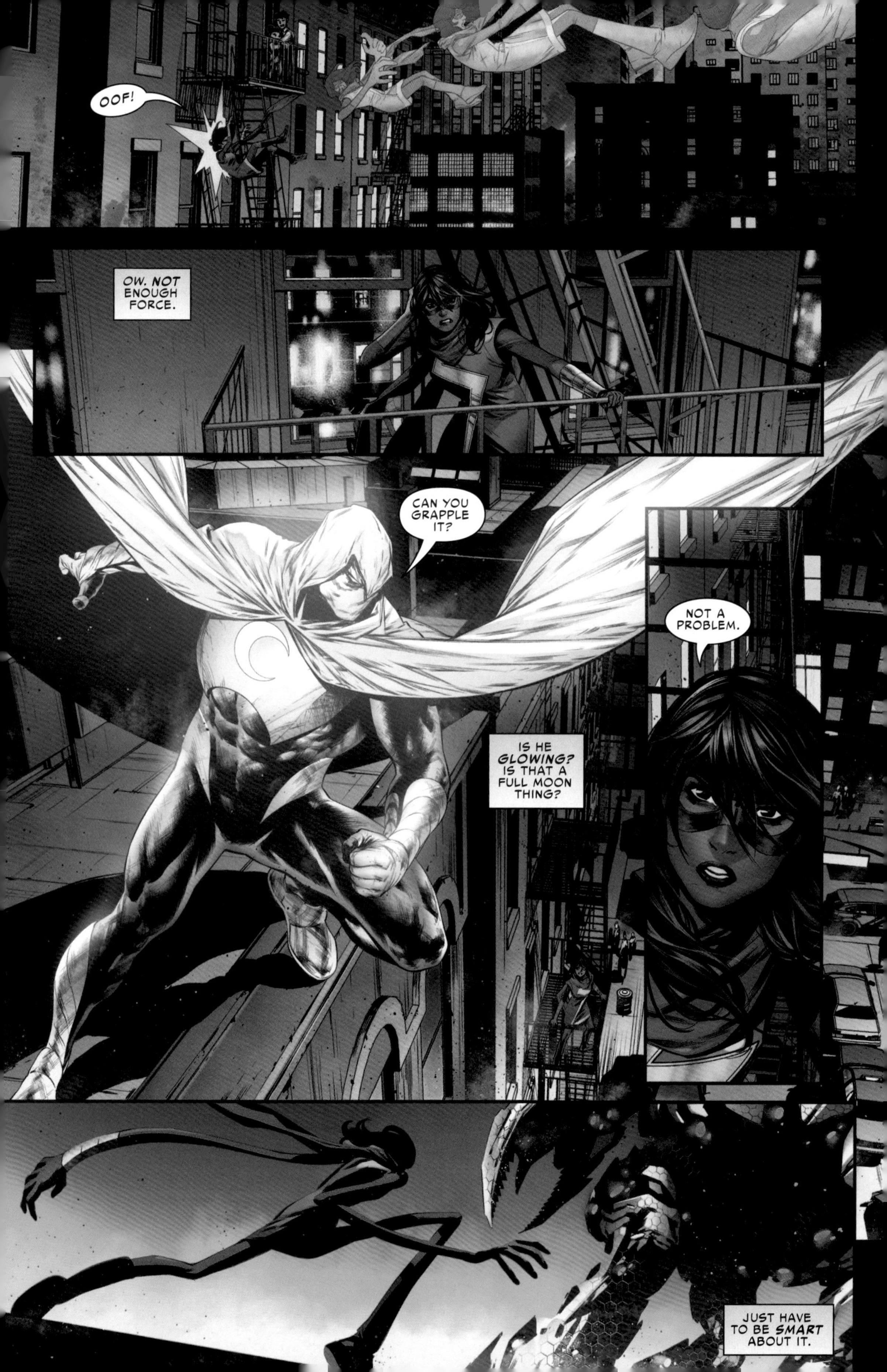
OOF!
OW. NOT ENOUGH FORCE.
CAN YOU GRAPPLE IT?
NOT A PROBLEM.
IS HE GLOWING? IS THAT A FULL MOON THING?
JUST HAVE TO BE SMART ABOUT IT.

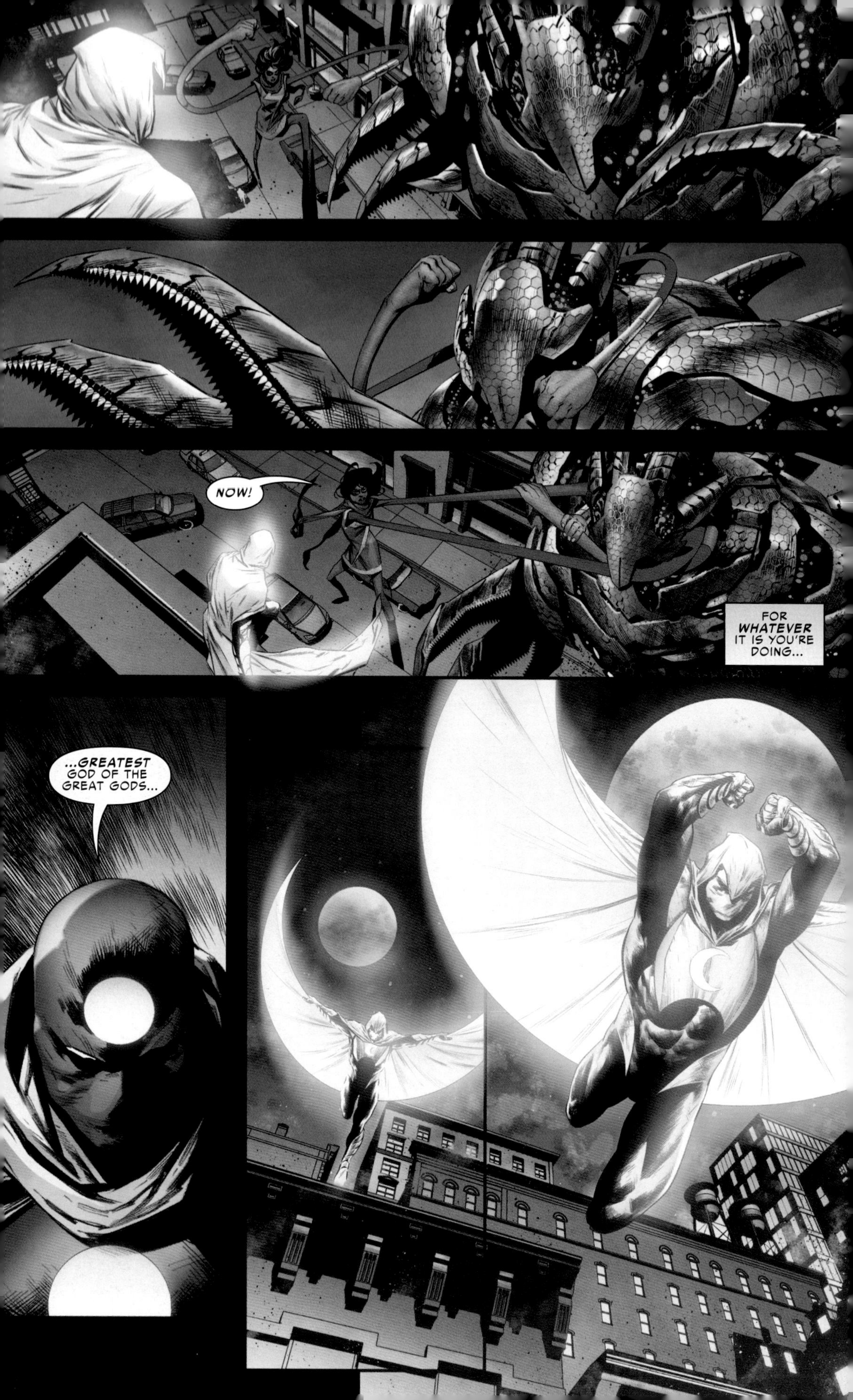

NOW!
FOR WHATEVER IT IS YOU'RE DOING...
...GREATEST GOD OF THE GREAT GODS...

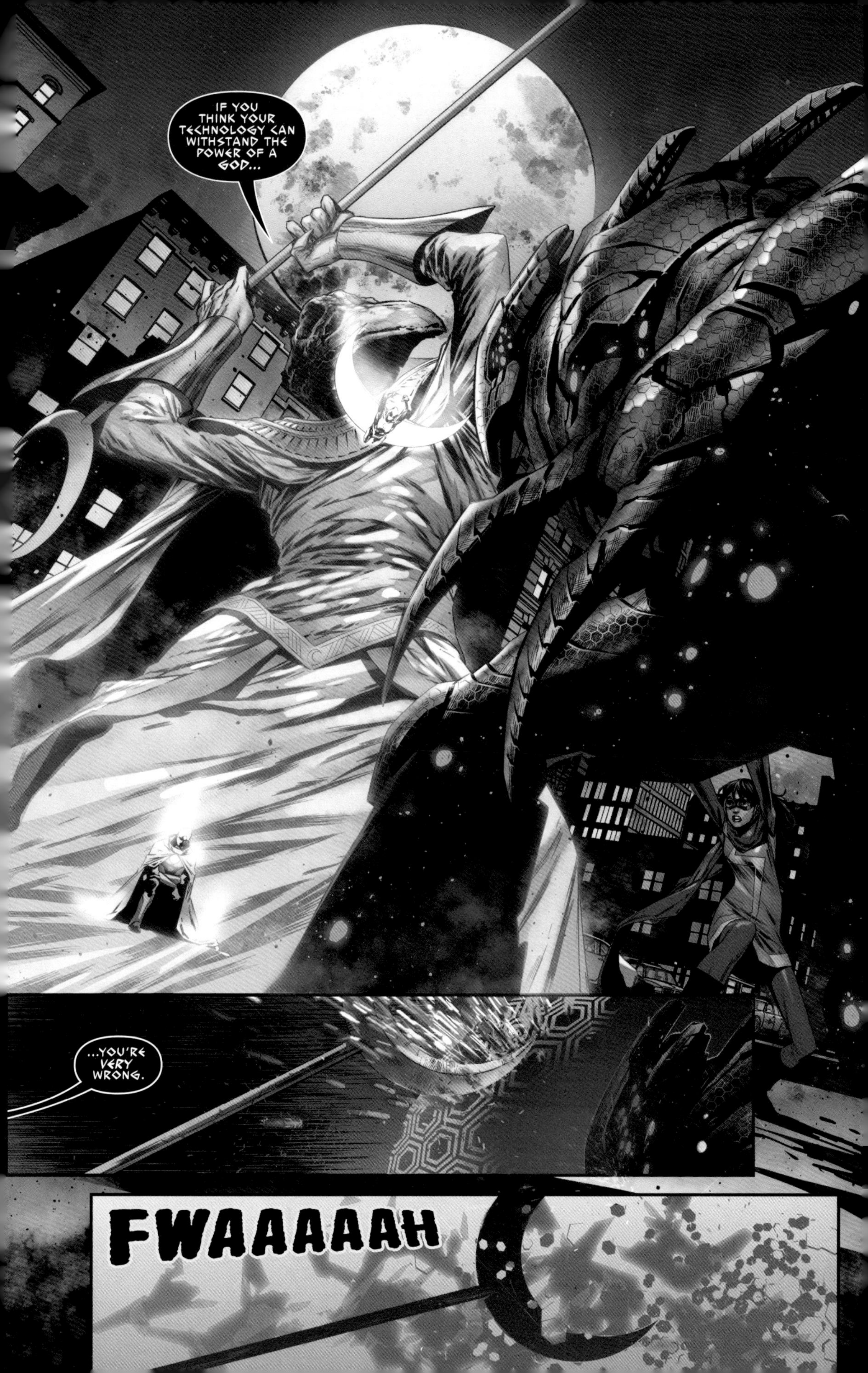
IF YOU THINK YOUR TECHNOLOGY CAN WITHSTAND THE POWER OF A GOD...
...YOU'RE VERY WRONG.
FWAAAAAH

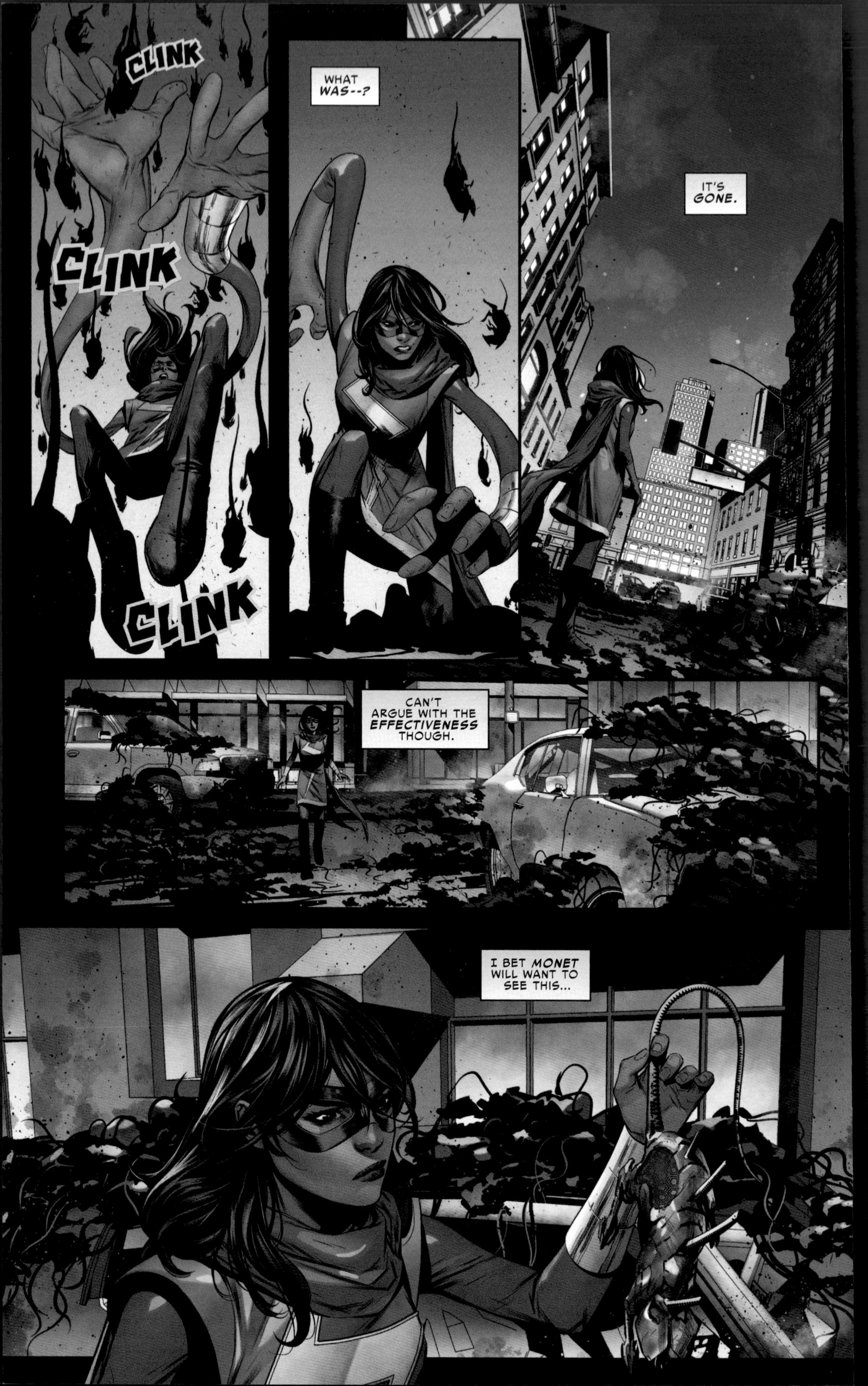
CLINK
CLINK
CLINK
WHAT WAS--?
IT'S GONE.
CAN'T ARGUE WITH THE EFFECTIVENESS THOUGH.
I BET MONET WILL WANT TO SEE THIS...

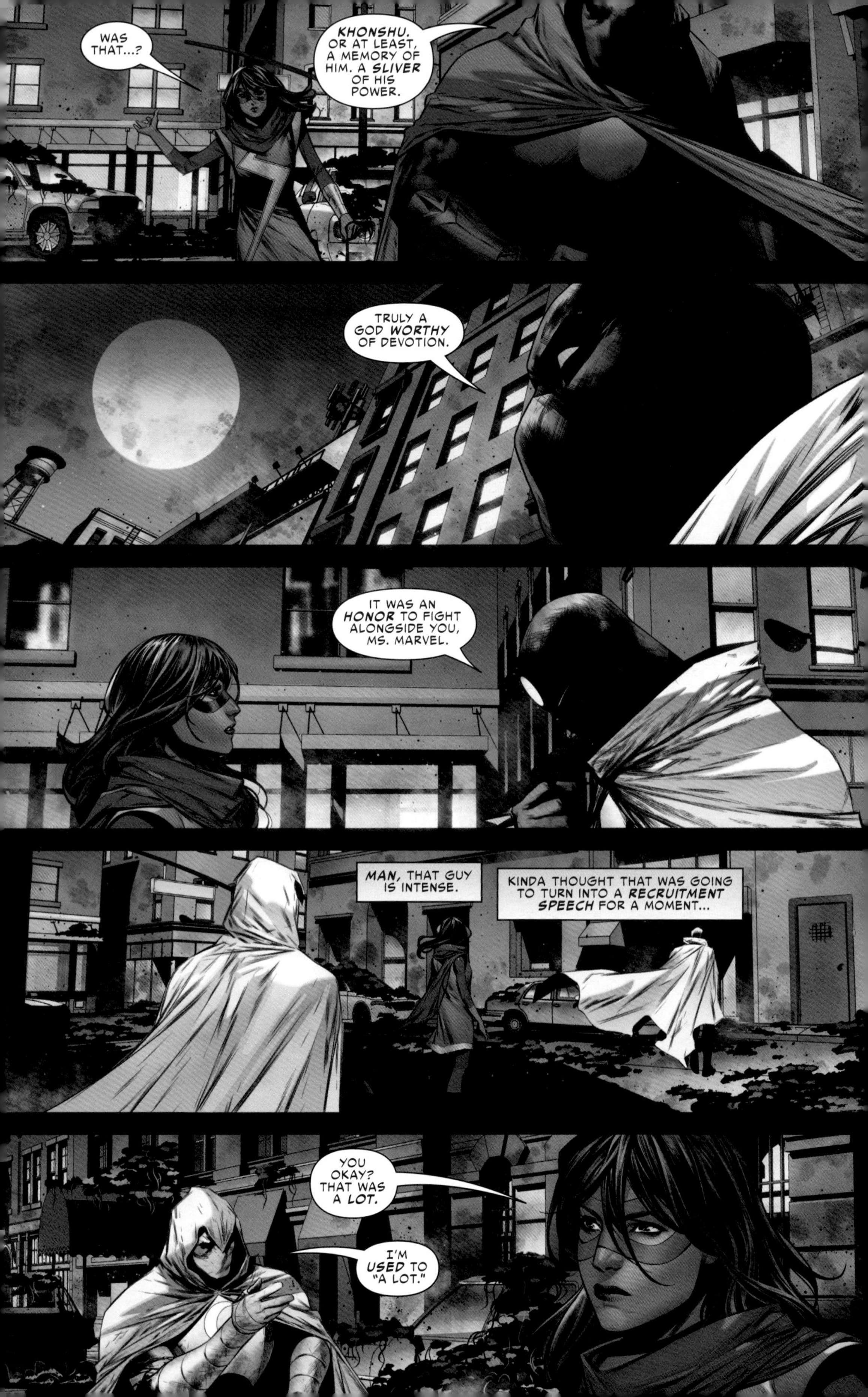
WAS THAT...?
KHONSHU. OR AT LEAST, A MEMORY OF HIM. A SLIVER OF HIS POWER.
TRULY A GOD WORTHY OF DEVOTION.
IT WAS AN HONOR TO FIGHT ALONGSIDE YOU, MS. MARVEL.
MAN, THAT GUY IS INTENSE.
KINDA THOUGHT THAT WAS GOING TO TURN INTO A RECRUITMENT SPEECH FOR A MOMENT...
YOU OKAY? THAT WAS A LOT.
I'M USED TO "A LOT."

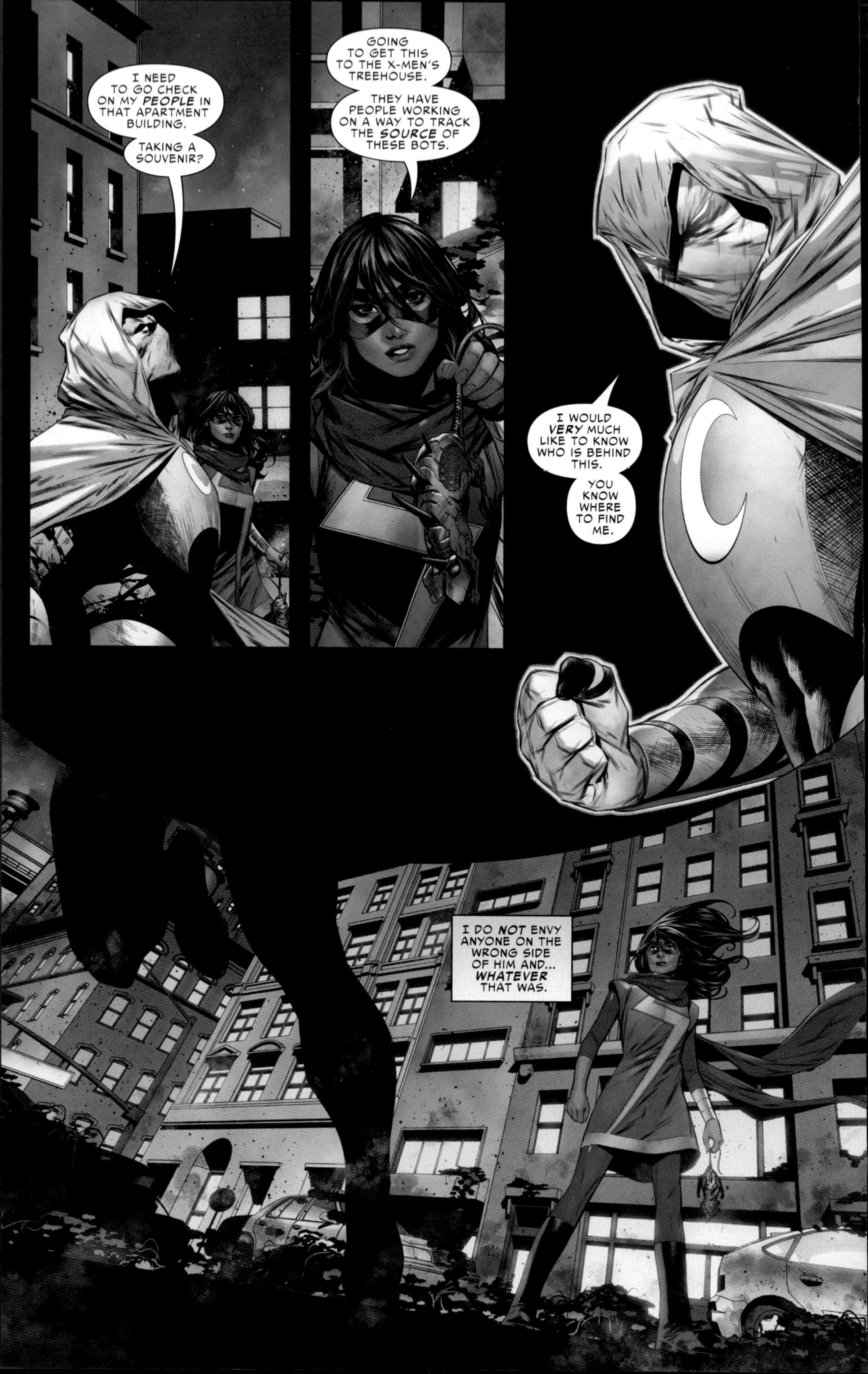
I NEED TO GO CHECK ON MY PEOPLE IN THAT APARTMENT BUILDING.
TAKING A SOUVENIR?
GOING TO GET THIS TO THE X-MEN'S TREEHOUSE.
THEY HAVE PEOPLE WORKING ON A WAY TO TRACK THE SOURCE OF THESE BOTS.
I WOULD VERY MUCH LIKE TO KNOW WHO IS BEHIND THIS.
YOU KNOW WHERE TO FIND ME.
I DO NOT ENVY ANYONE ON THE WRONG SIDE OF HIM AND... WHATEVER THAT WAS.

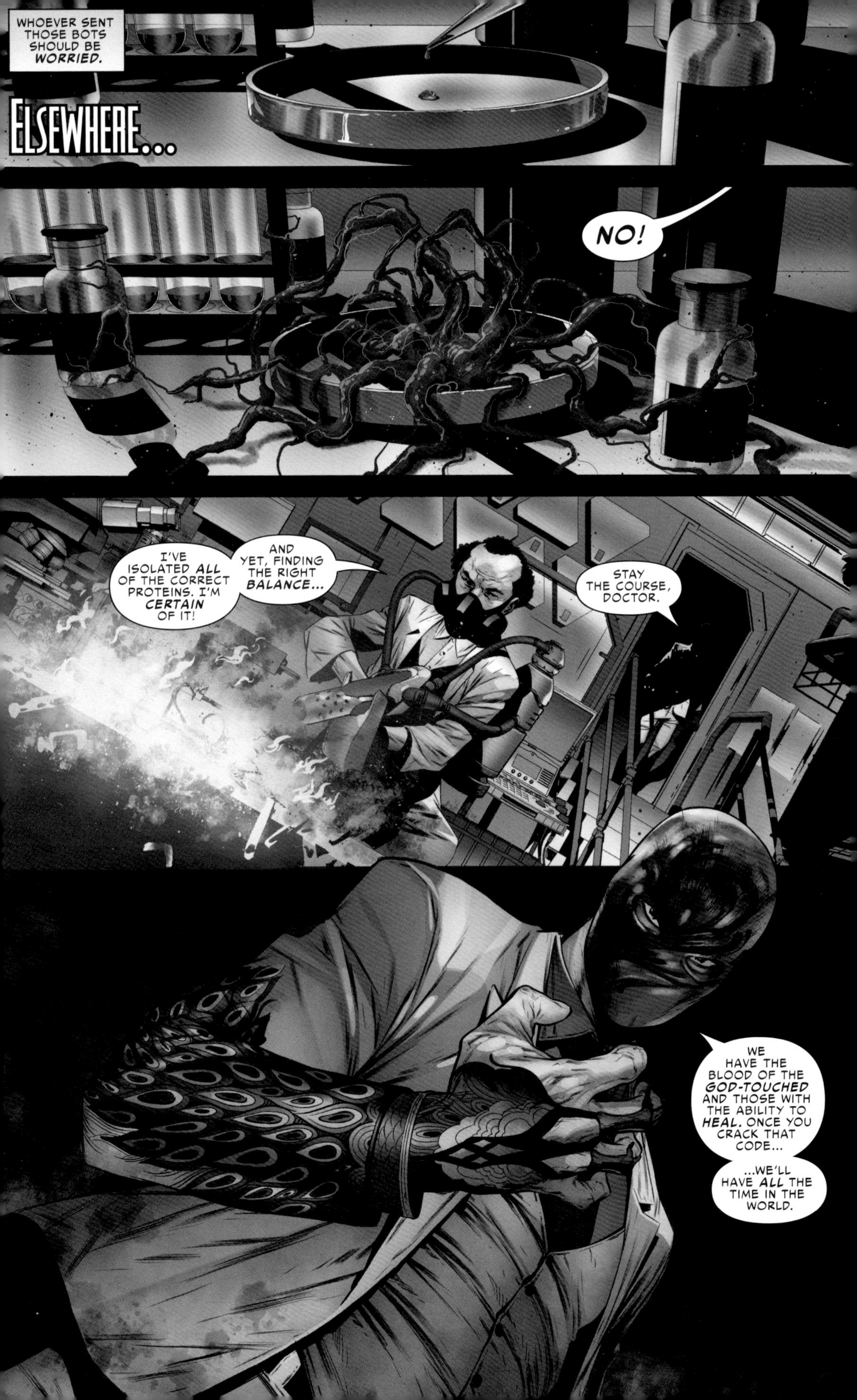
WHOEVER SENT THOSE BOTS SHOULD BE WORRIED.
ELSEWHERE...
NO!
I'VE ISOLATED ALL OF THE CORRECT PROTEINS. I'M CERTAIN OF IT!
AND YET, FINDING THE RIGHT BALANCE...
STAY THE COURSE, DOCTOR.
WE HAVE THE BLOOD OF THE GOD-TOUCHED AND THOSE WITH THE ABILITY TO HEAL. ONCE YOU CRACK THAT CODE...
...WE'LL HAVE ALL THE TIME IN THE WORLD.

MS. MARVEL & VENOM

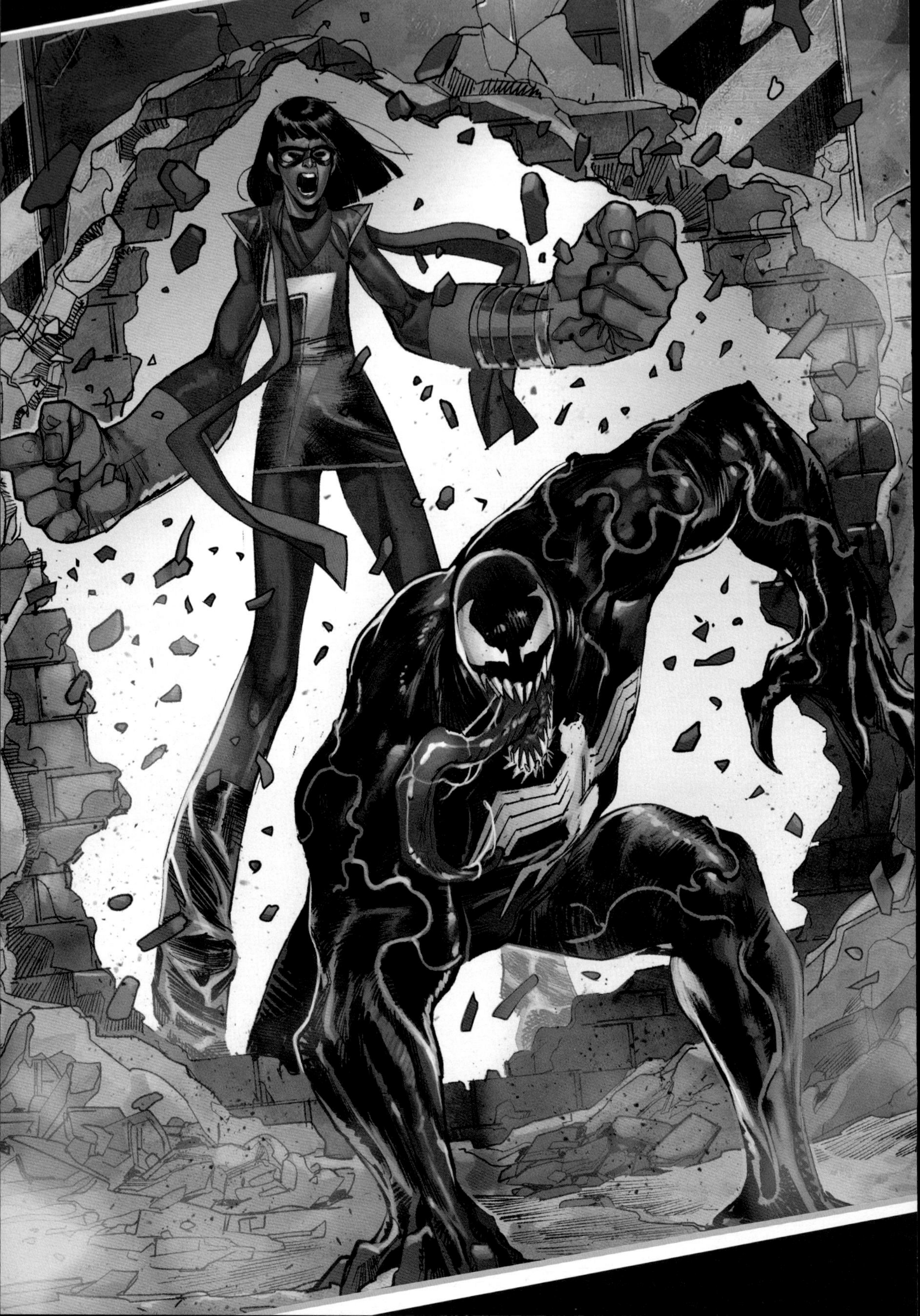

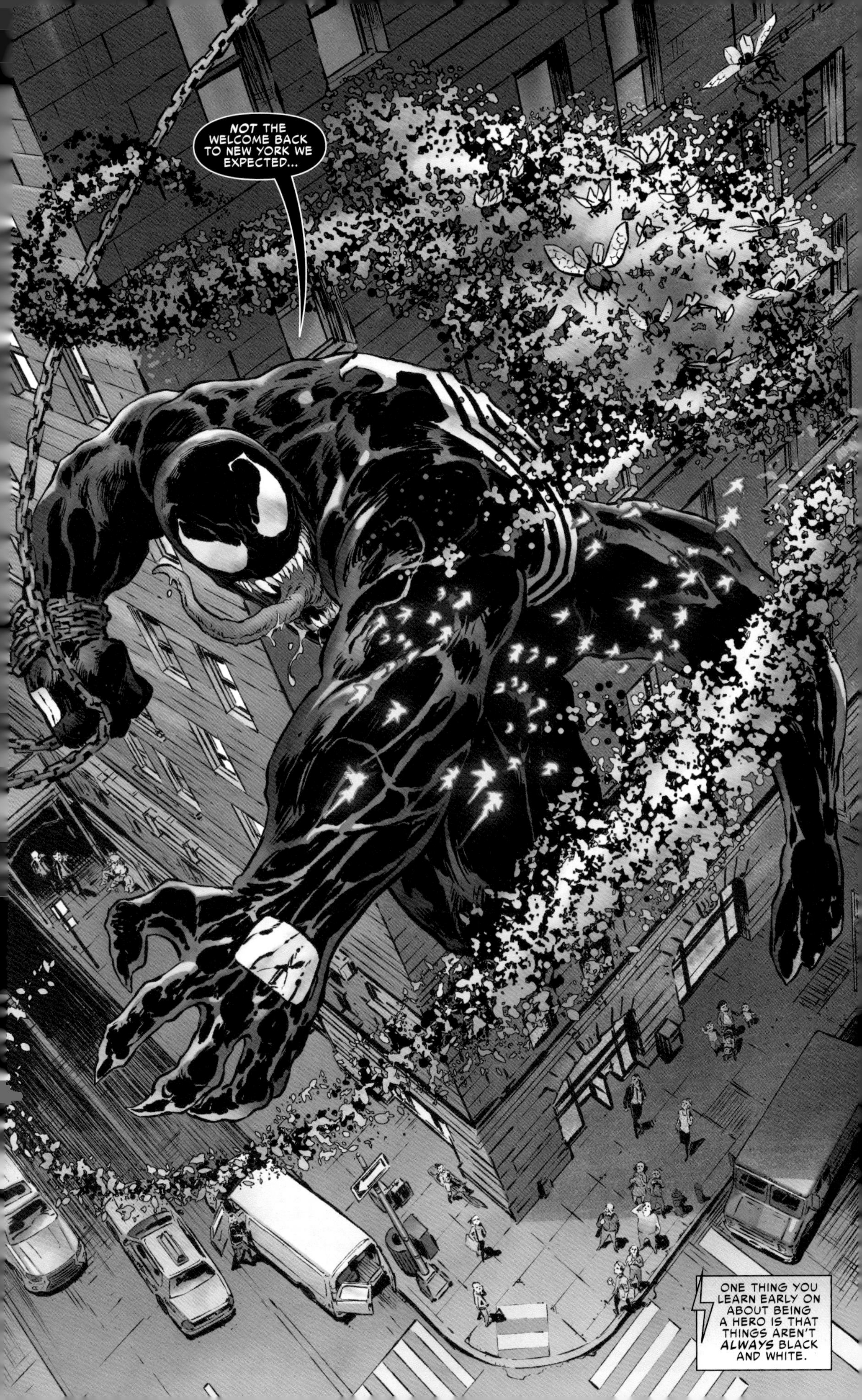
NOT THE WELCOME BACK TO NEW YORK WE EXPECTED...
ONE THING YOU LEARN EARLY ON ABOUT BEING A HERO IS THAT THINGS AREN'T ALWAYS BLACK AND WHITE.

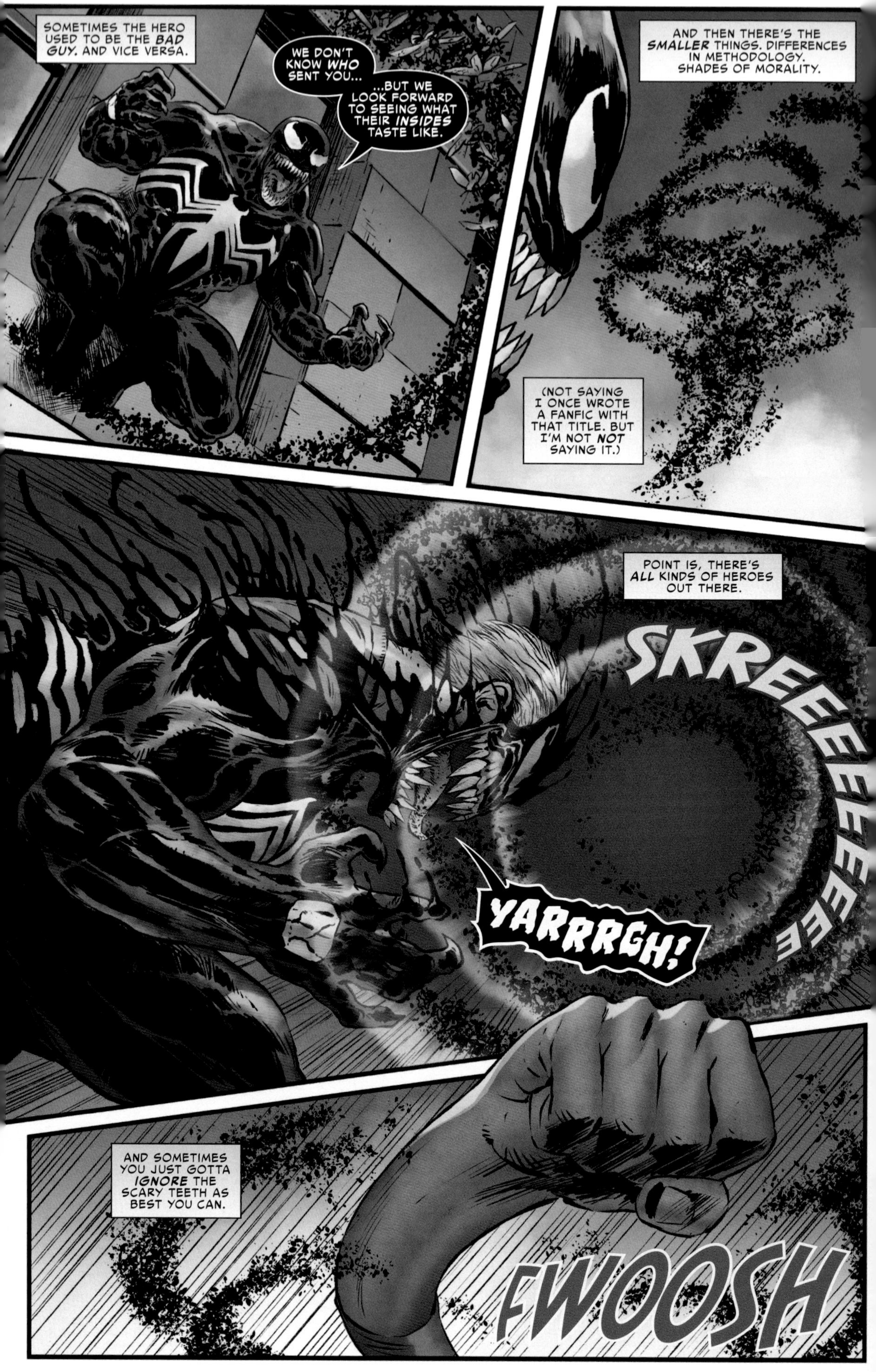
SOMETIMES THE HERO USED TO BE THE *BAD GUY.* AND VICE VERSA.
WE DON'T KNOW *WHO* SENT YOU...
...BUT WE LOOK FORWARD TO SEEING WHAT THEIR *INSIDES* TASTE LIKE.
AND THEN THERE'S THE *SMALLER* THINGS. DIFFERENCES IN METHODOLOGY. SHADES OF MORALITY.
(NOT SAYING I ONCE WROTE A FANFIC WITH THAT TITLE. BUT I'M NOT *NOT* SAYING IT.)
POINT IS, THERE'S *ALL* KINDS OF HEROES OUT THERE.
SKREEEEEEEEEEE
YARRRGH!
AND SOMETIMES YOU JUST GOTTA *IGNORE* THE SCARY TEETH AS BEST YOU CAN.
FWOOSH

YES! PROBABLY THE *ONLY* HIT I'M GETTING IN ON THOSE BUGS BEFORE THEY DO THE STUPID ADAPT-O-BOT THING.

GLAD IT WAS A *GOOD* ONE.

MORE IMPORTANTLY, IT LOOKS LIKE MONET'S TECH TRACKER *WORKS.*

WHOEVER IS BEHIND THESE WEIRD ROBOT SWARMS TARGETED THE *X-MEN'S* HOME FIRST.

PUNCHED A FEW HOLES IN *WOLVERINE.**

#MS. MARVEL & WOLVERINE #1!

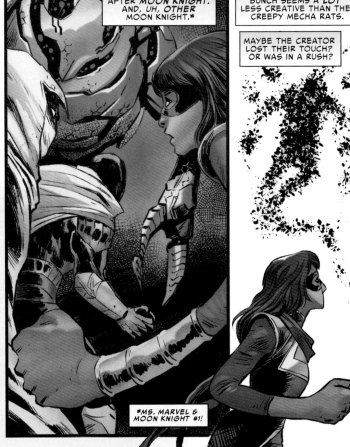

THEN THEY WENT AFTER *MOON KNIGHT.* AND, UH, *OTHER* MOON KNIGHT.**

HAVE TO SAY, THIS BUNCH SEEMS A *LOT* LESS CREATIVE THAN THE CREEPY MECHA RATS.

MAYBE THE CREATOR LOST THEIR TOUCH? OR WAS IN A RUSH?

#MS. MARVEL & MOON KNIGHT #1!

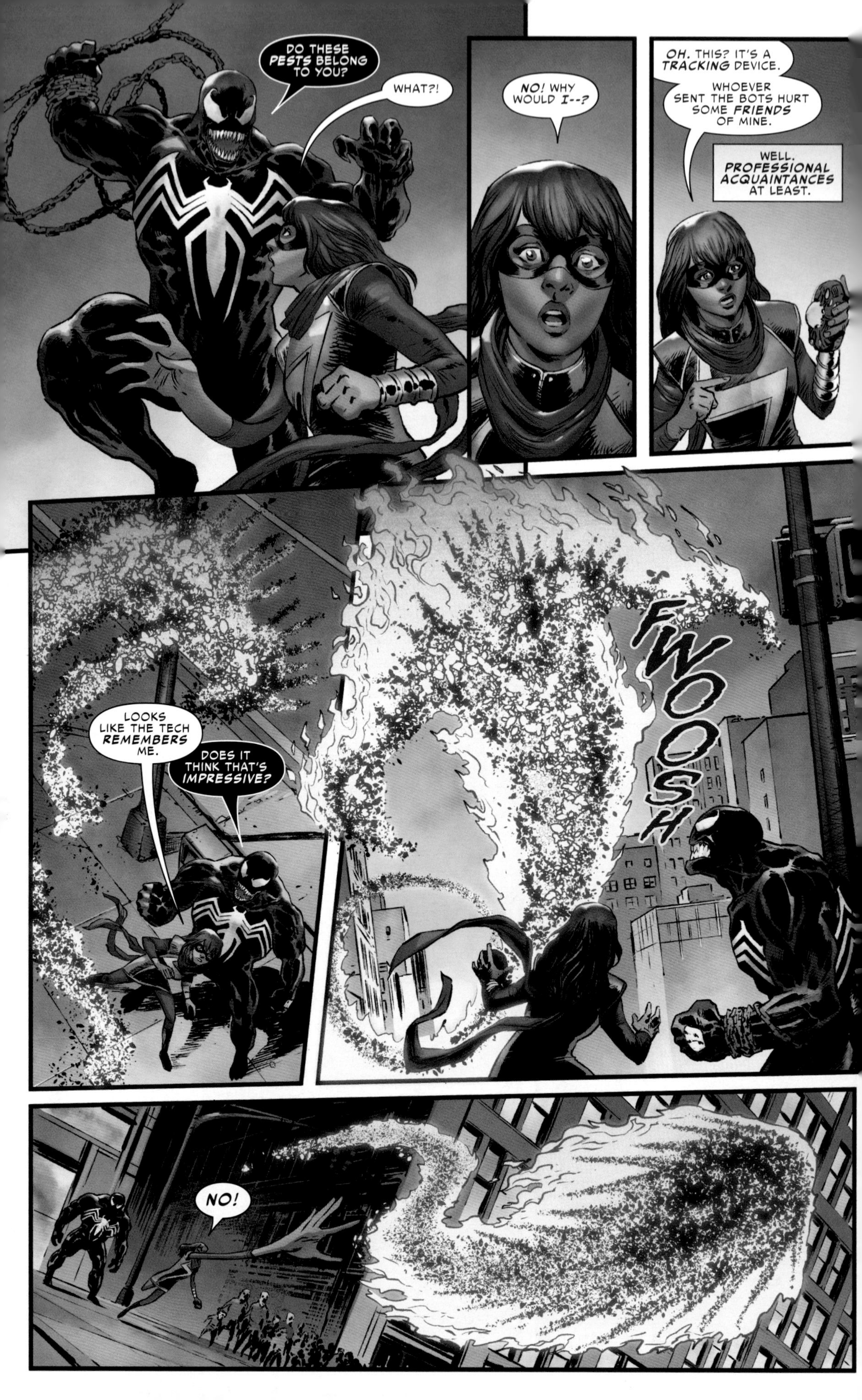

DO THESE PESTS BELONG TO YOU?
WHAT?!
NO! WHY WOULD I--?
OH. THIS? IT'S A TRACKING DEVICE.
WHOEVER SENT THE BOTS HURT SOME FRIENDS OF MINE.
WELL. PROFESSIONAL ACQUAINTANCES AT LEAST.
LOOKS LIKE THE TECH REMEMBERS ME.
DOES IT THINK THAT'S IMPRESSIVE?
FWOOSH
NO!

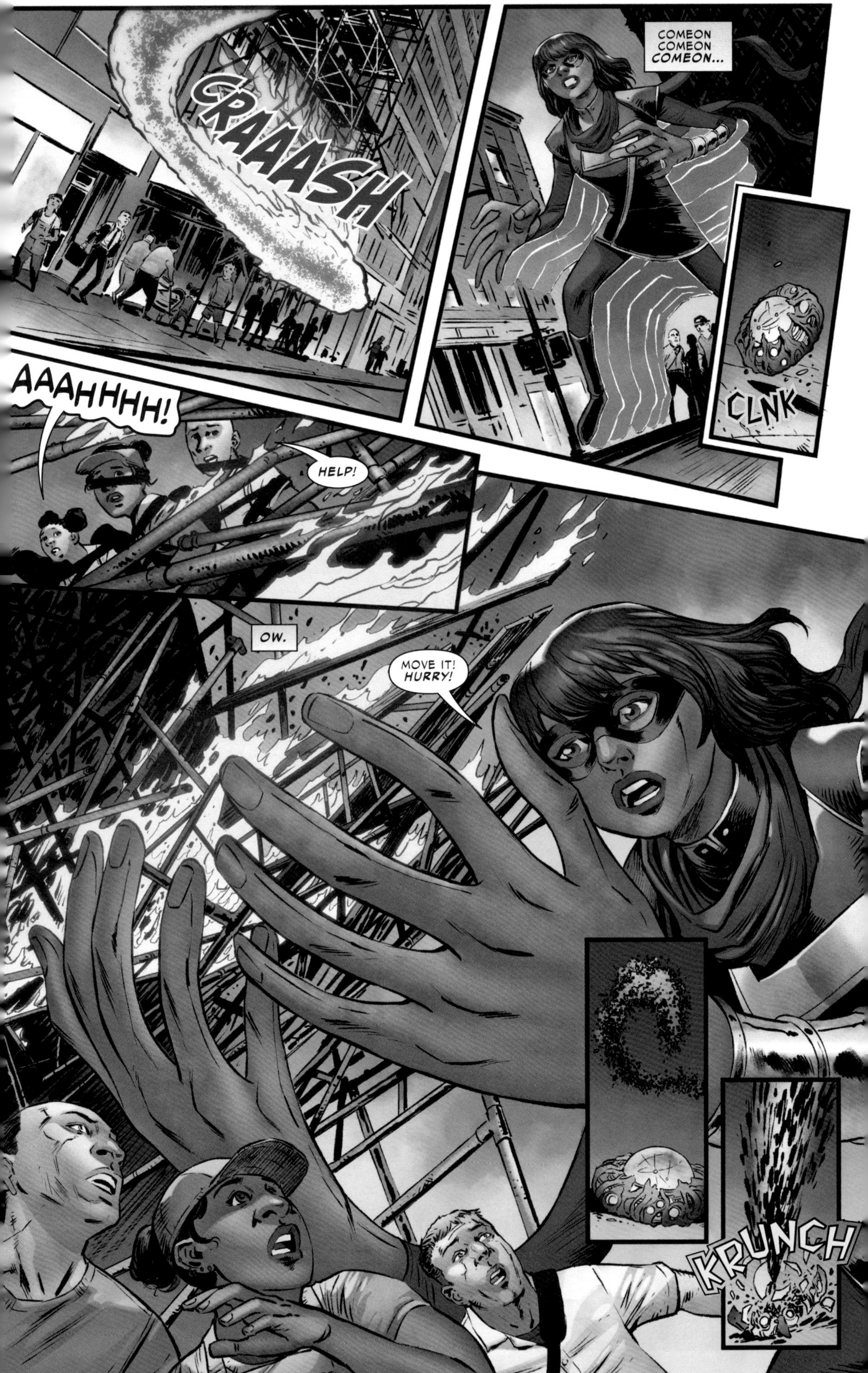
CRAAASH
COMEON
COMEON
COMEON...
CLNK
AAAHHHH!
HELP!
OW.
MOVE IT!
HURRY!
KRUNCH

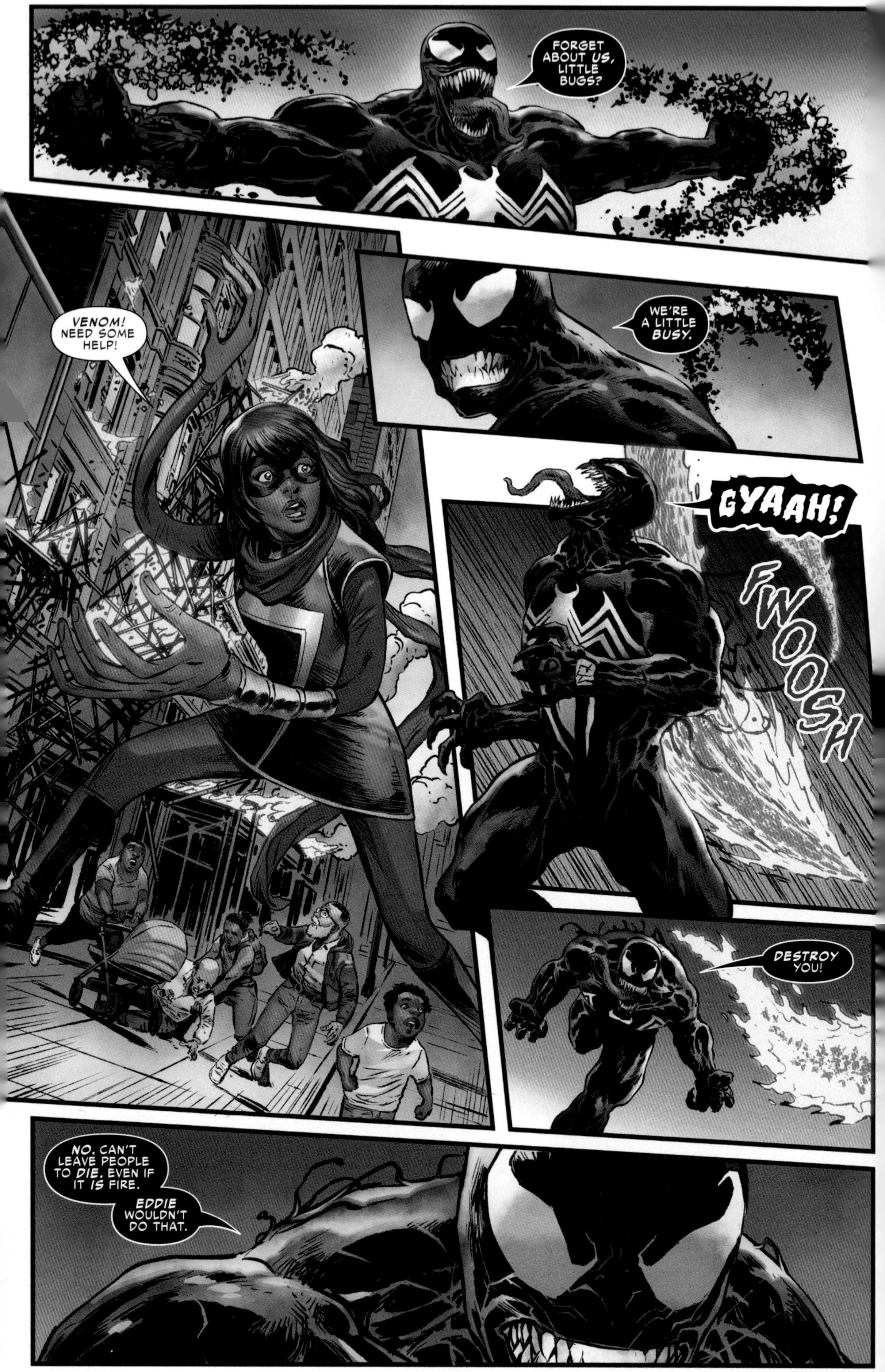
FORGET ABOUT US, LITTLE BUGS?
VENOM! NEED SOME HELP!
WE'RE A LITTLE BUSY.
GYAAH!
FWOOSH
DESTROY YOU!
NO. CAN'T LEAVE PEOPLE TO DIE. EVEN IF IT IS FIRE.
EDDIE WOULDN'T DO THAT.

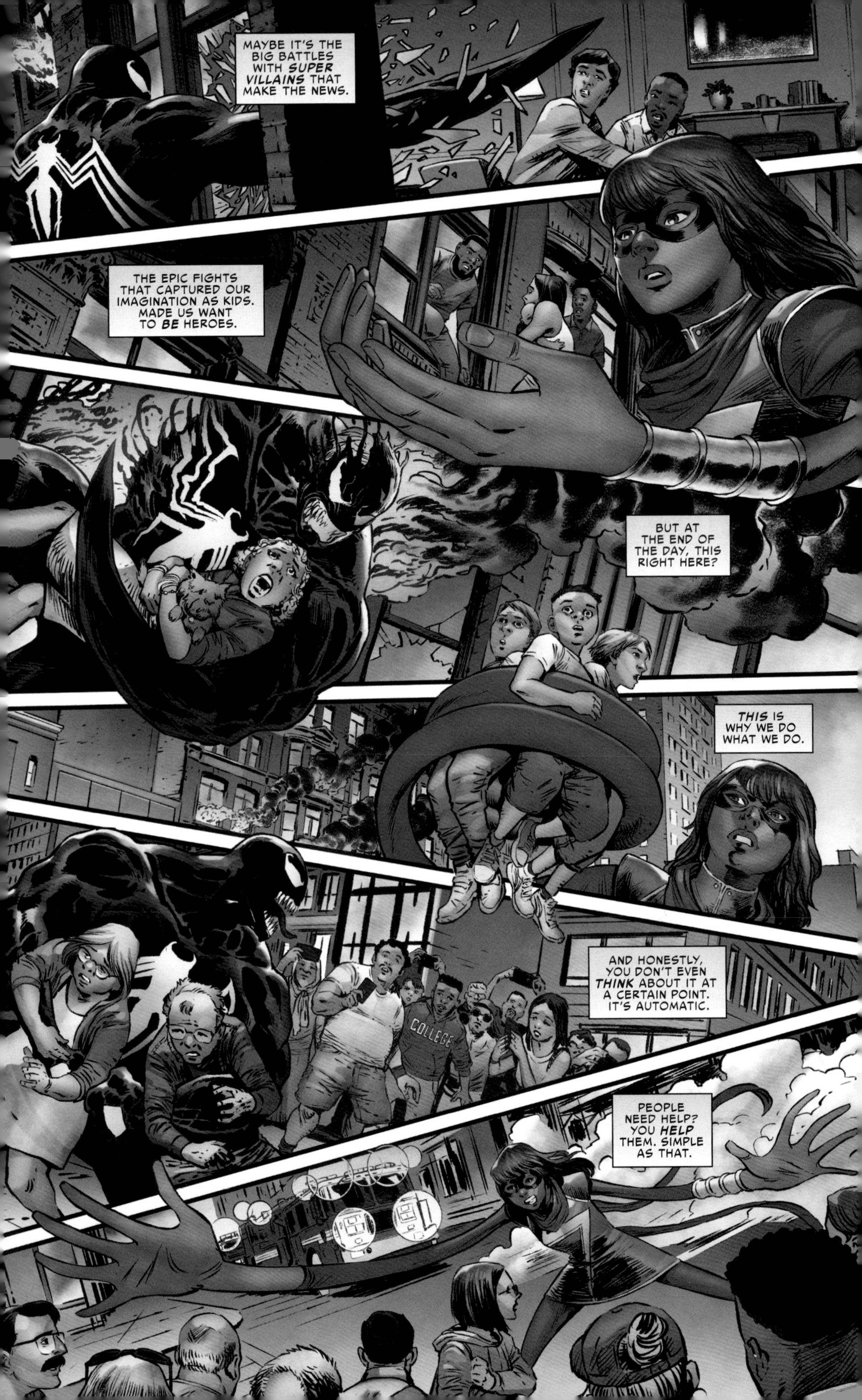
MAYBE IT'S THE BIG BATTLES WITH SUPER VILLAINS THAT MAKE THE NEWS.
THE EPIC FIGHTS THAT CAPTURED OUR IMAGINATION AS KIDS. MADE US WANT TO BE HEROES.
BUT AT THE END OF THE DAY, THIS RIGHT HERE?
THIS IS WHY WE DO WHAT WE DO.
COLLEGE
AND HONESTLY, YOU DON'T EVEN THINK ABOUT IT AT A CERTAIN POINT. IT'S AUTOMATIC.
PEOPLE NEED HELP? YOU HELP THEM. SIMPLE AS THAT.

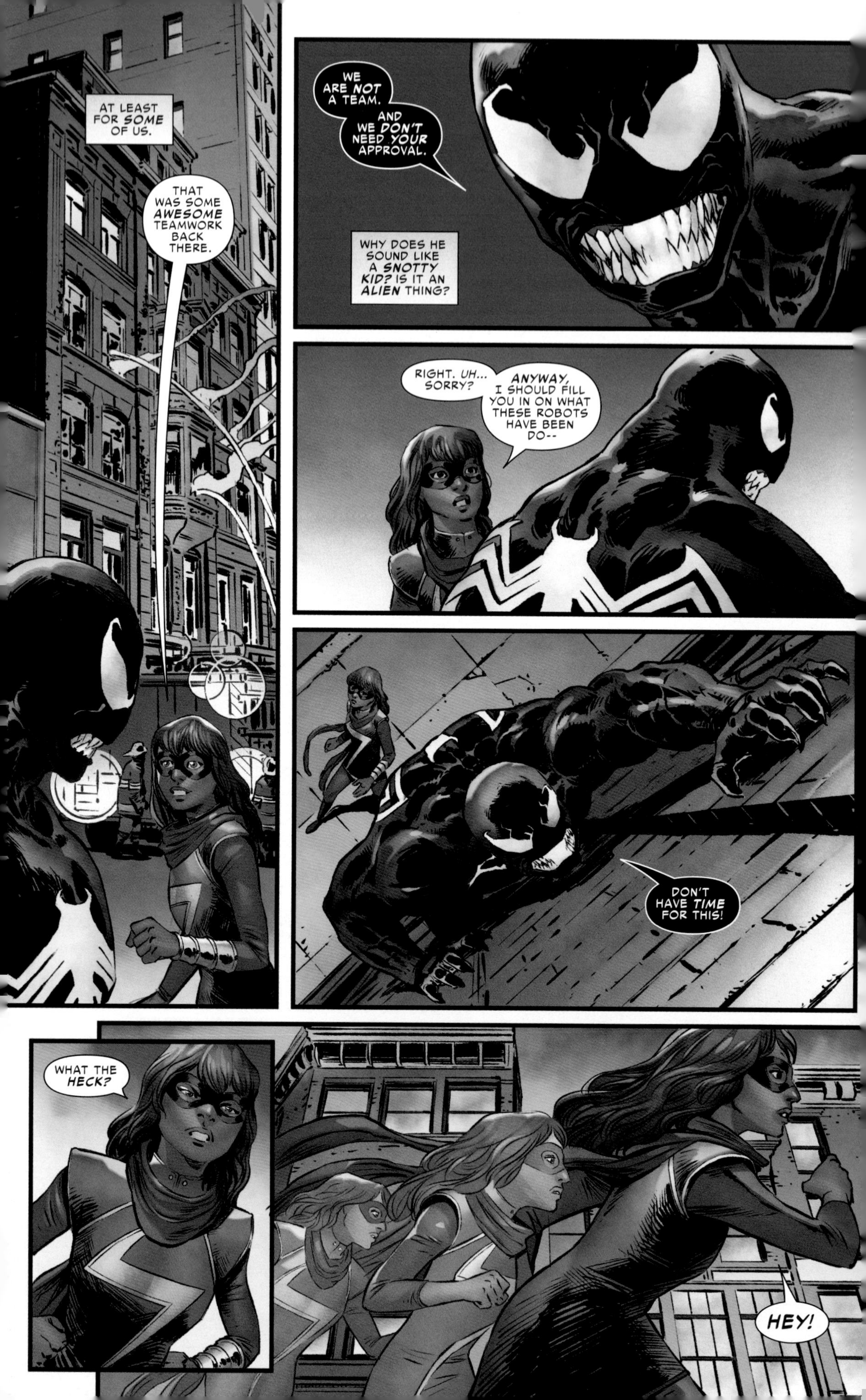
AT LEAST FOR SOME OF US.
THAT WAS SOME AWESOME TEAMWORK BACK THERE.
WE ARE NOT A TEAM.
AND WE DON'T NEED YOUR APPROVAL.
WHY DOES HE SOUND LIKE A SNOTTY KID? IS IT AN ALIEN THING?
RIGHT. UH... SORRY?
ANYWAY, I SHOULD FILL YOU IN ON WHAT THESE ROBOTS HAVE BEEN DO--
DON'T HAVE TIME FOR THIS!
WHAT THE HECK?
HEY!

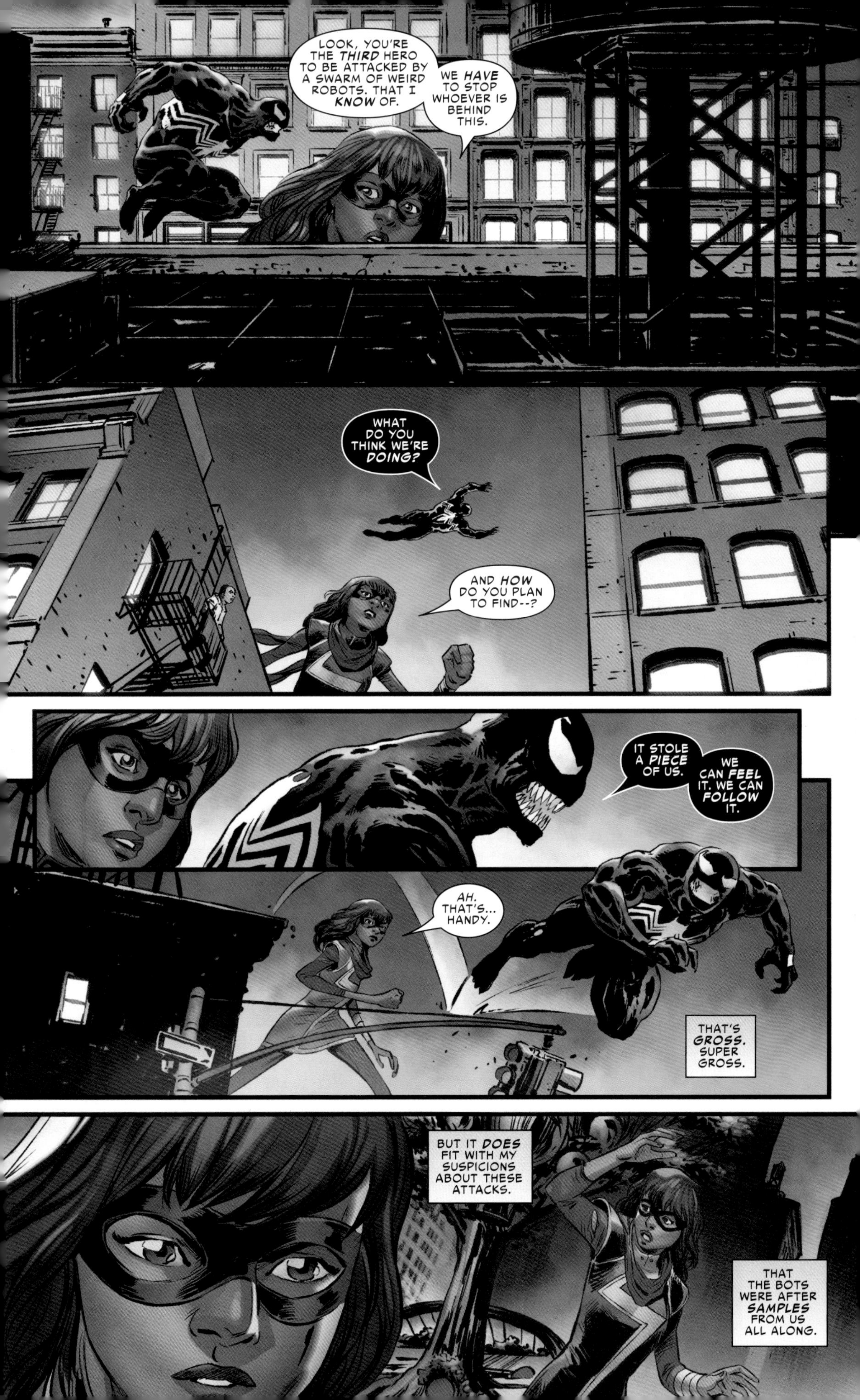
LOOK, YOU'RE THE THIRD HERO TO BE ATTACKED BY A SWARM OF WEIRD ROBOTS. THAT I KNOW OF.
WE HAVE TO STOP WHOEVER IS BEHIND THIS.
WHAT DO YOU THINK WE'RE DOING?
AND HOW DO YOU PLAN TO FIND--?
IT STOLE A PIECE OF US.
WE CAN FEEL IT. WE CAN FOLLOW IT.
AH. THAT'S... HANDY.
THAT'S GROSS. SUPER GROSS.
BUT IT DOES FIT WITH MY SUSPICIONS ABOUT THESE ATTACKS.
THAT THE BOTS WERE AFTER SAMPLES FROM US ALL ALONG.

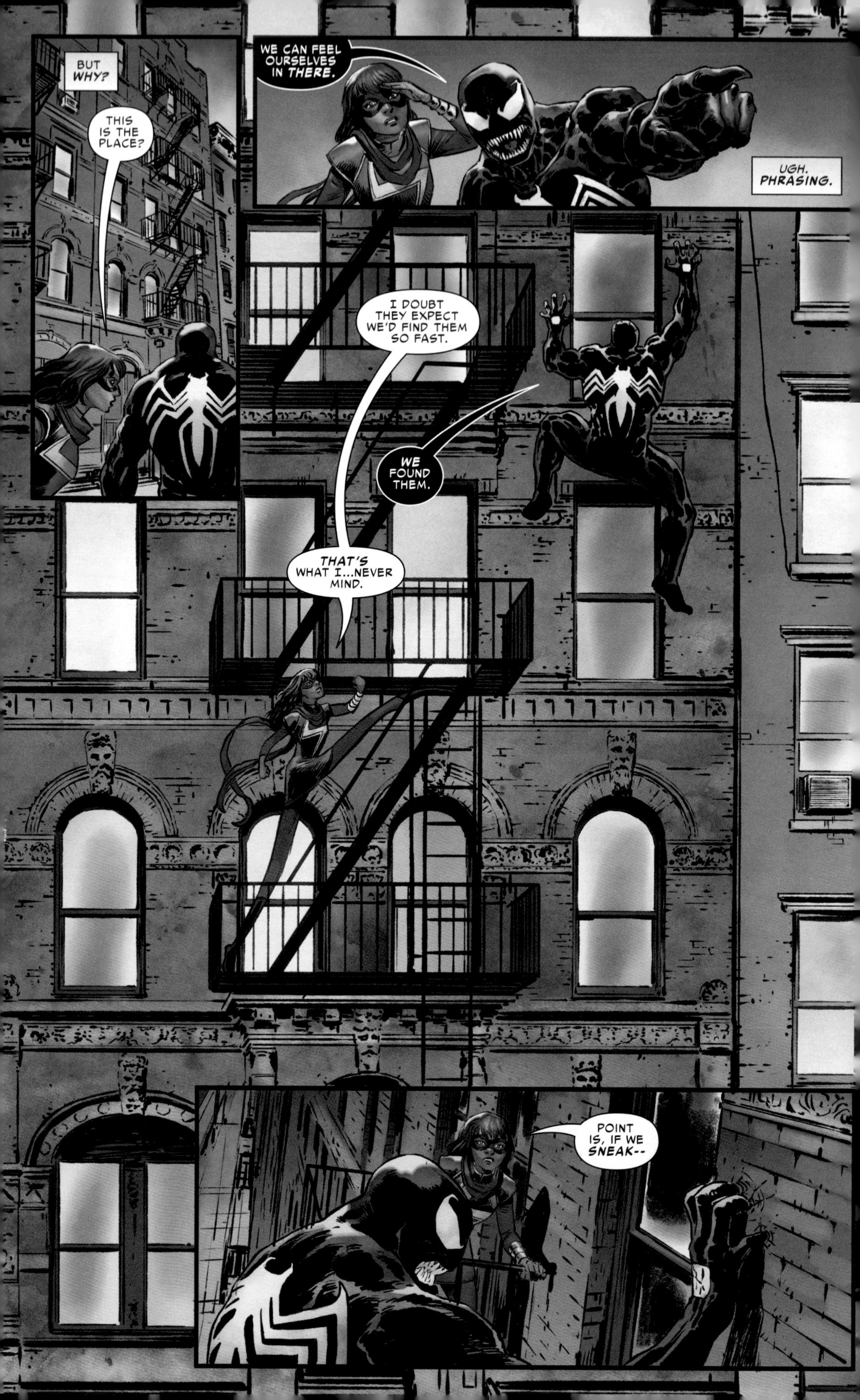

THIS IS THE PLACE?
BUT WHY?
WE CAN FEEL OURSELVES IN THERE.
UGH. PHRASING.
I DOUBT THEY EXPECT WE'D FIND THEM SO FAST.
WE FOUND THEM.
THAT'S WHAT I...NEVER MIND.
POINT IS, IF WE SNEAK--

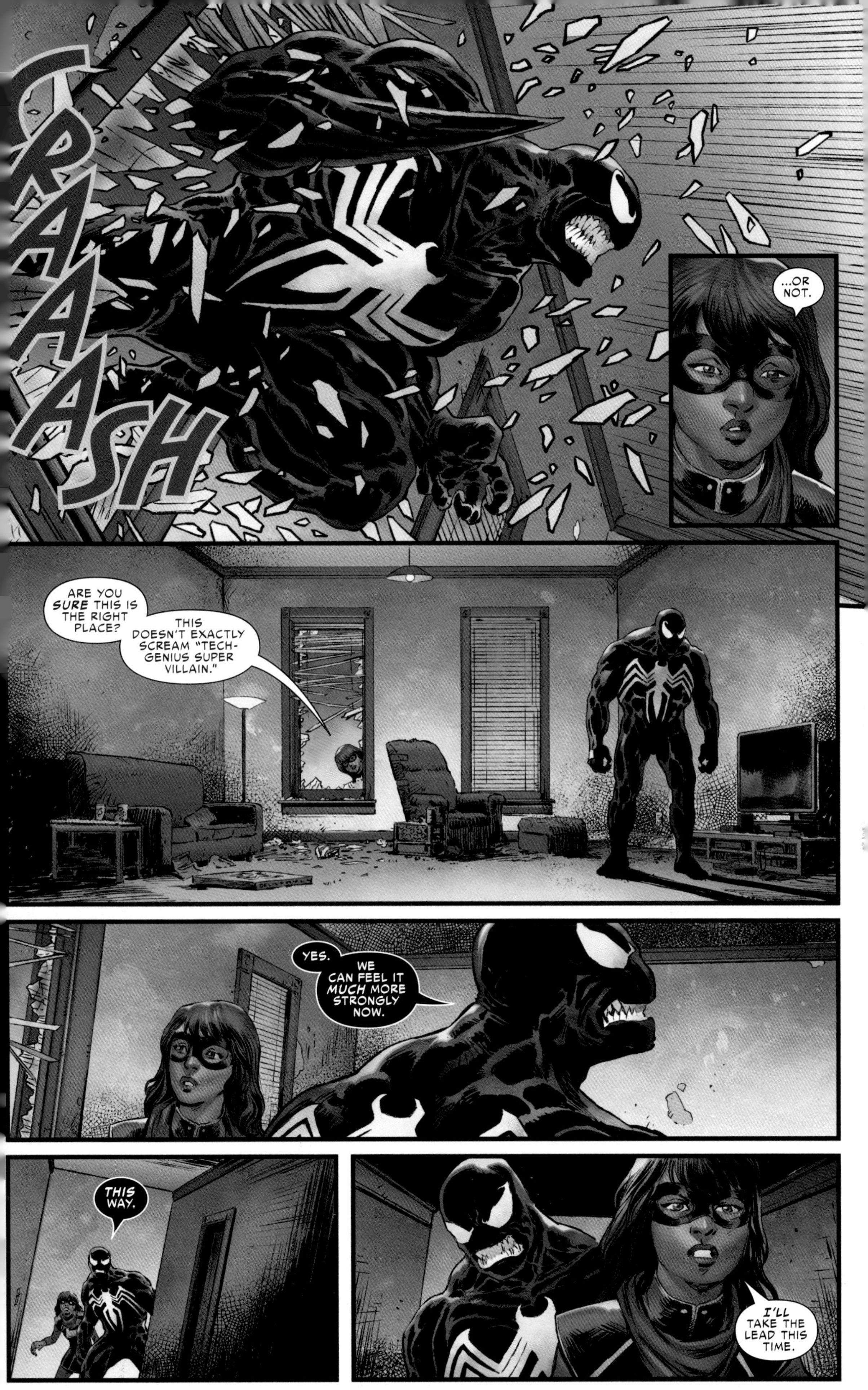
CRAAAASH
...OR NOT.
ARE YOU SURE THIS IS THE RIGHT PLACE?
THIS DOESN'T EXACTLY SCREAM "TECH-GENIUS SUPER VILLAIN."
YES.
WE CAN FEEL IT MUCH MORE STRONGLY NOW.
THIS WAY.
I'LL TAKE THE LEAD THIS TIME.

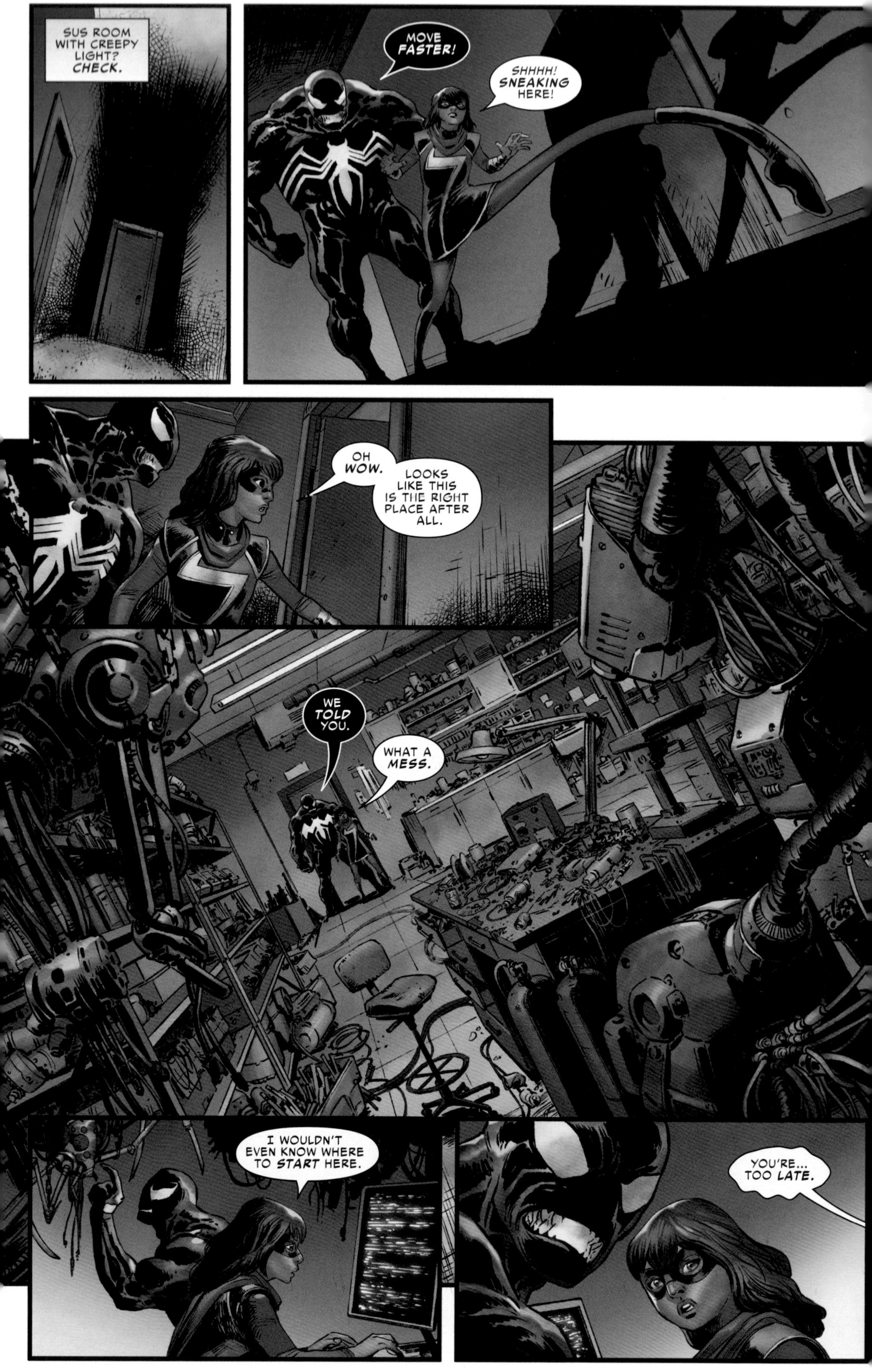

SUS ROOM WITH CREEPY LIGHT? CHECK.
MOVE FASTER!
SHHHH! SNEAKING HERE!
OH WOW.
LOOKS LIKE THIS IS THE RIGHT PLACE AFTER ALL.
WE TOLD YOU.
WHAT A MESS.
I WOULDN'T EVEN KNOW WHERE TO START HERE.
YOU'RE... TOO LATE.

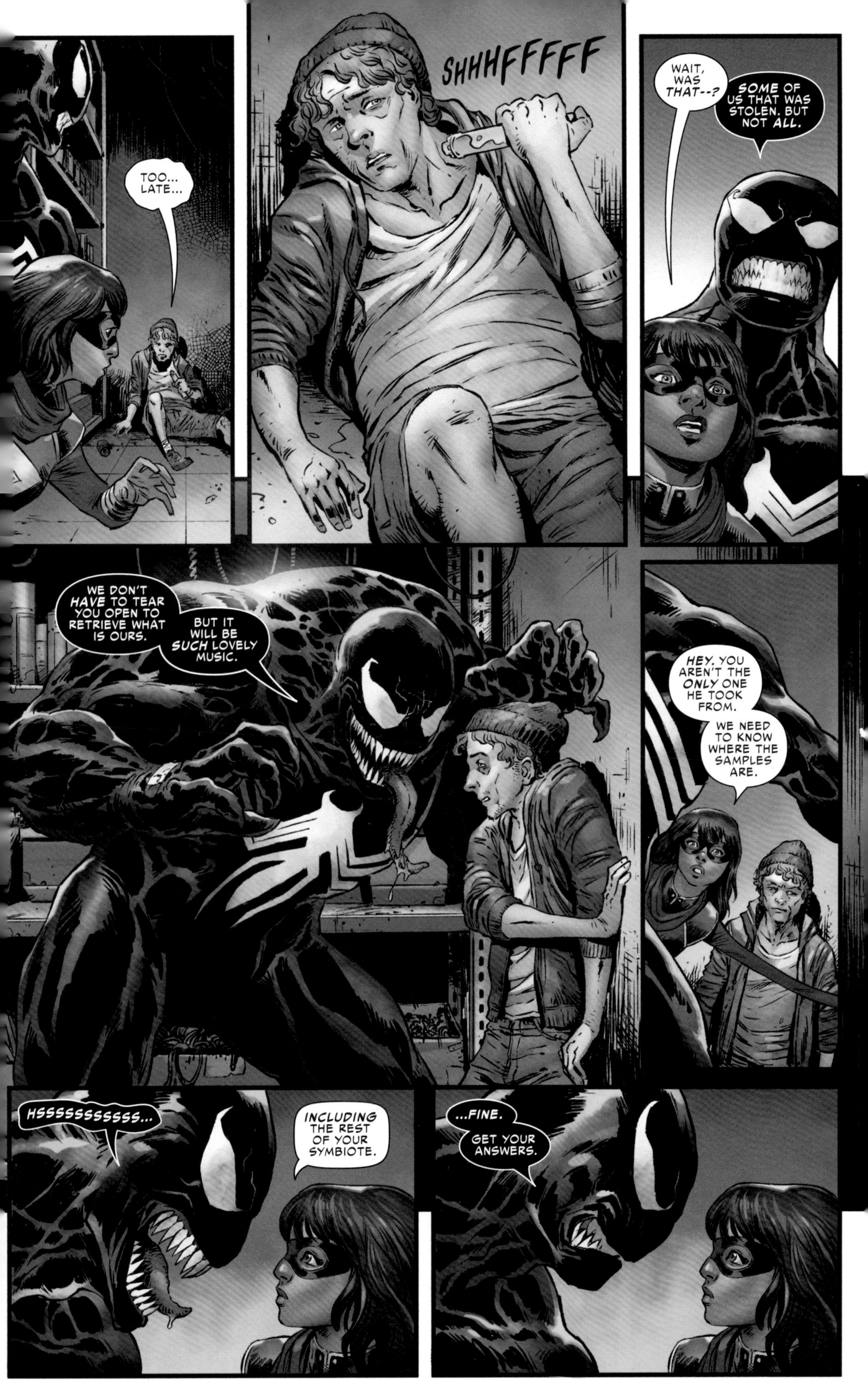
TOO... LATE...
SHHHFFFFF
WAIT, WAS THAT--?
SOME OF US THAT WAS STOLEN. BUT NOT ALL.
WE DON'T HAVE TO TEAR YOU OPEN TO RETRIEVE WHAT IS OURS.
BUT IT WILL BE SUCH LOVELY MUSIC.
HEY. YOU AREN'T THE ONLY ONE HE TOOK FROM.
WE NEED TO KNOW WHERE THE SAMPLES ARE.
HSSSSSSSSSS...
INCLUDING THE REST OF YOUR SYMBIOTE.
...FINE.
GET YOUR ANSWERS.

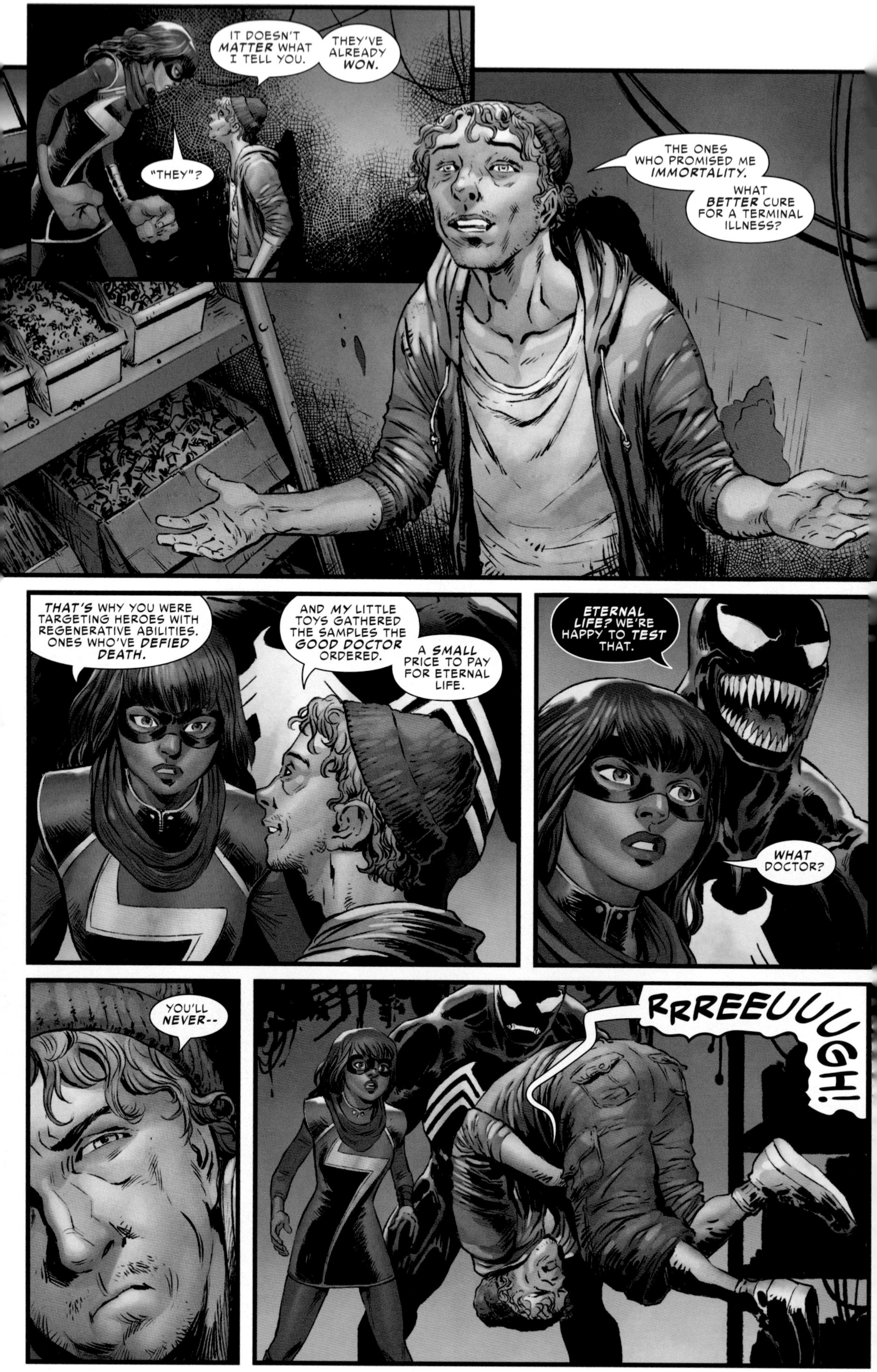
IT DOESN'T MATTER WHAT I TELL YOU.
THEY'VE ALREADY WON.
"THEY"?
THE ONES WHO PROMISED ME IMMORTALITY.
WHAT BETTER CURE FOR A TERMINAL ILLNESS?
THAT'S WHY YOU WERE TARGETING HEROES WITH REGENERATIVE ABILITIES. ONES WHO'VE DEFIED DEATH.
AND MY LITTLE TOYS GATHERED THE SAMPLES THE GOOD DOCTOR ORDERED.
A SMALL PRICE TO PAY FOR ETERNAL LIFE.
ETERNAL LIFE? WE'RE HAPPY TO TEST THAT.
WHAT DOCTOR?
YOU'LL NEVER--
RRREEUUUGH!

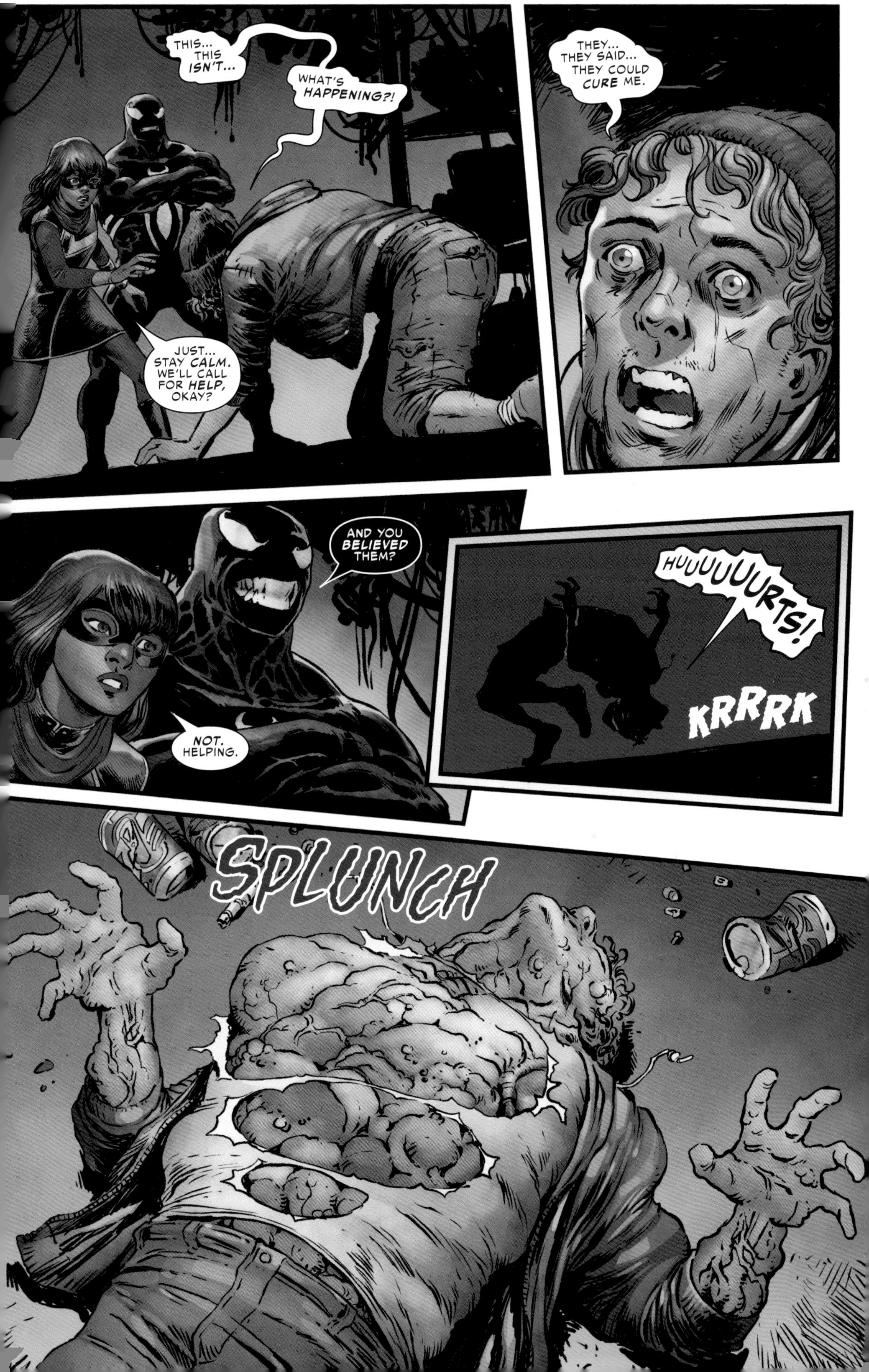

THIS... THIS ISN'T...
WHAT'S HAPPENING?!
JUST... STAY CALM. WE'LL CALL FOR HELP, OKAY?
THEY... THEY SAID... THEY COULD CURE ME.
AND YOU BELIEVED THEM?
NOT. HELPING.
HUUUUUURTS!
KRRRK
SPLUNCH

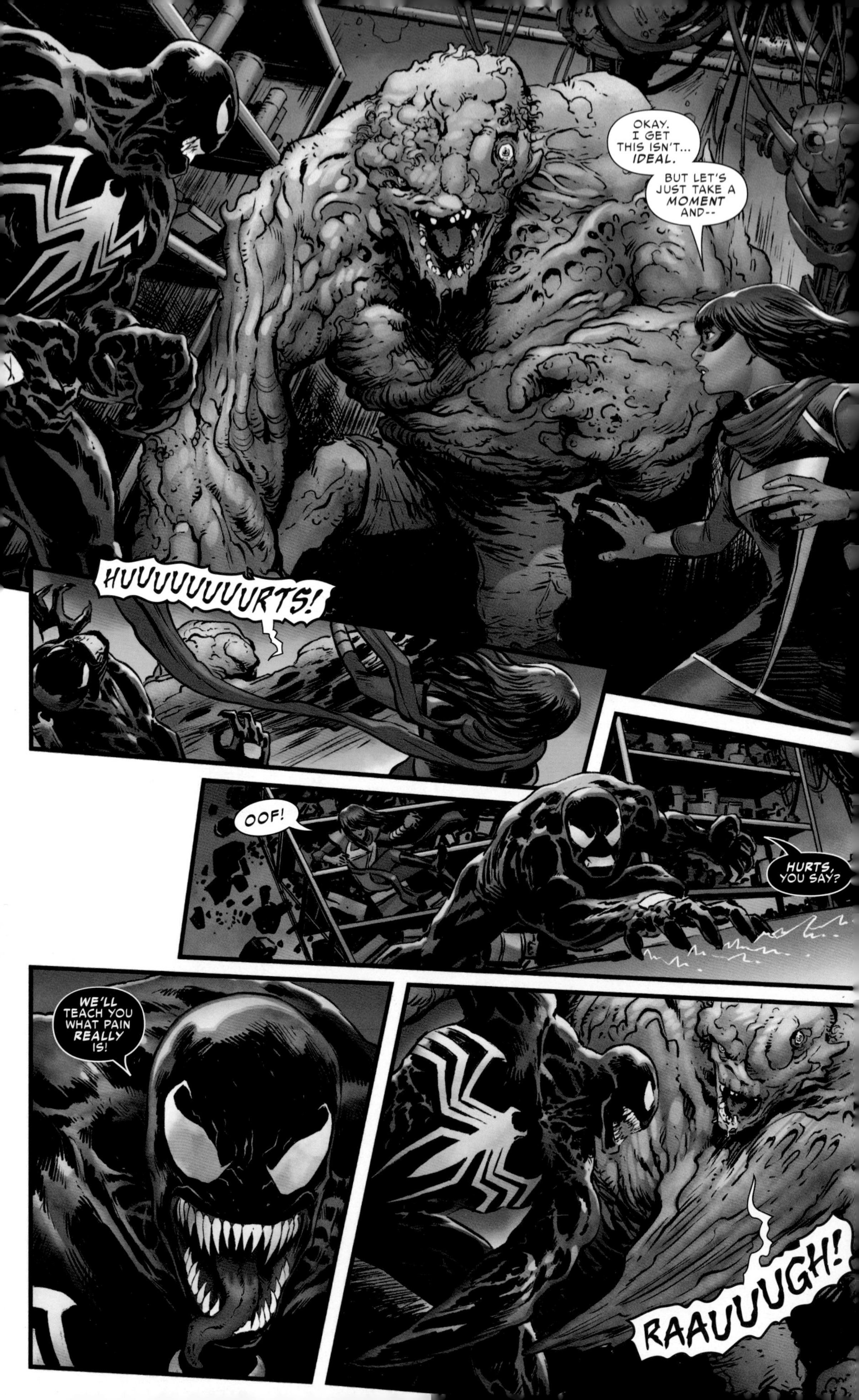
OKAY. I GET THIS ISN'T... IDEAL.
BUT LET'S JUST TAKE A MOMENT AND--
HUUUUUUUUURTS!
OOF!
HURTS, YOU SAY?
WE'LL TEACH YOU WHAT PAIN REALLY IS!
RAAUUUGH!

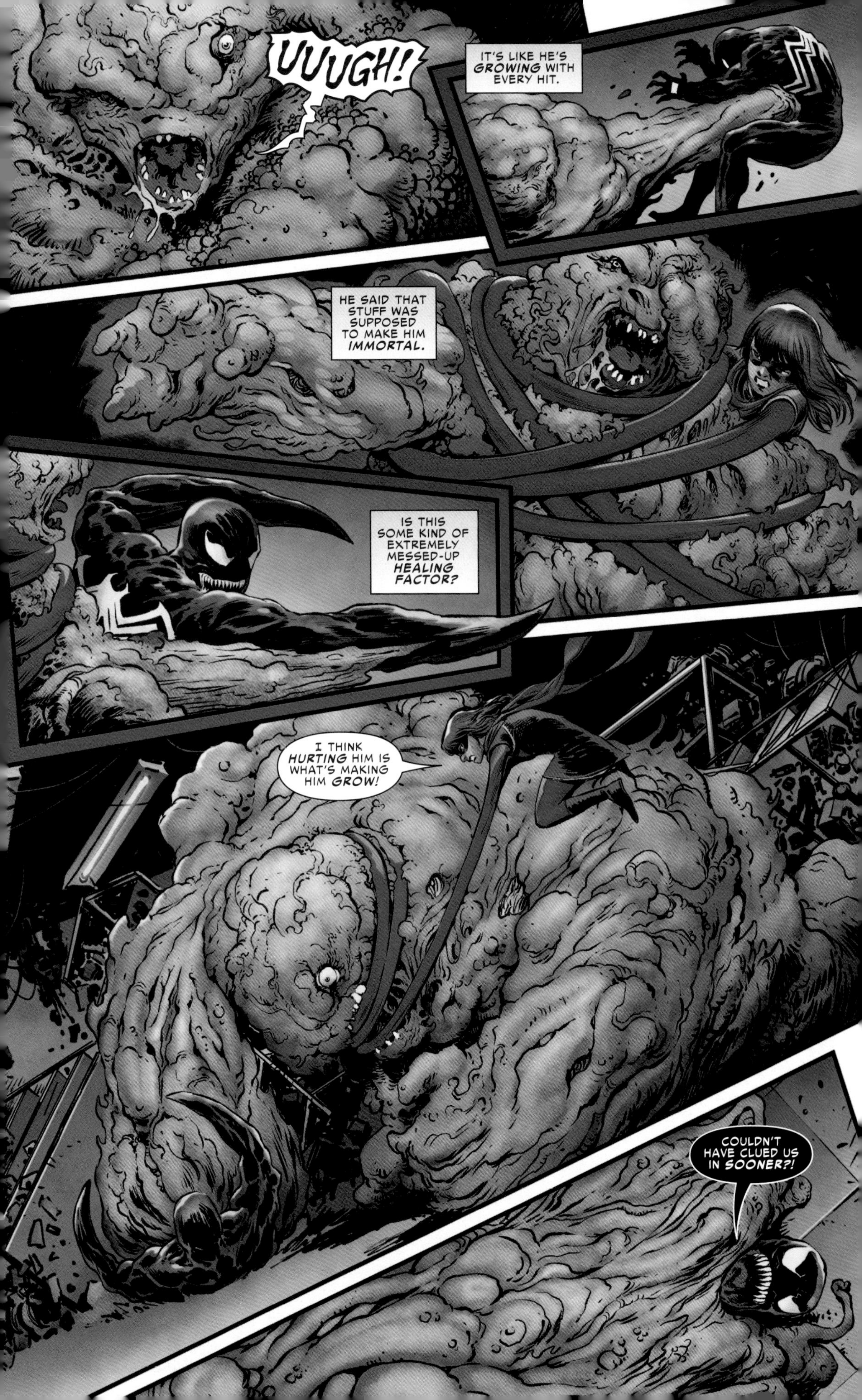
UUUGH!
IT'S LIKE HE'S GROWING WITH EVERY HIT.
HE SAID THAT STUFF WAS SUPPOSED TO MAKE HIM IMMORTAL.
IS THIS SOME KIND OF EXTREMELY MESSED-UP HEALING FACTOR?
I THINK HURTING HIM IS WHAT'S MAKING HIM GROW!
COULDN'T HAVE CLUED US IN SOONER?!

NNNGH! CAN'T MOVE!

CRUSHED BY AN EXPERIMENTAL FLESH MONSTER WOULD BE A *STUPID* WAY TO DIE.

MAYBE IF I CAN EMBIGGEN ENOUGH, PUSH BACK *WITHOUT* DAMAGING HIM TOO MUCH...

HUH?

IS HE--?

OH MAN...

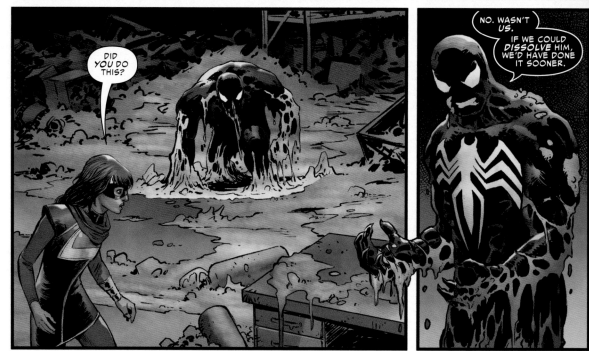

DID *YOU DO* THIS?

NO. WASN'T *US.* IF WE COULD *DISSOLVE* HIM, WE'D HAVE DONE IT SOONER.

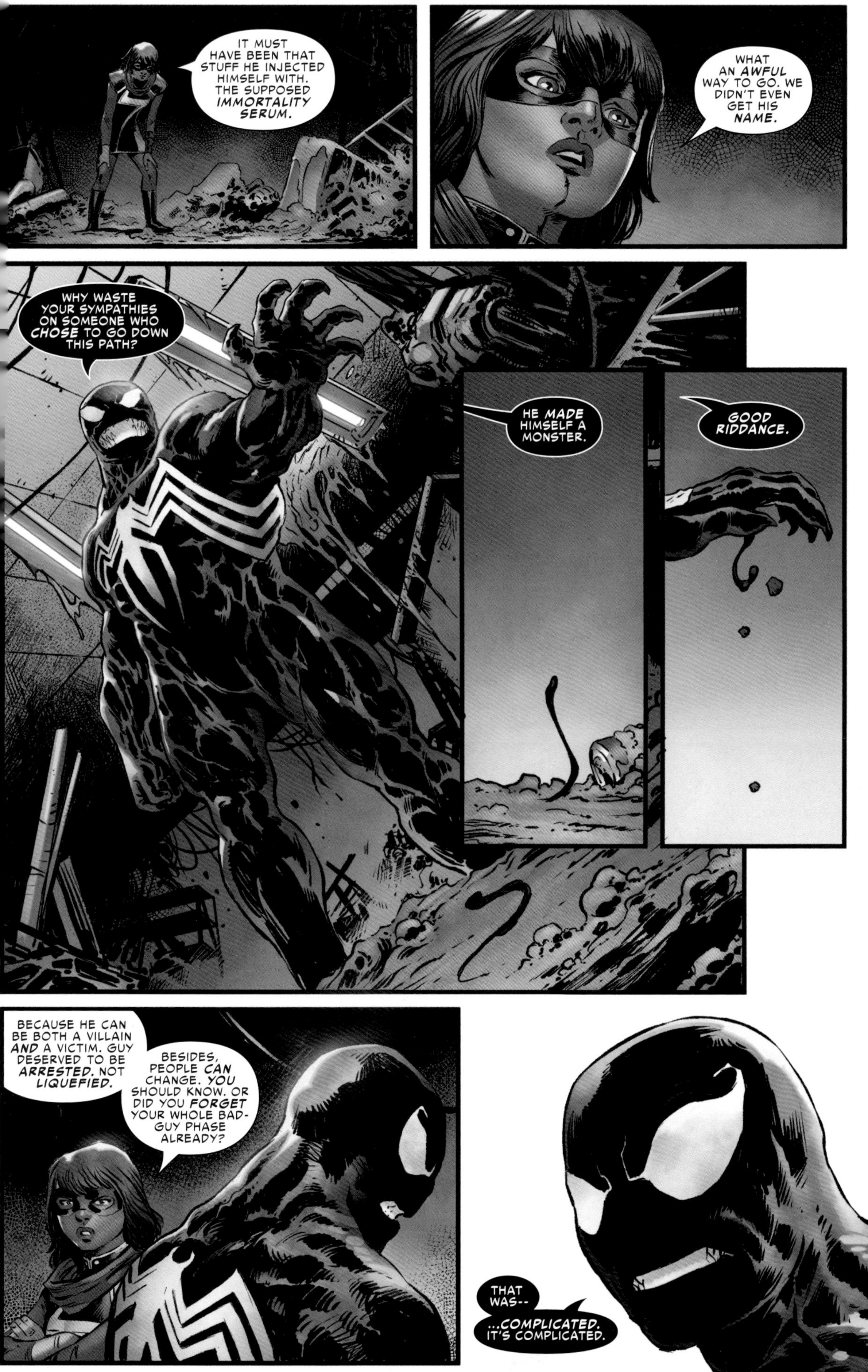
IT MUST HAVE BEEN THAT STUFF HE INJECTED HIMSELF WITH. THE SUPPOSED IMMORTALITY SERUM.
WHAT AN AWFUL WAY TO GO. WE DIDN'T EVEN GET HIS NAME.
WHY WASTE YOUR SYMPATHIES ON SOMEONE WHO CHOSE TO GO DOWN THIS PATH?
HE MADE HIMSELF A MONSTER.
GOOD RIDDANCE.
BECAUSE HE CAN BE BOTH A VILLAIN AND A VICTIM. GUY DESERVED TO BE ARRESTED. NOT LIQUEFIED.
BESIDES, PEOPLE CAN CHANGE. YOU SHOULD KNOW. OR DID YOU FORGET YOUR WHOLE BAD-GUY PHASE ALREADY?
THAT WAS--
...COMPLICATED. IT'S COMPLICATED.

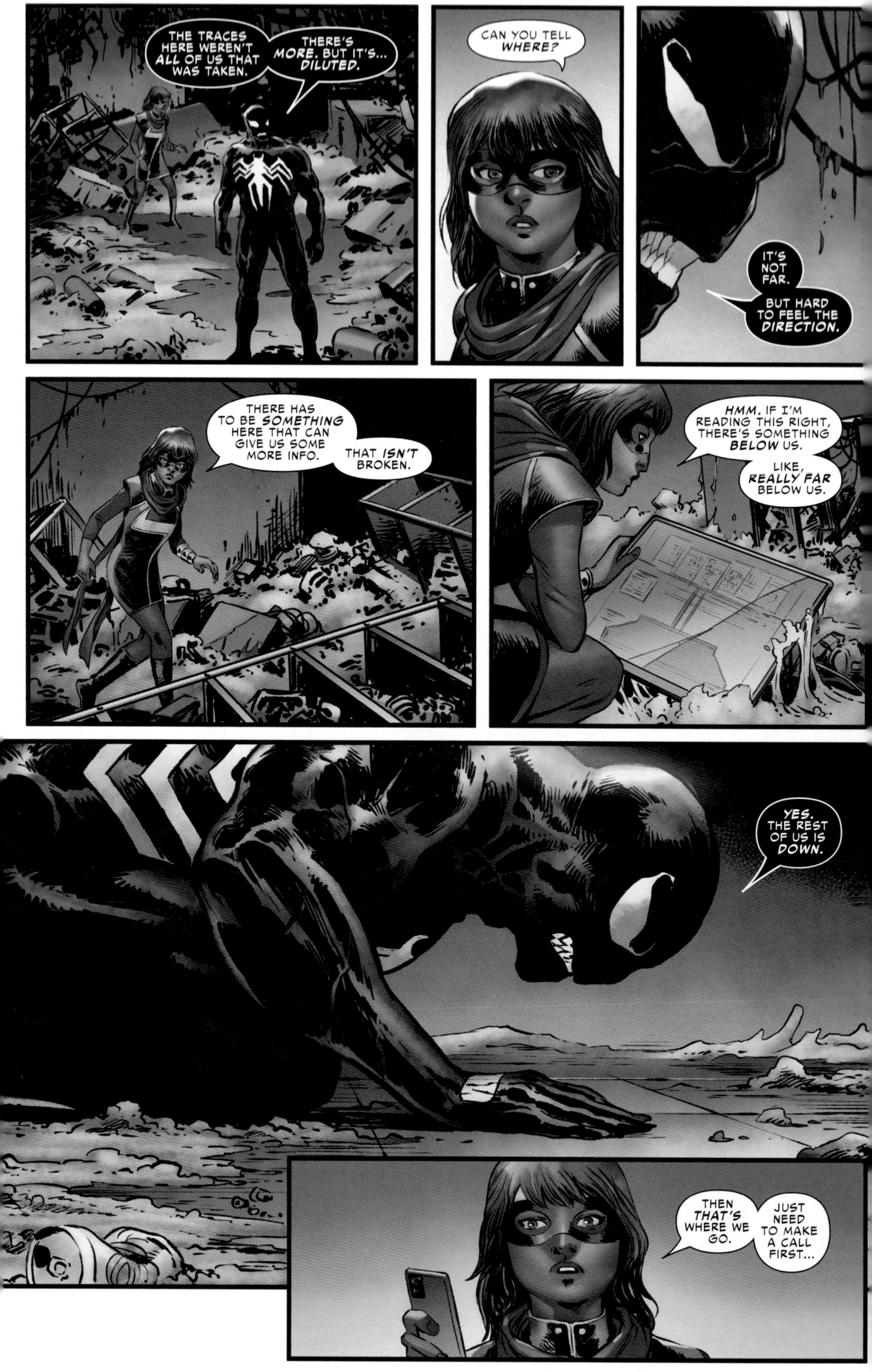
THE TRACES HERE WEREN'T ALL OF US THAT WAS TAKEN.
THERE'S MORE. BUT IT'S... DILUTED.
CAN YOU TELL WHERE?
IT'S NOT FAR.
BUT HARD TO FEEL THE DIRECTION.
THERE HAS TO BE SOMETHING HERE THAT CAN GIVE US SOME MORE INFO.
THAT ISN'T BROKEN.
HMM. IF I'M READING THIS RIGHT, THERE'S SOMETHING BELOW US.
LIKE, REALLY FAR BELOW US.
YES. THE REST OF US IS DOWN.
THEN THAT'S WHERE WE GO.
JUST NEED TO MAKE A CALL FIRST...

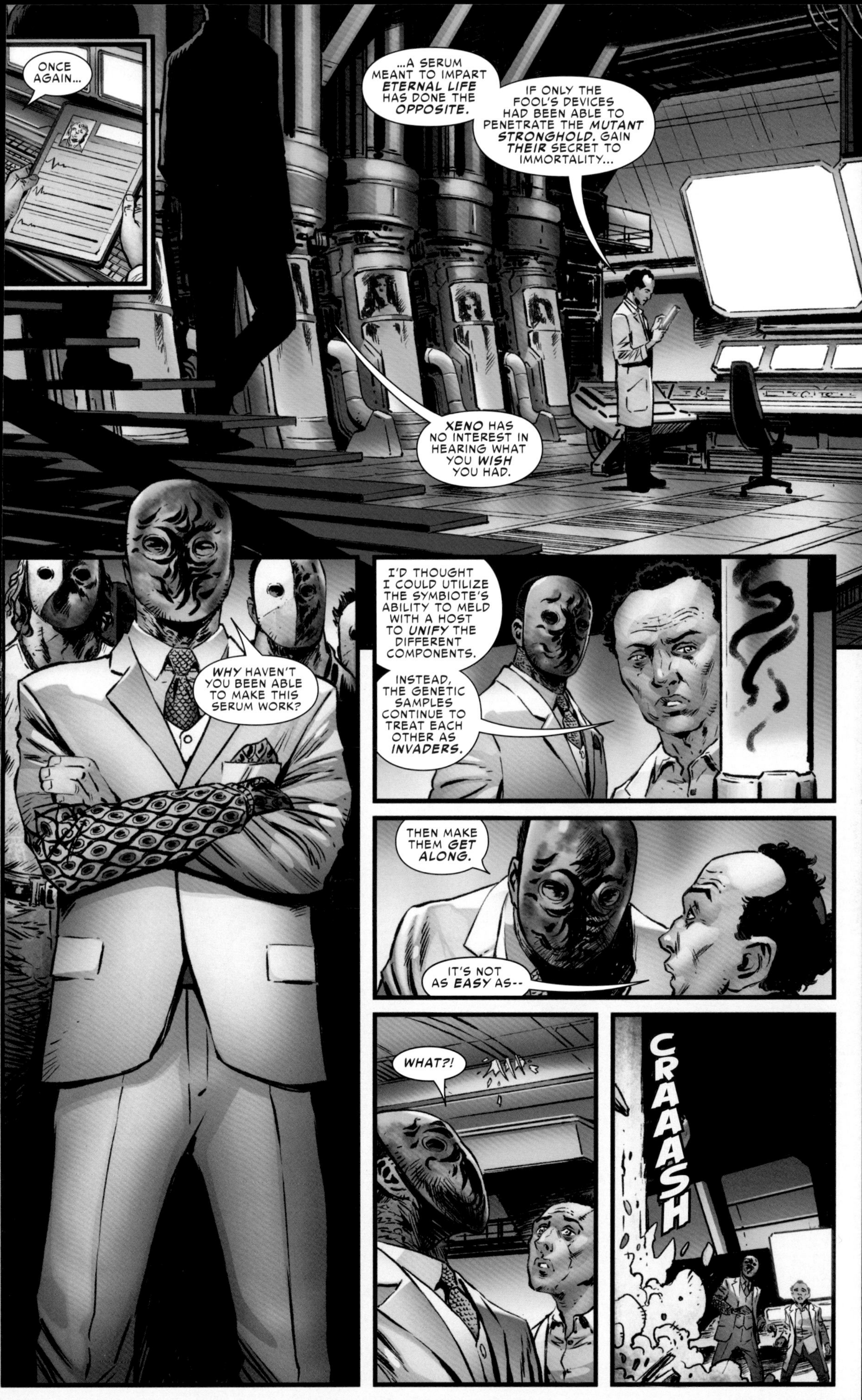
ONCE AGAIN...
...A SERUM MEANT TO IMPART ETERNAL LIFE HAS DONE THE OPPOSITE.
IF ONLY THE FOOL'S DEVICES HAD BEEN ABLE TO PENETRATE THE MUTANT STRONGHOLD. GAIN THEIR SECRET TO IMMORTALITY...
XENO HAS NO INTEREST IN HEARING WHAT YOU WISH YOU HAD.
WHY HAVEN'T YOU BEEN ABLE TO MAKE THIS SERUM WORK?
I'D THOUGHT I COULD UTILIZE THE SYMBIOTE'S ABILITY TO MELD WITH A HOST TO UNIFY THE DIFFERENT COMPONENTS.
INSTEAD, THE GENETIC SAMPLES CONTINUE TO TREAT EACH OTHER AS INVADERS.
THEN MAKE THEM GET ALONG.
IT'S NOT AS EASY AS--
WHAT?!
CRAAASH

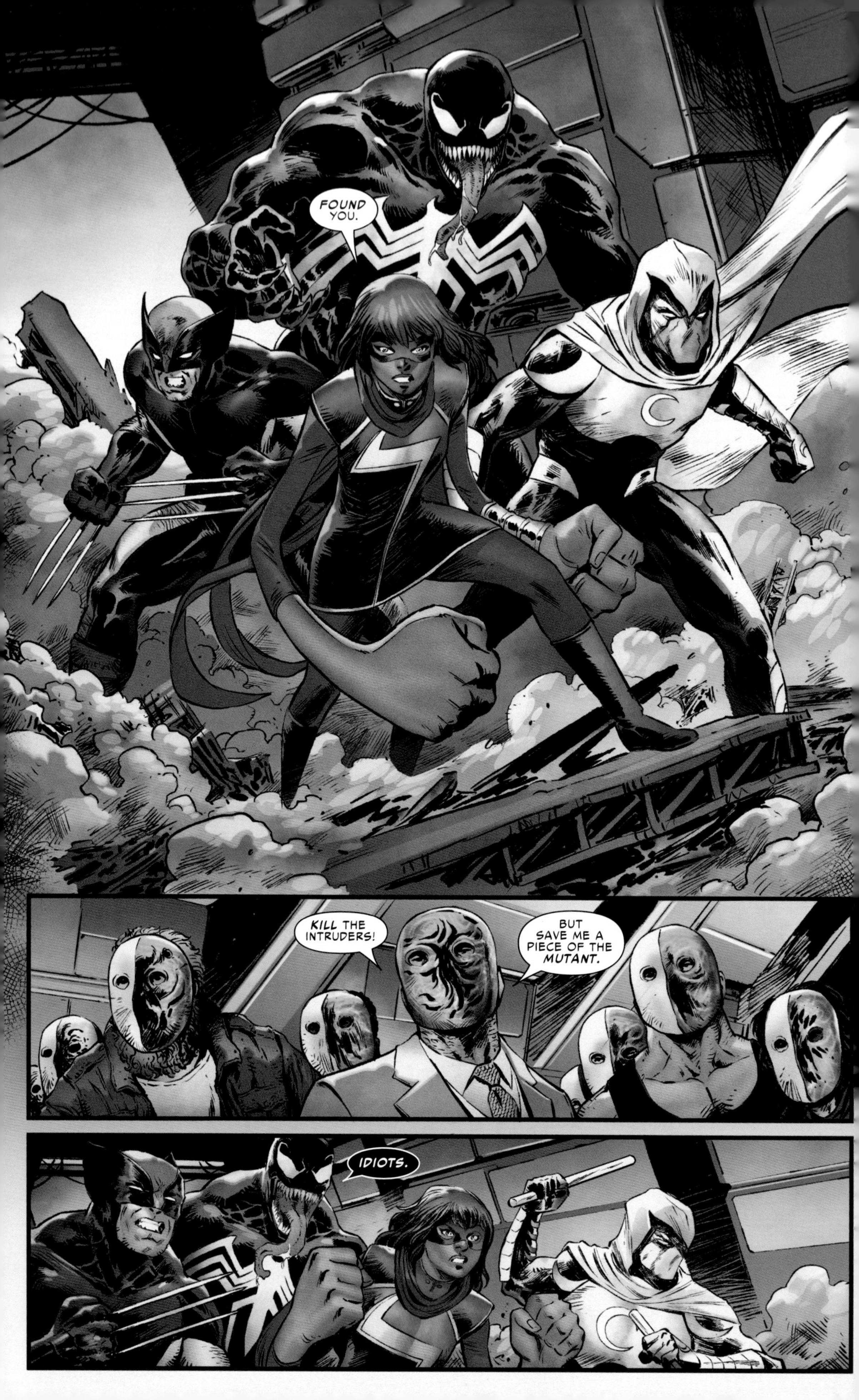
FOUND YOU.
KILL THE INTRUDERS!
BUT SAVE ME A PIECE OF THE MUTANT.
IDIOTS.

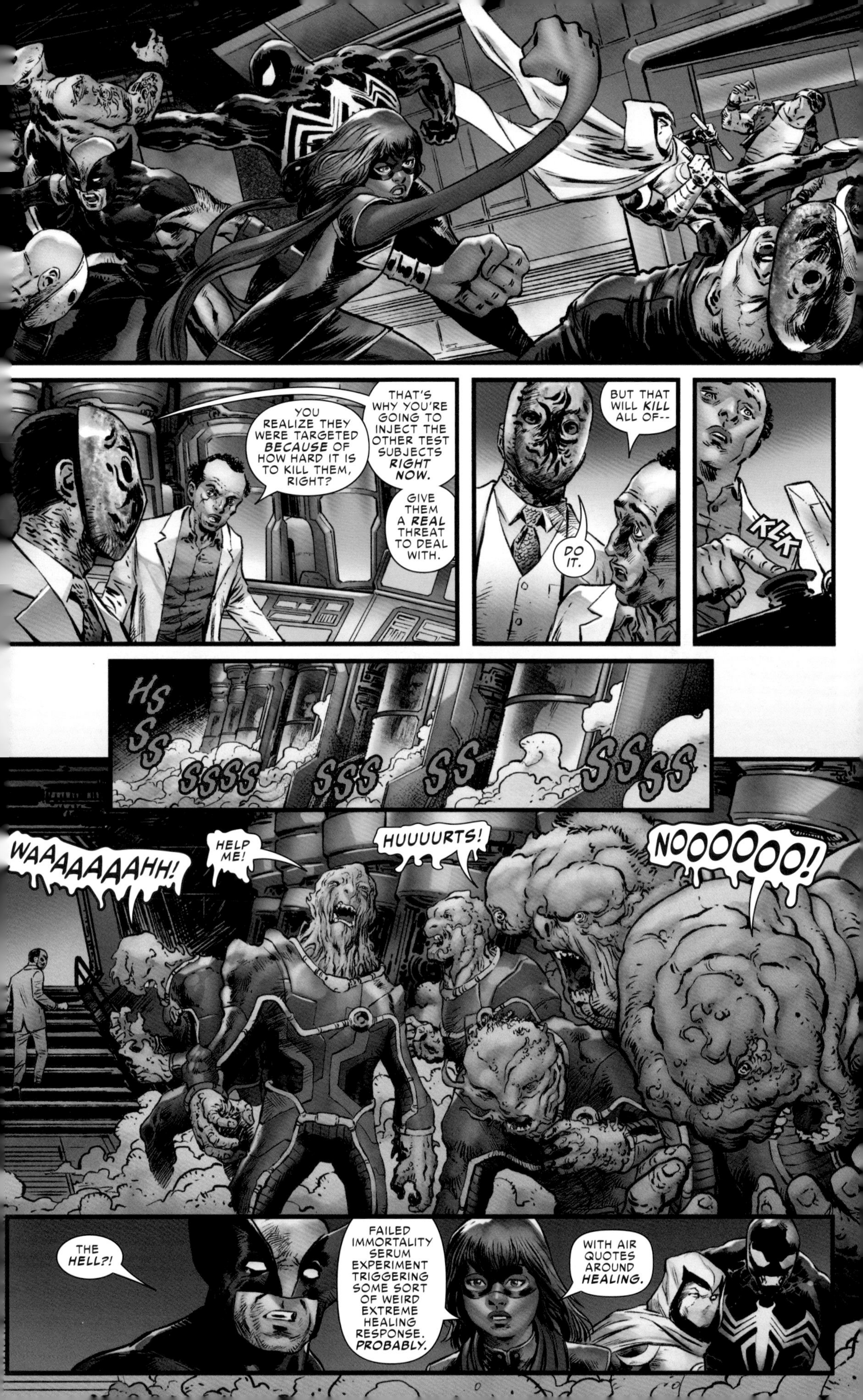

YOU REALIZE THEY WERE TARGETED BECAUSE OF HOW HARD IT IS TO KILL THEM, RIGHT?
THAT'S WHY YOU'RE GOING TO INJECT THE OTHER TEST SUBJECTS RIGHT NOW.
GIVE THEM A REAL THREAT TO DEAL WITH.
BUT THAT WILL KILL ALL OF--
DO IT.
KLIK
HSSSSSSSSSSSSSSSS
WAAAAAAAAHH!
HELP ME!
HUUUURTS!
NOOOOOO!
THE HELL?!
FAILED IMMORTALITY SERUM EXPERIMENT TRIGGERING SOME SORT OF WEIRD EXTREME HEALING RESPONSE. PROBABLY.
WITH AIR QUOTES AROUND HEALING.

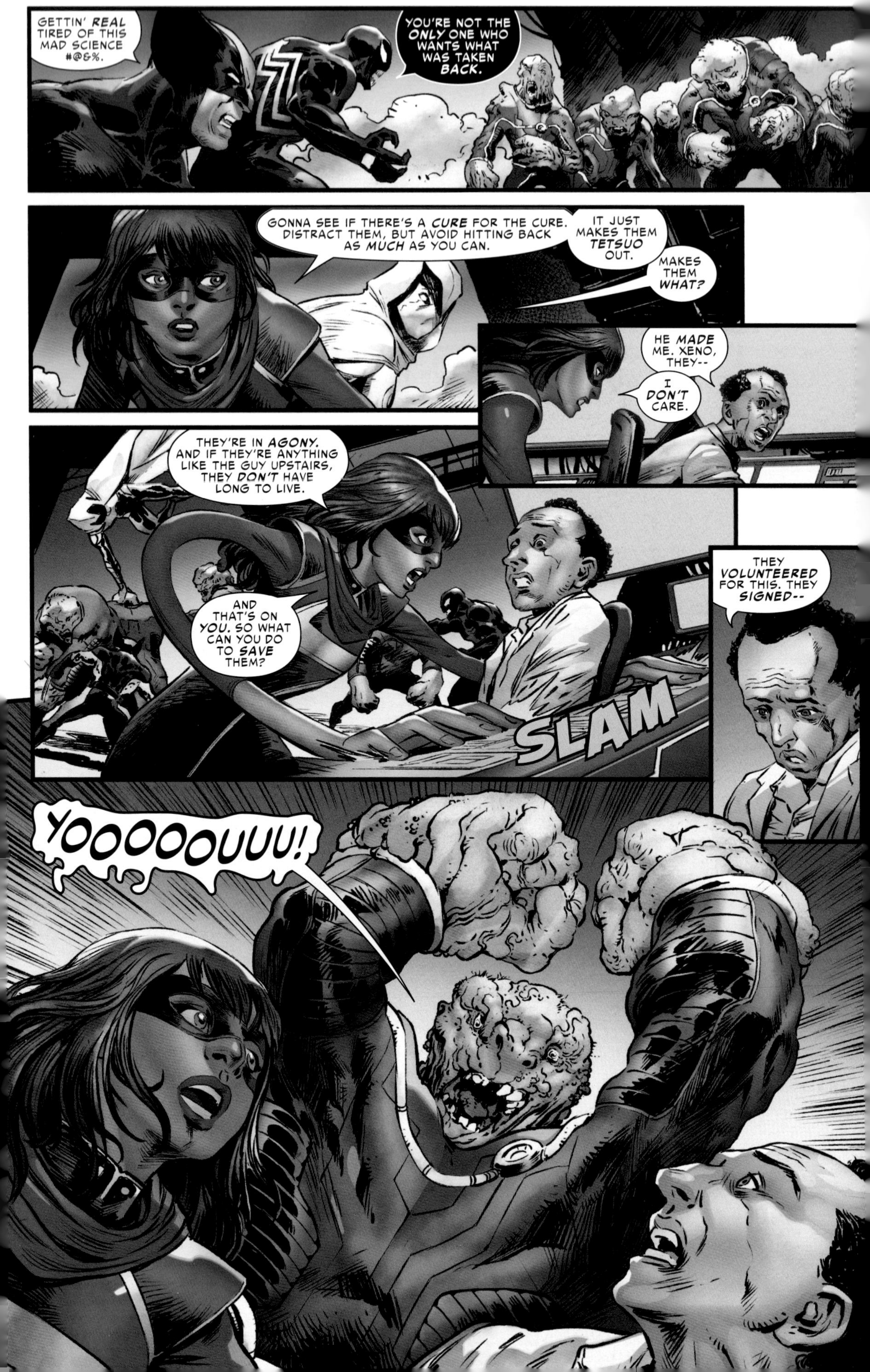
GETTIN' REAL TIRED OF THIS MAD SCIENCE #@&%.
YOU'RE NOT THE ONLY ONE WHO WANTS WHAT WAS TAKEN BACK.
GONNA SEE IF THERE'S A CURE FOR THE CURE. DISTRACT THEM, BUT AVOID HITTING BACK AS MUCH AS YOU CAN.
IT JUST MAKES THEM TETSUO OUT.
MAKES THEM WHAT?
HE MADE ME. XENO, THEY--
I DON'T CARE.
THEY'RE IN AGONY. AND IF THEY'RE ANYTHING LIKE THE GUY UPSTAIRS, THEY DON'T HAVE LONG TO LIVE.
AND THAT'S ON YOU. SO WHAT CAN YOU DO TO SAVE THEM?
SLAM
THEY VOLUNTEERED FOR THIS. THEY SIGNED--
YOOOOOUUU!

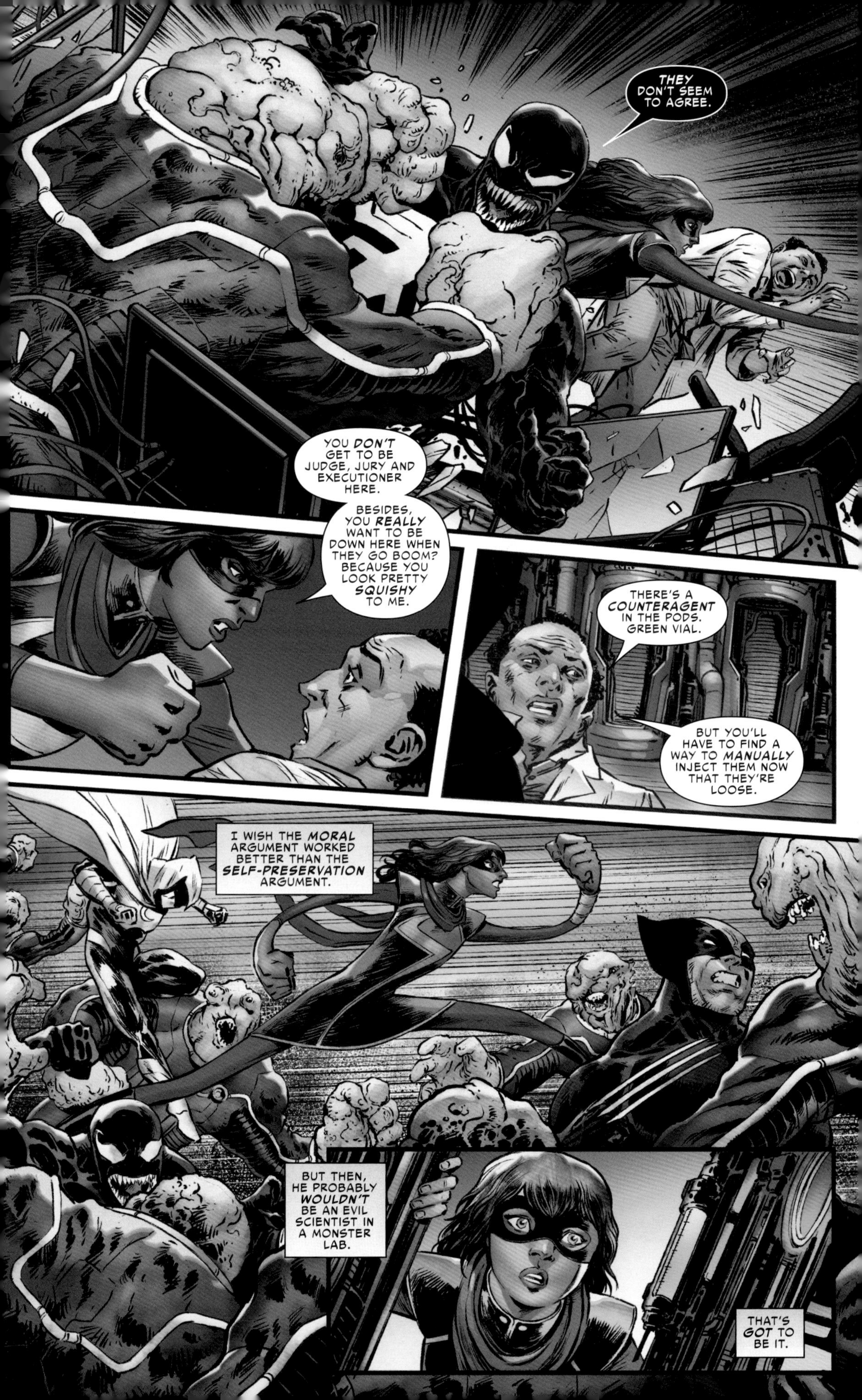
THEY DON'T SEEM TO AGREE.
YOU DON'T GET TO BE JUDGE, JURY AND EXECUTIONER HERE.
BESIDES, YOU REALLY WANT TO BE DOWN HERE WHEN THEY GO BOOM? BECAUSE YOU LOOK PRETTY SQUISHY TO ME.
THERE'S A COUNTERAGENT IN THE PODS. GREEN VIAL.
BUT YOU'LL HAVE TO FIND A WAY TO MANUALLY INJECT THEM NOW THAT THEY'RE LOOSE.
I WISH THE MORAL ARGUMENT WORKED BETTER THAN THE SELF-PRESERVATION ARGUMENT.
BUT THEN, HE PROBABLY WOULDN'T BE AN EVIL SCIENTIST IN A MONSTER LAB.
THAT'S GOT TO BE IT.

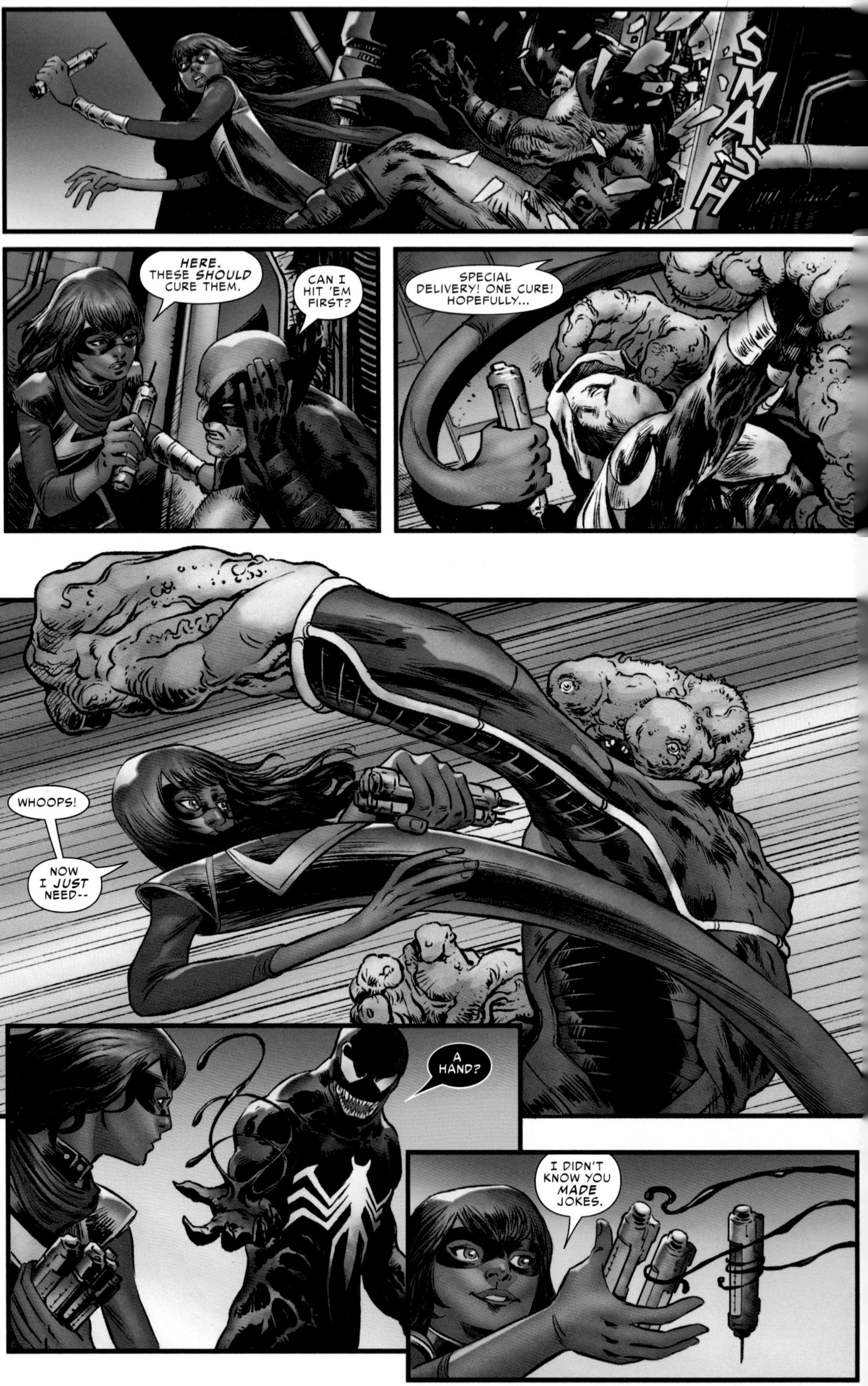
SMASH
HERE. THESE SHOULD CURE THEM.
CAN I HIT 'EM FIRST?
SPECIAL DELIVERY! ONE CURE! HOPEFULLY...
WHOOPS!
NOW I JUST NEED--
A HAND?
I DIDN'T KNOW YOU MADE JOKES.

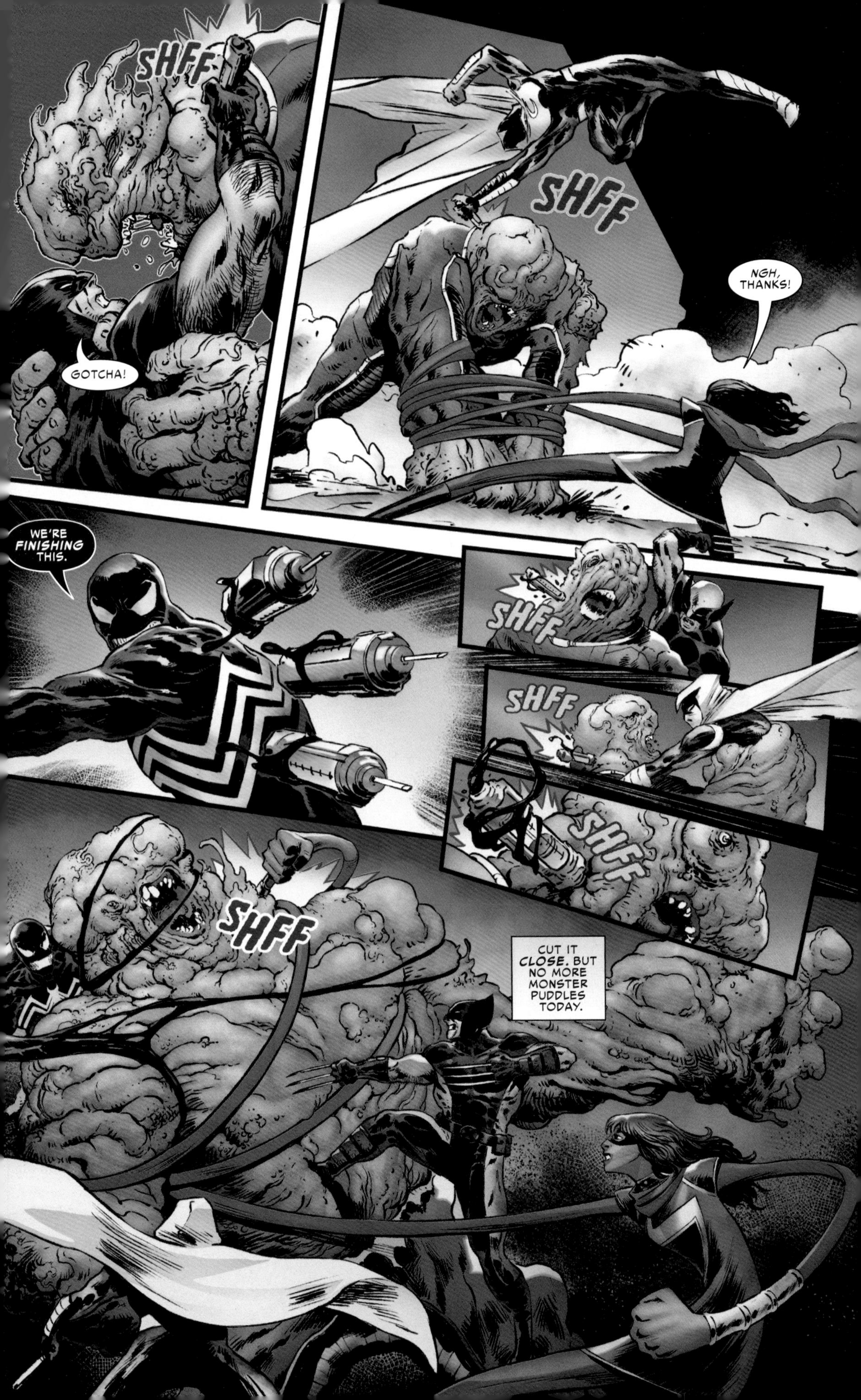
SHFF
GOTCHA!
SHFF
NGH, THANKS!
WE'RE FINISHING THIS.
SHFF
SHFF
SHFF
SHFF
CUT IT CLOSE. BUT NO MORE MONSTER PUDDLES TODAY.

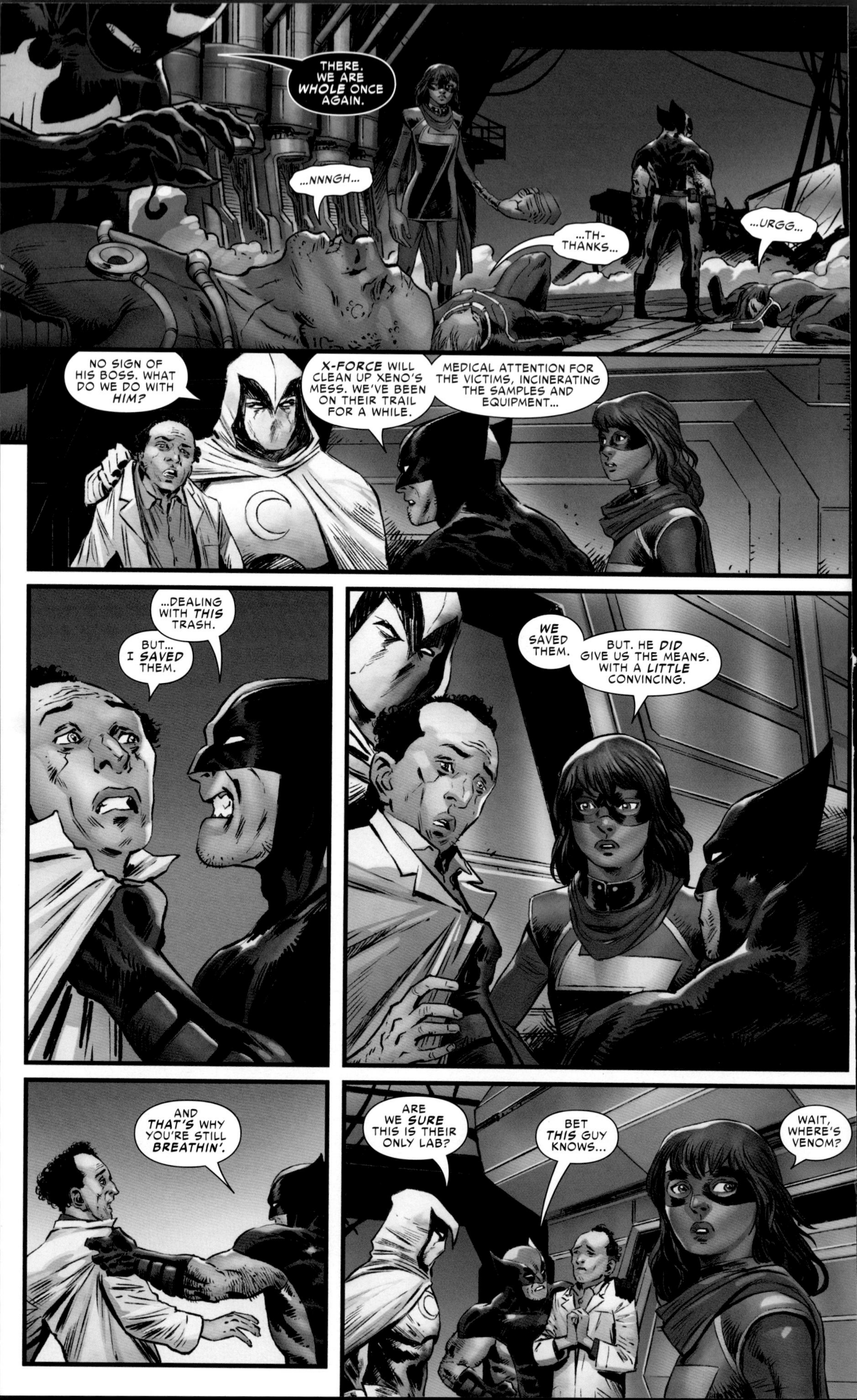
THERE. WE ARE WHOLE ONCE AGAIN.
...NNNGH...
...TH-THANKS...
...URGG...
NO SIGN OF HIS BOSS. WHAT DO WE DO WITH HIM?
X-FORCE WILL CLEAN UP XENO'S MESS. WE'VE BEEN ON THEIR TRAIL FOR A WHILE.
MEDICAL ATTENTION FOR THE VICTIMS, INCINERATING THE SAMPLES AND EQUIPMENT...
...DEALING WITH THIS TRASH.
BUT... I SAVED THEM.
WE SAVED THEM.
BUT. HE DID GIVE US THE MEANS. WITH A LITTLE CONVINCING.
AND THAT'S WHY YOU'RE STILL BREATHIN'.
ARE WE SURE THIS IS THEIR ONLY LAB?
BET THIS GUY KNOWS...
WAIT, WHERE'S VENOM?

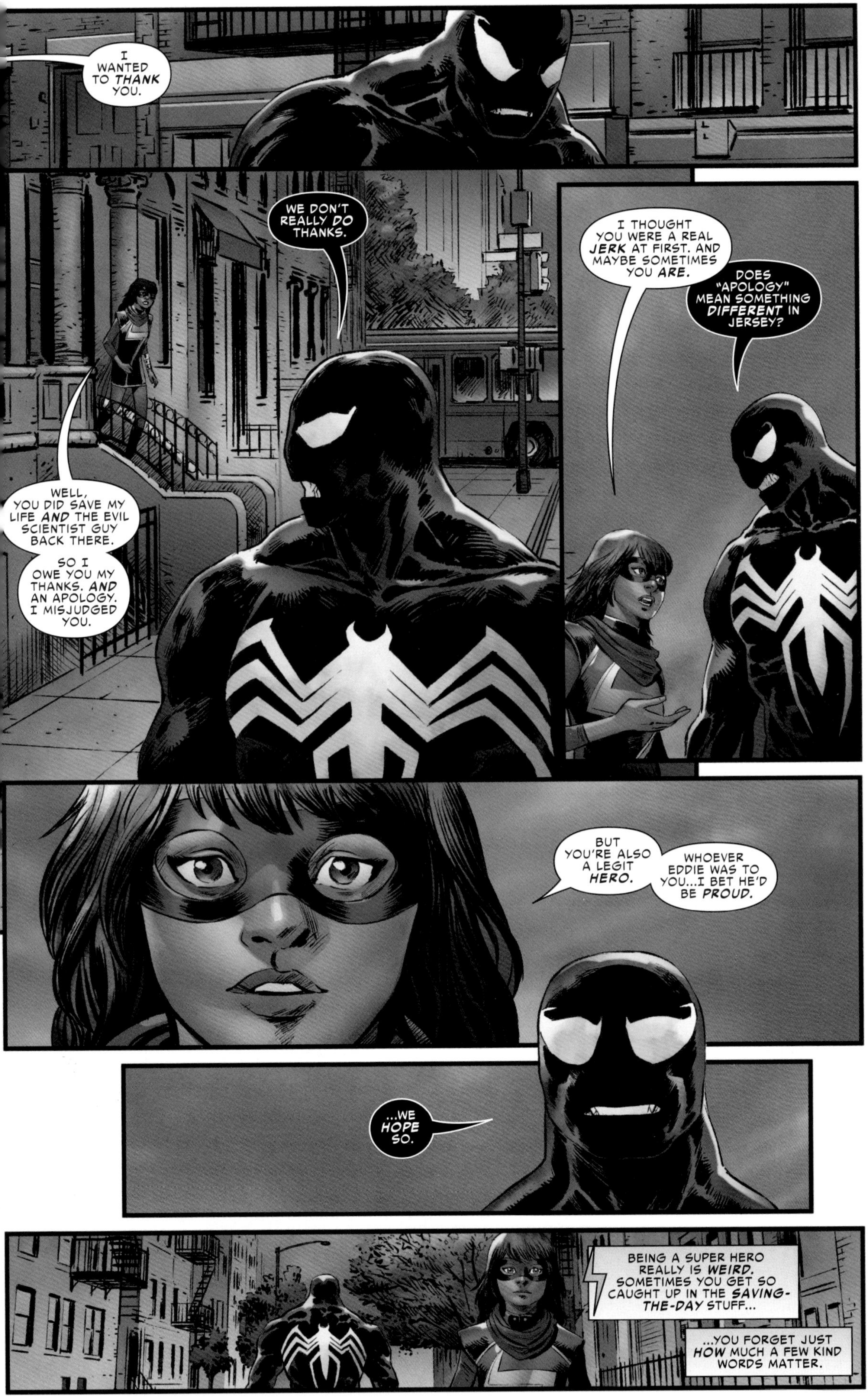

I WANTED TO THANK YOU.
WE DON'T REALLY DO THANKS.
WELL, YOU DID SAVE MY LIFE AND THE EVIL SCIENTIST GUY BACK THERE.
SO I OWE YOU MY THANKS. AND AN APOLOGY. I MISJUDGED YOU.
DOES "APOLOGY" MEAN SOMETHING DIFFERENT IN JERSEY?
I THOUGHT YOU WERE A REAL JERK AT FIRST. AND MAYBE SOMETIMES YOU ARE.
BUT YOU'RE ALSO A LEGIT HERO.
WHOEVER EDDIE WAS TO YOU...I BET HE'D BE PROUD.
...WE HOPE SO.
BEING A SUPER HERO REALLY IS WEIRD. SOMETIMES YOU GET SO CAUGHT UP IN THE SAVING-THE-DAY STUFF...
...YOU FORGET JUST HOW MUCH A FEW KIND WORDS MATTER.

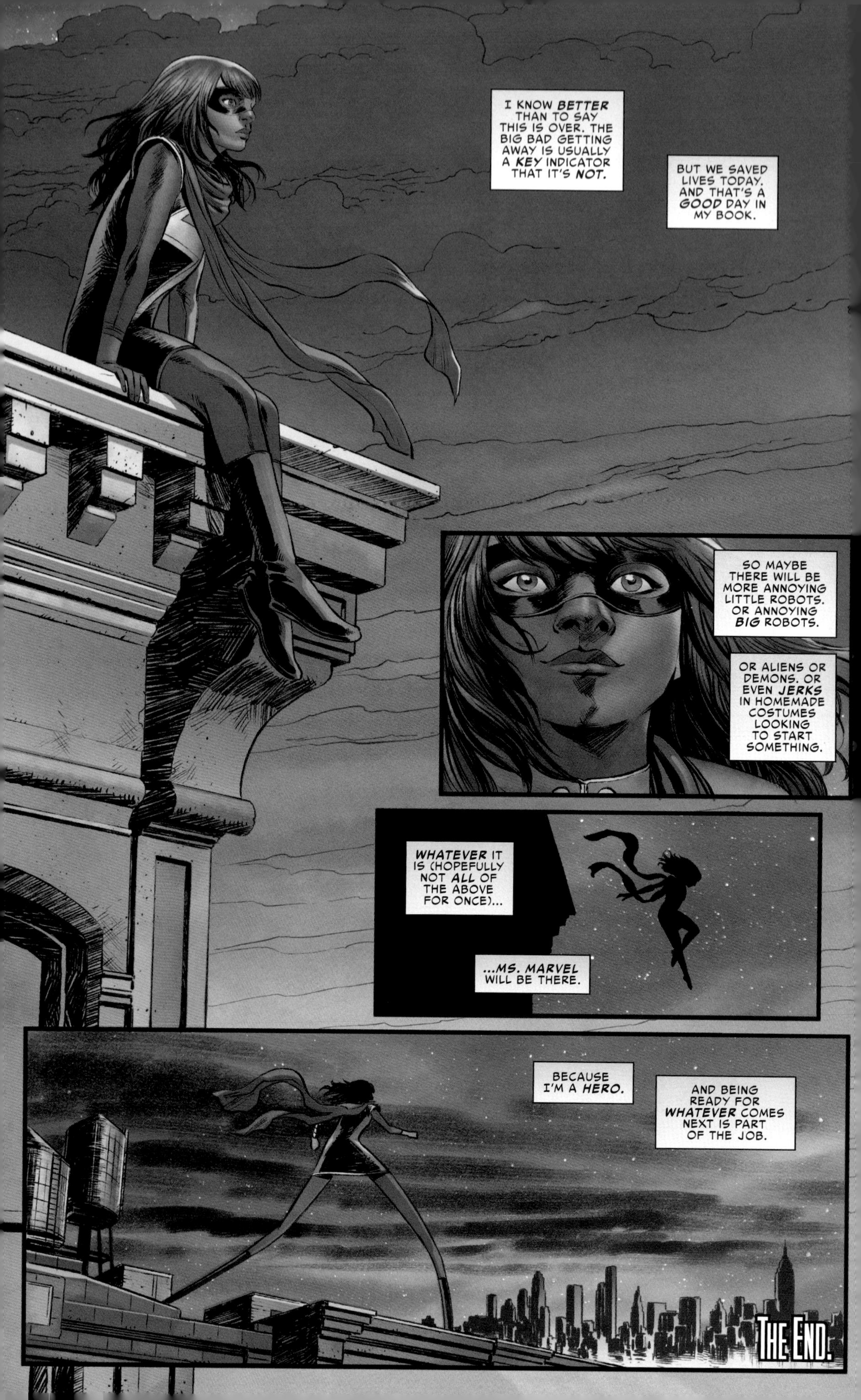
I KNOW BETTER THAN TO SAY THIS IS OVER. THE BIG BAD GETTING AWAY IS USUALLY A KEY INDICATOR THAT IT'S NOT.
BUT WE SAVED LIVES TODAY. AND THAT'S A GOOD DAY IN MY BOOK.
SO MAYBE THERE WILL BE MORE ANNOYING LITTLE ROBOTS. OR ANNOYING BIG ROBOTS.
OR ALIENS OR DEMONS. OR EVEN JERKS IN HOMEMADE COSTUMES LOOKING TO START SOMETHING.
WHATEVER IT IS (HOPEFULLY NOT ALL OF THE ABOVE FOR ONCE)...
...MS. MARVEL WILL BE THERE.
BECAUSE I'M A HERO.
AND BEING READY FOR WHATEVER COMES NEXT IS PART OF THE JOB.
THE END.

MS. MARVEL & WOLVERINE VARIANT BY MAHMUD ASRAR & EDGAR DELGADO

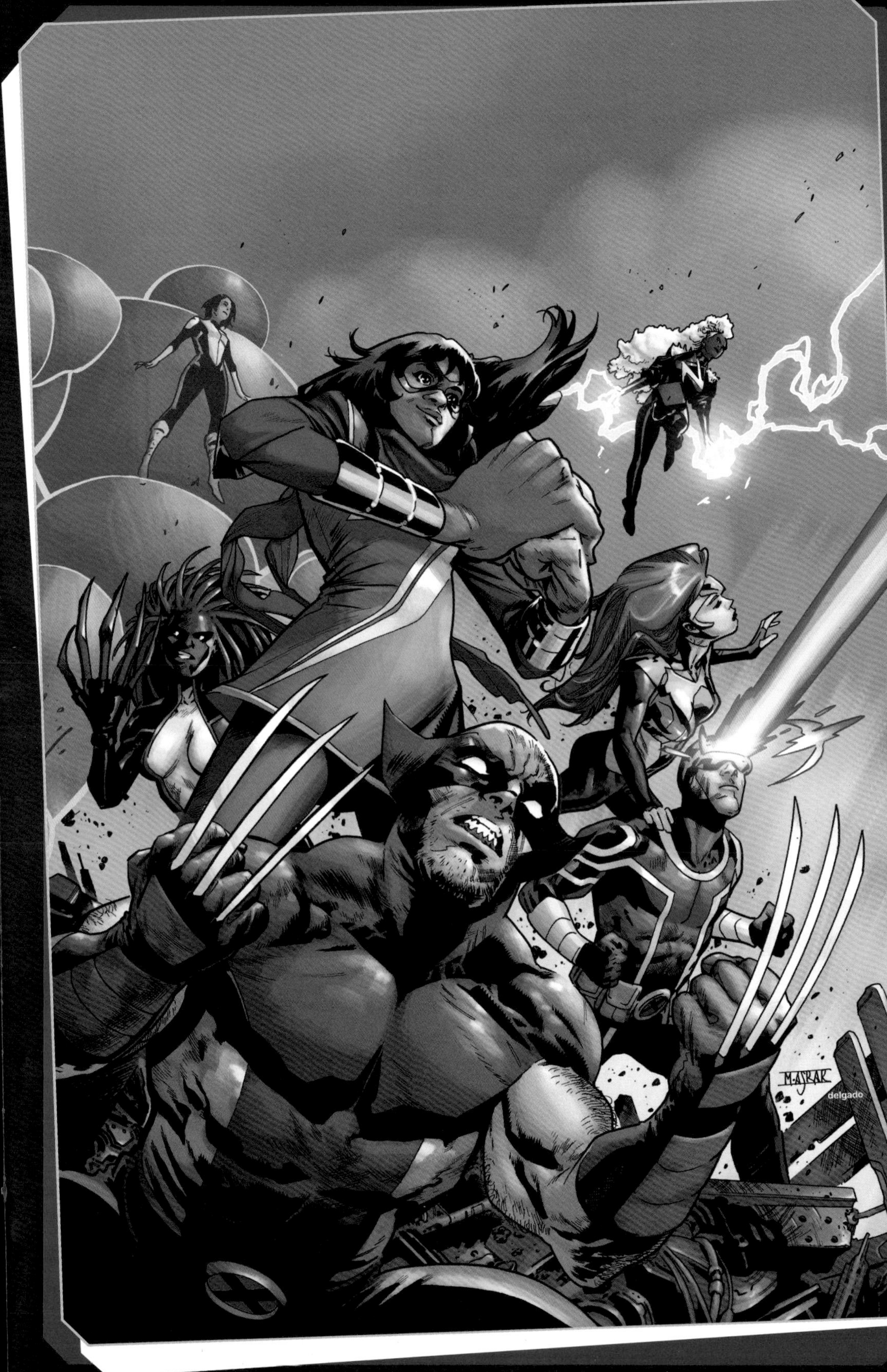
M. ASRAR
delgado

MS. MARVEL & WOLVERINE VARIANT BY PEACH MOMOKO

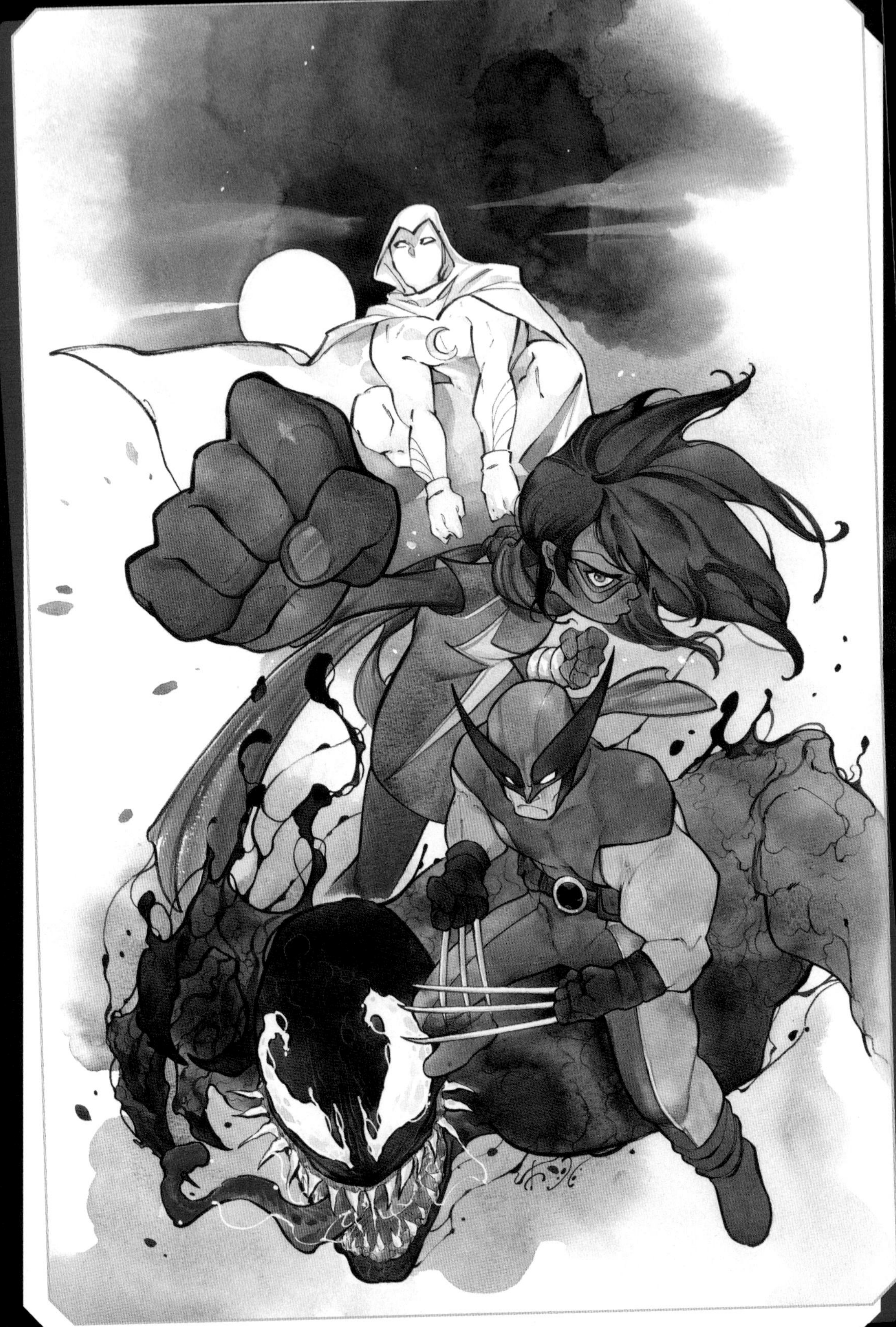

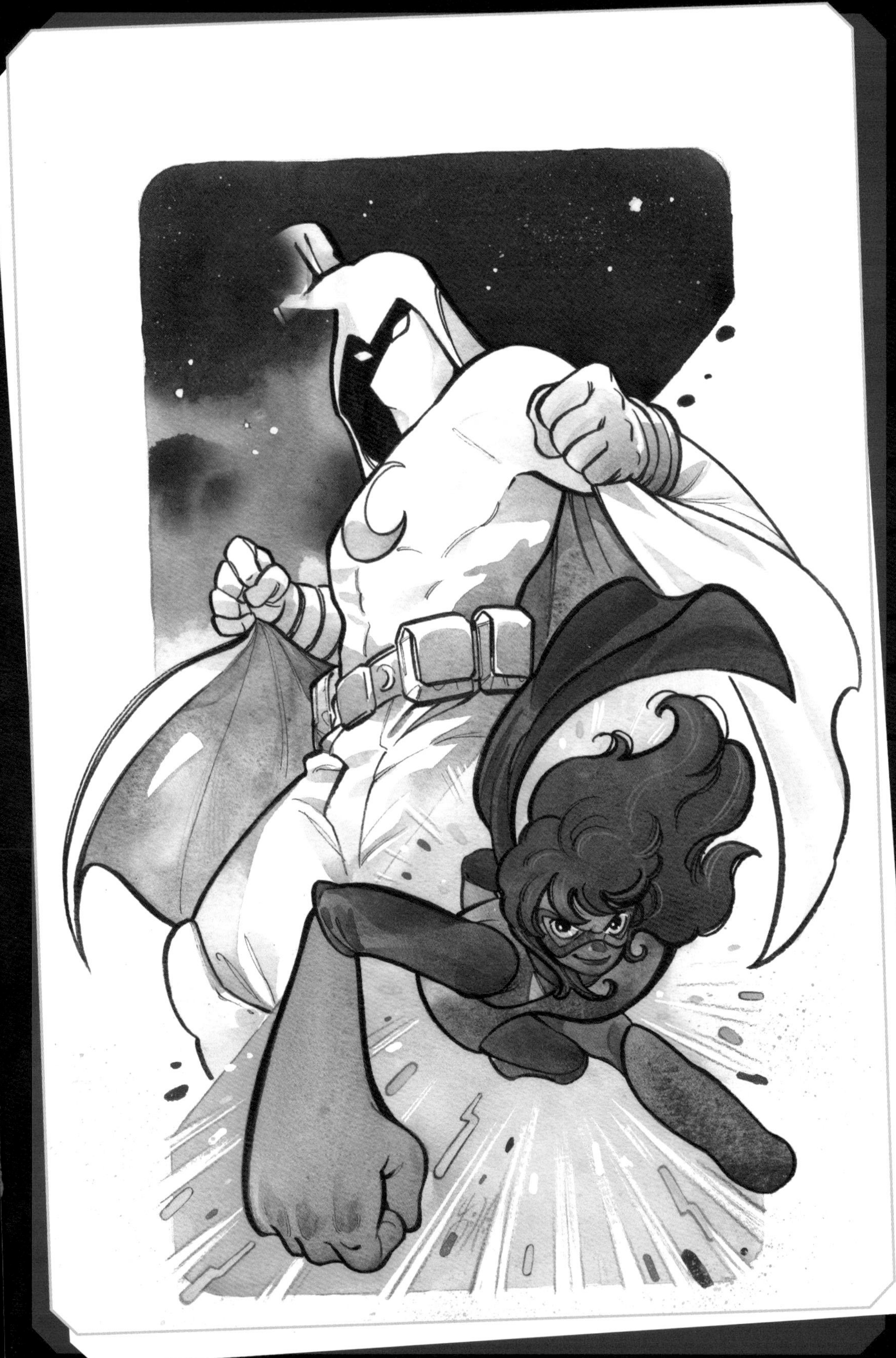

MS. MARVEL & MOON KNIGHT VARIANT BY **DECLAN SHALVEY**

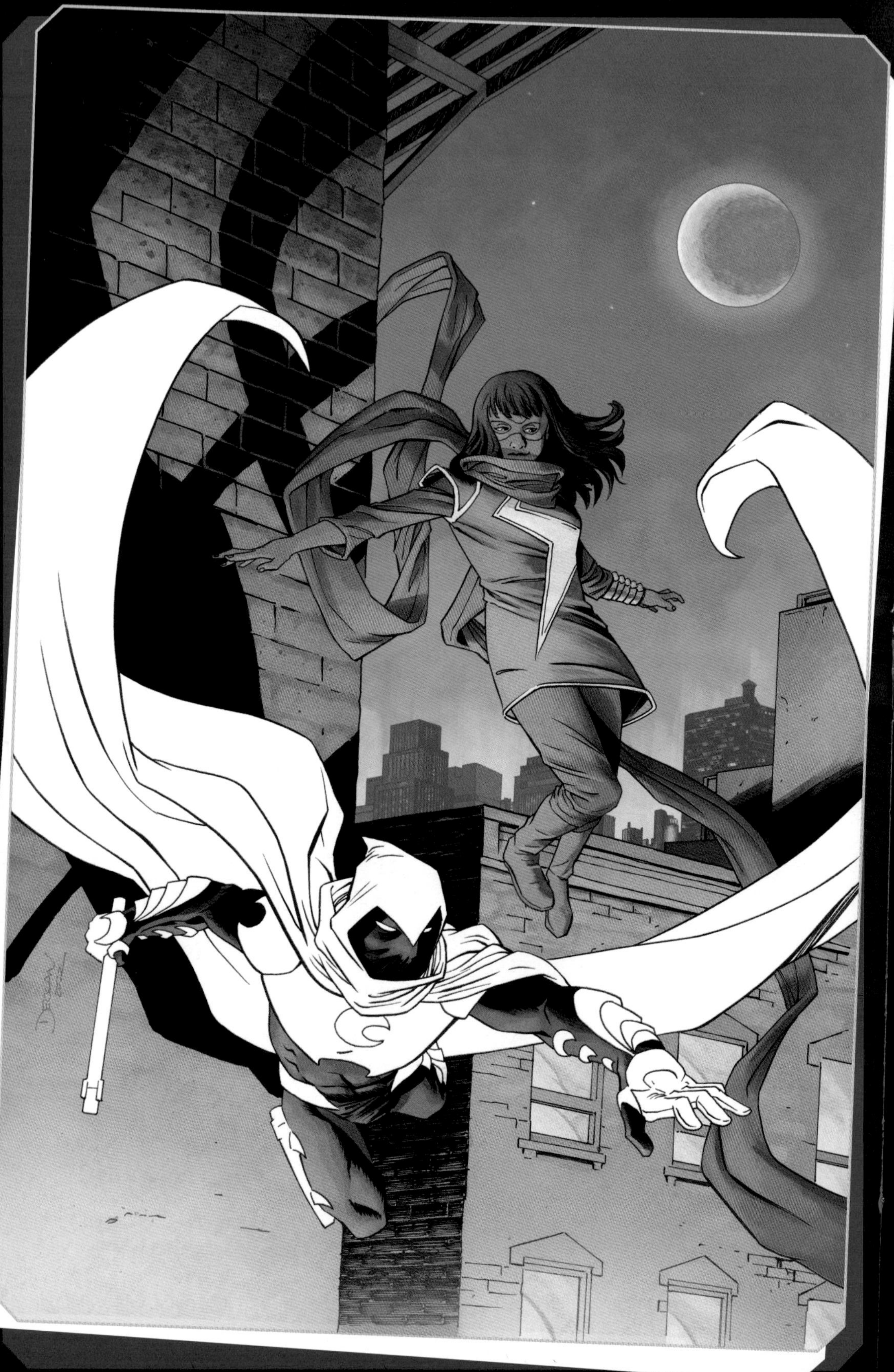

MS. MARVEL & VENOM VARIANT BY **PEACH MOMOKO**

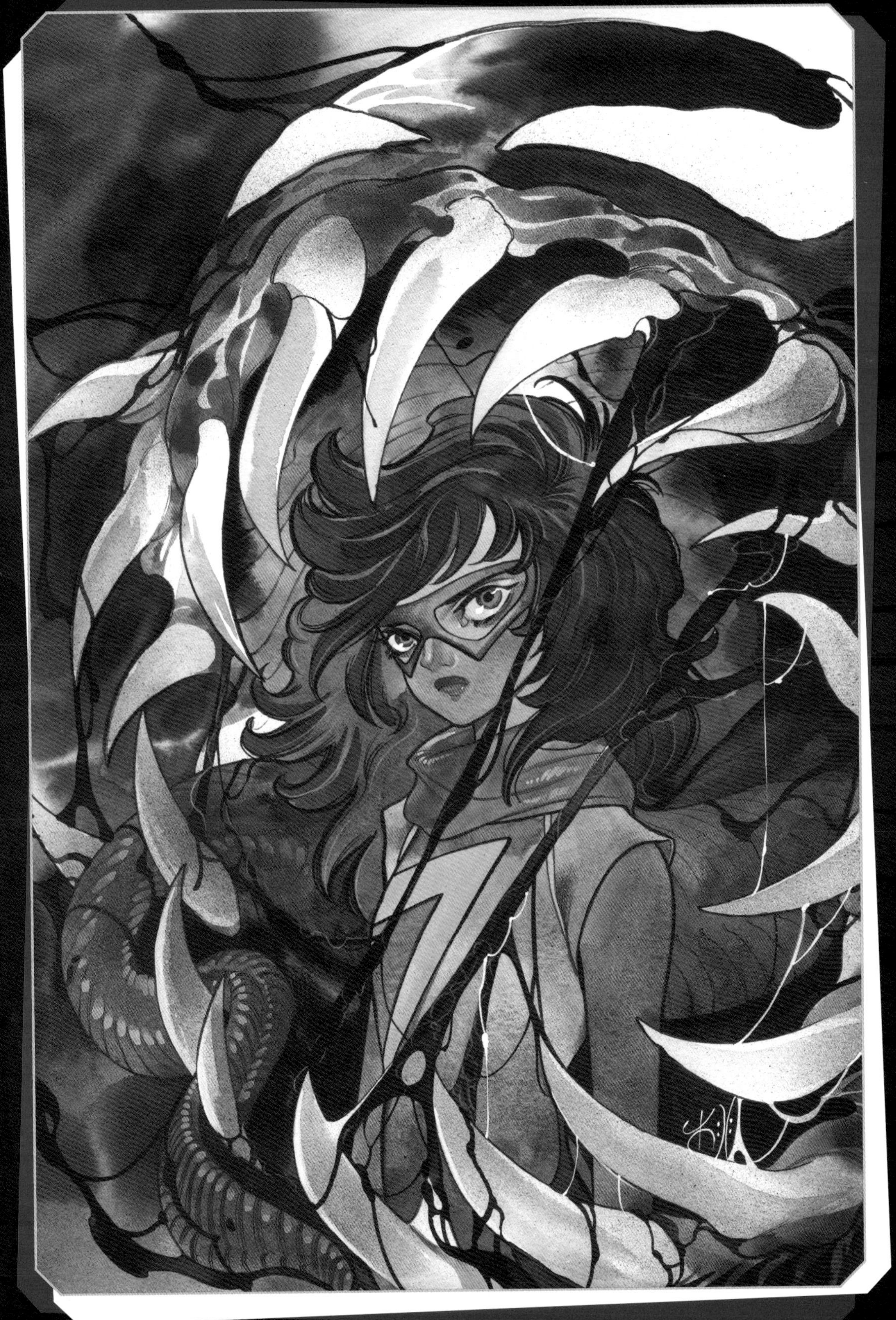

MS. MARVEL & VENOM VARIANT BY **WALTER SIMONSON** & **EDGAR DELGADO**

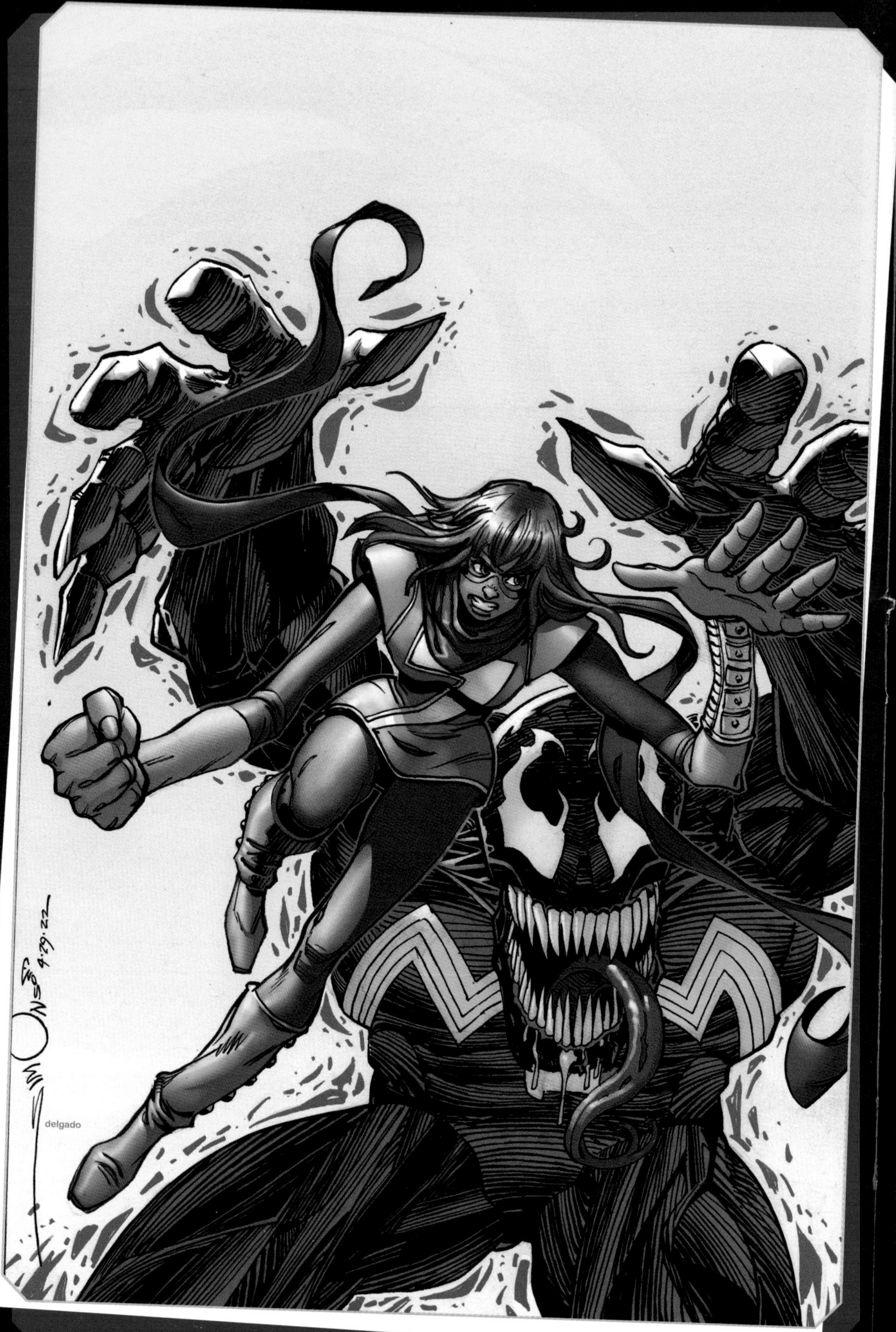

4·29·22
delgado

MS. MARVEL & WOLVERINE COVER SKETCH BY **SARA PICHELLI**

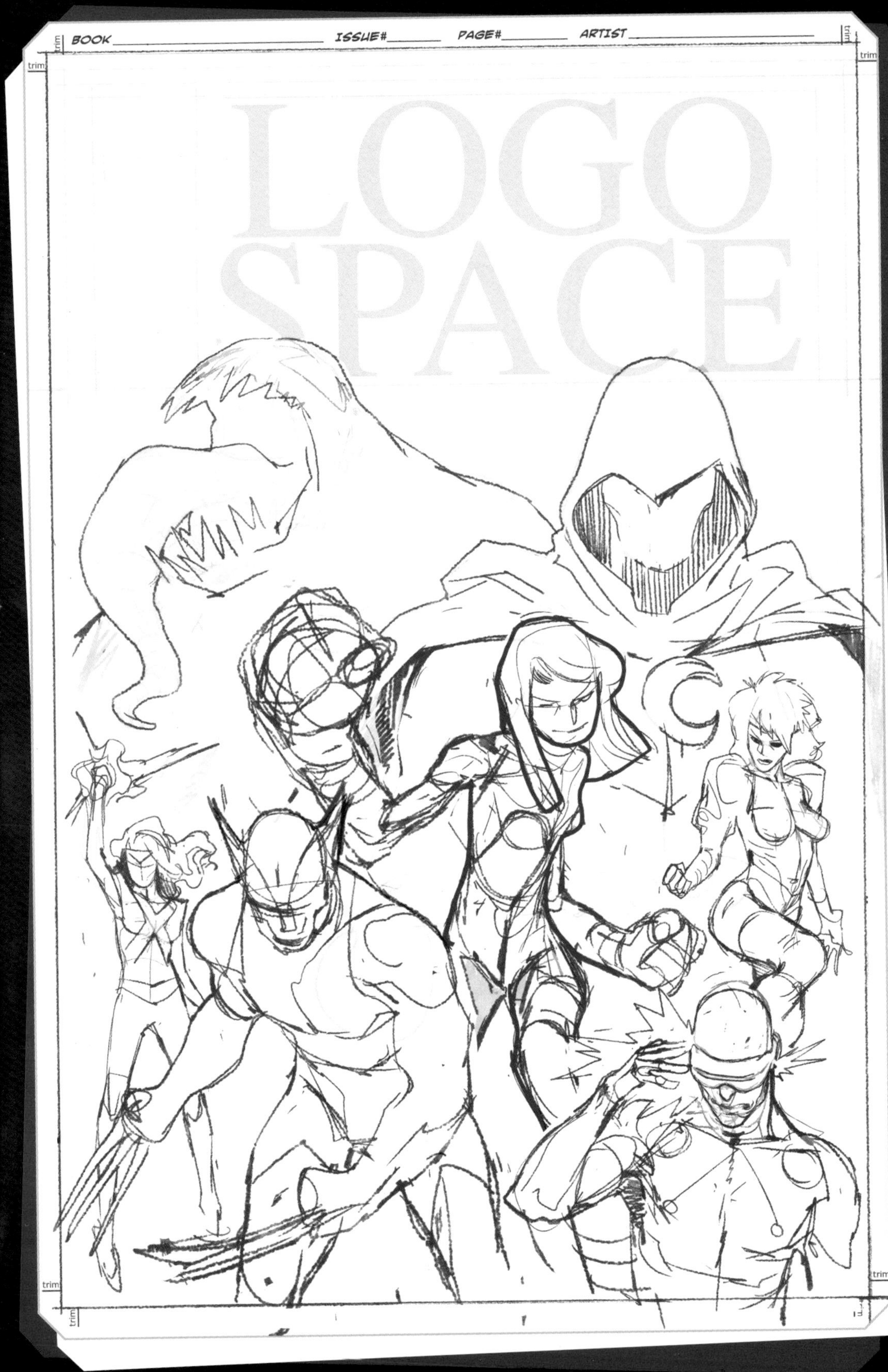
BOOK
ISSUE#
PAGE#
ARTIST
LOGO
SPACE

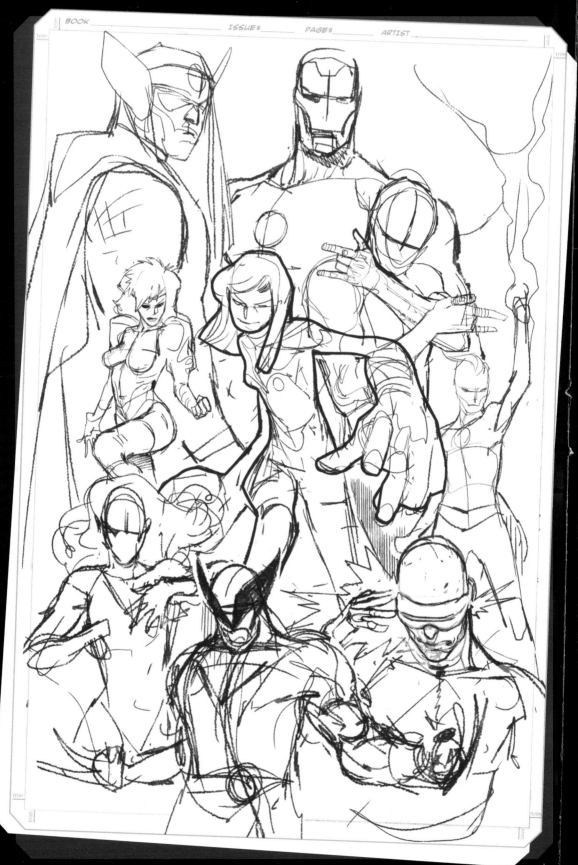